THE URBAN DOG

THE URBAN DOG

How to understand, enjoy, and care for a dog in the city

PATRICIA CURTIS

BANTAM BOOKS

TORONTO · NEW YORK · LONDON · SYDNEY · AUCKLAND

THE URBAN DOG

A Bantam Book / August 1986

Library of Congress Cataloging-in-Publication Data

Curtis, Patricia, 1923–
  The urban dog.

  Includes index.
  1. Dogs. I. Title.
SF426.C87 1986   636.7   85-48238
ISBN 0-553-34270-3

Published simultaneously in the United States and Canada

PRINTED IN THE UNITED STATES OF AMERICA

FG   0 9 8 7 6 5 4 3 2 1

ACKNOWLEDGMENTS

I am indebted to many knowledgeable people who extended help and encouragement to me when I was writing this book, but several deserve special mention.

First, I owe much to Dr. Audrey Hayes, Diplomate of the American College of Veterinary Internal Medicine and Staff Veterinarian of the Animal Medical Center in New York City. Audrey carefully advised me on the medical information in this book.

I was greatly helped by William Berloni of Berloni Theatrical Animals. Bill truly knows and loves dogs and generously shared with me much of his experience and insights into dog behavior.

And I am deeply grateful to Jane Sapinsky, photographer, who gave hours of her time and contributed some of the best pictures in this book.

A big thanks also to the following: Attorneys Jolene Marion of the

Animal Legal Defense Fund and Elinor Molbegott, Legal Counsel
of the ASPCA; groomer Jim Stewart of Caniche; dog trainer Job
Michael Evans; Dr. Mark Lerman; and Dr. Ben E. Sheffy, Assistant
Director of the James A. Baker Institute for Animal Health, Cornell
University.

I'd like Dr. William J. Kay, Chief of Staff of the Animal Medical
Center, to know that I am honored and grateful to him for writing the
Foreword. And I wish to thank my friend Grace Bechtold for
helping make this book possible, and my fine editor Jeanne
Bernkopf for making it a lot better.

Lastly, a pat on the head to all the many dogs I know, for being
themselves.

P.C.

CONTENTS

PREFACE

When you read this book, you'll notice that I use the pronoun "it" when referring to a dog. Of course, no dog is an "it." My use of this word stems from the failure of the English language to provide a singular pronoun that applies to both genders, as the plural pronoun "them" does very nicely. To avoid the tiresome repetition of "he and she," "him and her," and "his and hers," I had to fall back on *it* and *its*. My apologies to all dogs and their owners for this.

I also wish there were a word other than "owner" to use when referring to the person responsible for a dog. The law still considers our dogs property, even though we all know that they are much more than that. "Parent" is certainly too coy, although in a way we do parent our pets.

As yet, there is no satisfactory word that clearly fits our relationship with our dogs; perhaps one will evolve in the light of the new interest in this animal's meaning to us. Meanwhile, for referring to their people as owners, my apologies to dogs.

FOREWORD

Urbanization in the United States has created the need for dog owners, as well as people planning or contemplating dog ownership, to learn much more about the many issues that must be considered in order to create a truly enjoyable relationship with dogs in a city environment. Success with our canine friends is not automatic. This book, a compilation of excellent data and good story, is packed with useful information. Just about any issue that a city dog owner, experienced or otherwise, needs to know is here.

As a veterinarian, I have observed and experienced thousands of dogs and their owners. Here at the Animal Medical Center, we treat 64,000 animals a year, including 35,000 dogs. I can tell you that the human/dog relationship can be wonderful, or it can be less than satisfying. Both the hazards and the delights are covered in *The Urban Dog*. Whether you are a many-dog person, with several canine pets already in your household, or a novice contemplating your first, this book is a must.

I particularly enjoyed the chapter entitled "The Urban Dog: Choosing the best for you." Many people make mistakes by obtaining the wrong dog (for them) at the wrong time in their lives.

The chapters on diet, health, and first aid are clear and accurate.

Ms. Curtis has written extensively in the book about the problems of dogs in urban housing. Her description of the battles between landlords and dog owners, and the recourses available to dog owners, alone are worth the price of her book.

Patricia Curtis is particularly well qualified to address the subject of the urban dog, for her love of animals and experience as a writer on animals are well known. I found the book easy to read and entertaining, as well as useful. Ms. Curtis writes with experience, perception, and deep affection for dogs. If we follow her guidelines and use even a few of the many wisdoms set forth in *The Urban Dog*, our relationship with man's best friend will be just that: best friends.

William J. Kay, D.V.M.

Diplomate, American
College of Veterinary
Internal Medicine

Chief of Staff,
The Animal Medical
Center, New York

CHAPTER 1

THE URBAN DOG:
Choosing the Best for You

Dog: a four-legged carnivorous animal whose natural habitat, in most parts of the world, is the human home. The creature comes in various sizes and shapes and is sometimes beloved, sometimes mistreated, and often wrongly taken for granted.

The early canids evolved in such close association with the first human beings that nobody knows for certain just when or how the relationship began. Presumably, wild dogs hung around the caves or campsites and scavenged for the remains of meals. According to early cave paintings, primitive people trained these wild dogs to hunt with them; the animals' keen hearing, sense of smell, and speed were no doubt useful.

But those humans took from their environment only what they needed for survival and were gatherers as much as hunters, so dogs must have performed other functions as well. They probably gave warning when strangers approached. Perhaps their pups were playmates for the children. They also might have filled a need for companionship, as they most definitely do today.

The way I imagine it, one cold wet day when a cave man (or

woman) returned from a successful hunt, the dog stopped as usual at the entrance of the warm cave and looked in hopefully.

"Oh, all right, come on in," the man (or woman) said, and made a gesture inviting the animal in out of the bad weather.

When the dog walked warily across the threshold, it took a giant step that affected the lives of all dogs thereafter. It cast its lot with us and became domesticated. It may have had cause to regret it many times since.

When people were little more than barbarians, they probably treated dogs worse than they did each other. Eventually, certain fortunate dogs were upgraded to the status of pets and fared better, though in some societies they were still looked upon as little more than vermin. Certainly, references to the dog in the Bible are contemptuous.

I will spare you the details of the brutal general treatment of dogs from the Middle Ages up until the first anticruelty laws of the nineteenth century. And even today, dogs endure monstrous cruelty in many places, and not just in poor and backward countries—they may be abused and neglected even in the genteel neighborhoods of modern America.

Nevertheless, millions of dogs live with us in our caves in cities. Over half of all American households have dogs or cats, or both. The animals have adapted to our ways and made themselves indispensable to us.

Let me tell you how I got my first urban dog.

One Sunday afternoon many years ago I was walking with some friends in Central Park in New York City, where I live, when we met a little brown dog running loose. Heartless people who want to get rid of dogs frequently use Central Park as a dumping ground. It's said that packs of feral dogs (former pets that are now homeless and have more or less reverted to a wild state) exist there, though I have never seen any such packs, and the survival rate among them, like that of most abandoned dogs, can't be very high.

However, many people let their dogs run off the leash in the park, in spite of the city ordinance against it. And so we looked around for any possible owner of the brown dog and did not encourage him to follow us, especially since he didn't look particularly starved or unkempt.

But follow us he did. His behavior was extremely anxious and humble—a telltale sign of an abandoned dog.

Two little boys materialized; the dog seemed to know them. "He used to be our dog," one replied to our question. "But our father got a German Shepherd he liked better."

So that was it—the kids had been told to lose the dog in the park. One child picked up the dog in his arms. "Here, lady," he said to me.

Just like that, I became a dog owner. I borrowed the drawstring from a companion's parka and put it around the dog's neck as a makeshift leash. He acted willing, even relieved, to come along with us.

When I got him home, my family's two cats eyed him suspiciously, though without fear. He sized them up, and realizing that they lived there, he apparently guessed, correctly, that if he was to live there also, it would not be smart to chase them. So he kept his distance. From then on, his behavior toward them was the height of decorum.

I named the Central Park dog Benjy. He looked rather like a small deer—short brown coat, big eyes, big ears, slender longish legs. His ancestry must have included some Basenji, though unlike the true Basenji he had a perfectly serviceable bark.

Benjy was our good dog for nine years, and when he died, I missed him terribly. I could see him lying in all his favorite spots; I could hear the tick-tack of his nails across the floor. Unconsciously, I expected to find him waiting inside the door each time I returned home.

Ten days later, I couldn't stand being dogless any longer, so I answered an ad in the *Village Voice*. A young couple living in a garden apartment with a whole passel of dogs and cats wanted to pare down.

Poor two-year-old Dandy was the dog fingered for giveaway, and suddenly, as I was sitting in the apartment talking to the couple, she *knew*. She crawled into a corner under the bed. Her former owner had to pull her out, drag her from the house, and stuff her into a taxicab with me.

Dandy was depressed for a few days, but settled in bravely. Today, this minute, twelve years later, she is lying by my chair. She is a beloved pet, one of the great delights of my life, friend to my family, cats, friends, and the entire neighborhood.

Dandy illustrates another time-honored way of acquiring a pet. Perhaps it was just marvelous luck that both dogs, Benjy and Dandy, for whom there was almost no calculated choice on my part, turned out to be perfect city dogs. Or maybe they are both examples of the triumph of environment over heredity.

Dogs, like people, owe their temperaments and intelligence to a complex combination of their genes and the interaction of their genetic programming with their individual life experiences. And there's one additional factor in dogs: They have a strong desire to adjust to the people they love, so they are amazingly flexible.

If you already have a dog—have taken in a stray, adopted one from an animal shelter or a private home, or gone out and bought one—you may have acquired a winner and be reading this book just for additional information and, I hope, pleasure. I'll try to provide you with ideas for steps you can take to make living with your pet in the city more comfortable and rewarding for both of you.

On the other hand, you may be about to choose a dog and wish to go about it in the most clear-eyed and sensible way possible. It is a serious commitment and should be permanent for the natural life of the dog. And I am here to help you make it. So let's get to the things you should be considering.

YOUR LIFESTYLE

There should be nothing tentative about acquiring a dog—it ought to be almost like adopting a child. You wouldn't keep in the back of your mind the notion that you could always return the baby to the adoption agency if it got too big, or you had to move, or it turned out to be a bother. Having a dog is a privilege and a joy, but if you aren't prepared to put up with the hassles, take the responsibility, and be its friend for life, you should forgo the pleasure.

Very few dogs are misfits in cities, but many are the wrong dogs for the homes they're in. Selecting an appropriate dog seems a matter of common sense, yet if it really is so self-evident, why do we see so many poorly matched pets and owners?

On my block, for instance, a frustrated young Giant Schnauzer pulls at the leash held by an elderly lady who loves him dearly but did not consider beforehand the exercise needs of this spirited animal—nor did she anticipate the difficulty she would have in controlling him. The problem with this dog is not that he lives in the city. He could thrive with a city dweller who took him for long, vigorous daily walks and trained him properly.

On the other hand, a muscular male jogger whipped by me the other evening accompanied by a panting little skeleton of a dog.

The lady and the jogger were oblivious to their pets' misery. Some owners wise up soon enough, but then there's an emotional strain on all concerned if the dog must be given away. The solution is to think well before you acquire a dog.

I once met a couple at a party who told me about a mistake they had made. They had thought it was a nifty idea to get a pair of glossy Irish Setter puppies. The couple were both at work all day, so the pups demolished the apartment. And as the dogs quickly grew into hyperactive adolescents, neither the wife nor the husband felt like walking the two maniacs for an hour at the end of a hard day, much less like taking them to obedience classes. It was not easy to find new homes for them, and in the end they had to be separated not only from the home and people they had grown to love, but from each other.

If the couple had devoted some time and consistent effort to training the two dogs, in a few months they probably could have had two well-behaved Irish Setters. Or, if they had thought more beforehand about their choice, they might have realized that a pair of older dogs, and a less high-strung breed or mixture of breeds, would have worked out very well.

Be realistic about what you wish in a dog and what your lifestyle is, don't have unfair expectations of the animal, and then try to get it all together.

One of your biggest considerations is, of course, the size of the dog. Dogs under 20 pounds are small; dogs 20 to more or less 60 pounds are considered medium-size; large dogs are roughly between 65 and 120 pounds; any dog that weighs in above 120 probably falls into the giant breed category. When you are deciding between big and little, remember that a small dog can be toted about the city in a carrier, even on public transportation. That's helpful when you want to take it to the veterinarian, to visit a friend, on a plane trip, maybe even to work with you as some people in rare and privileged circumstances can. Anyone who has ever tried to hail a taxi with a medium-size or large dog on the leash knows what a frustrating experience that can be.

Another basic consideration is whether to choose a puppy or an adult dog. A dog, by the way, is considered a puppy until it is nearly a year old, though very small breeds may reach their full growth at six months, while very large breeds may take as long as fourteen months. A puppy will require much, much more of your time, for many months, than an adult dog will. In a household of very busy people, the dog that will cause the least trouble and require the least amount of time, comparatively, is an older dog.

Nevertheless, if your idea of the dog for you is a large puppy, then that's what you should have, even in the city. But do yourself a favor and at least get one that's temperamentally suitable for city living, and be sure to obedience-train it.

Are you very fussy about your home and easily upset by mess? Though the great pleasure and comfort of having a dog far outweighs the nuisance of occasional clean-up jobs, the presence of a dog is bound to have some impact, especially in an apartment. Your feelings about shedding, paw prints, and the like should be a consideration in the type of dog you choose. So keep in mind the length of its fur as well as its trainability.

SPACE AND TIME

How big is your house or apartment? If you think I'm going to suggest that unless you own a big townhouse you should have nothing but a tiny dog, you're wrong. Much more depends on how much time you can give to your pet.

As a rule of thumb, small-to-medium-size dogs are probably more practical than large ones for busy city people who work outside the home. While some small breeds (certain terriers, for instance) do need quite a lot of exercise, they generally don't require the *distance* exercise that the retrievers and other big-chested, long-legged, active types need. To some people, this is a definite advantage. A little dog can let off steam running around indoors, and, to it, a turn around the block is a real excursion, while a large, spirited dog is just getting started.

However, if you want a running partner, or like to take long walks, you do want a big, hardy dog. A little short-legged canine is not for you—you'd have to carry it all the way home.

Even a Great Dane could live happily enough, even in a studio apartment, with an owner who could provide plenty of long, time-consuming walks. Let's say you do fall in love with a big lovable hulk of a dog and you're certain you'd like to live with it on a day-in, day-out basis in the confines of the city. I say go ahead, as long as you can devote lots of time to taking it out.

Time is especially important during a dog's first weeks in your home. Bill Berloni of Berloni Theatrical Animals, who earns his living largely by his ability to select and train dogs, recommends that you adopt a dog on a Friday and devote the entire first weekend to getting to know it and helping it to settle in with you. Some dogs learn faster than others; some may need several weekends of your undivided attention, with brush-up courses in between, to become truly good urban dogs.

SEX AND LIFE EXPECTANCY

Female dogs are said to be easier to train than males, and they are likely to be more docile than males, a desirable trait for city living. Some dog lovers consider females more affectionate and companionable, though in loyalty to the memory of my male dog Benjy, I have to question that. There's no evidence that one sex is more intelligent than the other.

Here's something you may not have thought of: A female dog can hold her urine longer than a male—some can wait as long as twelve hours if necessary—which might be an advantage in a household where no one is home during the day. Also, when you walk a female dog, she will empty her bladder all at once. A male dog urinates in little spurts here and there, and it takes him seemingly forever to relieve himself, especially on cold winter nights.

But you will certainly want to neuter your pet (see Chapter 6), and it's more expensive to neuter a female than a male.

As to life expectancy, you should be aware that the common belief that each year of a dog's life equals seven human years is highly inaccurate. A year-old dog is a sexually mature teenager, not a seven-year-old child. A two-year-old dog of any breed is comparable to a young adult person in his or her mid-twenties, certainly not a fourteen-year-old adolescent. After that, you might estimate that each year of a dog's life equals roughly four human years—but you have to figure the dog's life expectancy into the equation, and life spans vary considerably.

In general, the toy breeds and other small dogs live longest; many are still perky at fifteen years or more. A medium-size dog (Springer Spaniel, Bearded Collie, Husky, and mixed breeds of those approximate dimensions) can easily live to ten, and longer with luck and good care. Dandy, who is about the size of a Springer Spaniel, is fourteen—very elderly but in good health. A Great Dane or other specimen of the giant breeds has an average life span of six or seven years, and it's a miracle if one lives to ten.

THE COST FACTOR

Think hard to be sure you can afford a dog, now and in the foreseeable long-term future. I'm not talking about the initial outlay, but the cost of feeding and maintaining for years to come.

Big dogs of course cost more to feed than small ones, but they don't live as long.

You'll need a license every year. A collar, leash, shampoo, maybe a coat. If you like a fluffy or curly dog, better add professional grooming fees to your cost estimate, especially with certain purebreds.

Be sure to figure on veterinary bills, whether you choose a big or little dog, purebred or mixed breed. Even a dog that enjoys good health for most of its life will need neutering, checkups, annual vaccinations. In its old age, it will undoubtedly need expensive medical care from time to time.

And in case your pet has a serious accident or illness, would you mind sacrificing, if necessary, to get it well? Every animal shelter with a clinic can show you dogs that were brought in sick or injured and then abandoned when the owners learned what the vet bills would be.

One shelter I know tells the story of a beautiful young Husky whose owners brought her in to the veterinary clinic with fractured forelegs; she had been hit by a car. When her owners were told what the charges would be for setting the poor animal's legs, they balked.

"We'll give her up and adopt a new, healthy dog," they offered.

"Not from this shelter, you won't," said the outraged shelter manager. "This dog is hurt but not incurable. You don't bring in a broken dog and trade it in for a new one, like a vacuum cleaner or a radio."

The veterinarian set the Husky's legs, and the shelter publicized her case, complete with a picture in the newspaper. Sure enough, several prospective owners materialized, and the lucky dog went off with one as soon as her legs were out of the casts.

With proper care, your dog will be with you many years. If you contemplate retiring in a few years and living on a lowered or limited income, this should be a consideration in your choice of a pet. It might be wise to adopt a small, middle-aged dog.

CHILDREN

If you're acquiring a dog that's to be a pal to the children, think ahead to the time when the kids will be out of the nest for good.

I'll never forget seeing a Spaniel turned into an animal shelter by a man who, grinning sheepishly, explained that the dog was his daughter's, but she was off at college now, and he and his wife didn't want the trouble of keeping a dog. The frightened animal apparently guessed what was happening and had to be dragged bodily into the shelter, all the while trying frantically to ingratiate herself with the man and everybody else.

The Spaniel may have been a devoted, sweet-tempered, well-behaved pet, but no matter—she had outlived her usefulness and was no longer convenient to keep. So she was discarded like an outgrown toy. Her chances of being adopted from the shelter were nil. She was middle-aged and not particularly beautiful. The shelter was crowded with dogs that needed homes, dogs that were younger and more appealing than she. I learned later that she was killed within two days.

By contrast, for several years I saw in my neighborhood a gray-haired man walking a very old dog who, he told me, had been left behind by grown children. When this dog died, it was not replaced—but it had been allowed to live out its life comfortably in its own home.

Never get a dog for a child with the idea that the dog will "teach the child responsibility." Although a dog can be a wonderful companion, playmate, confidant, and comfort for a child, it should not be expected to be a teacher. It will not, by itself, transform a child into a responsible person, no matter how much wishful thinking on the parents' part. It is highly unfair for a dog to have to depend on a little kid for its food, walks, and other needs.

And while a dog is an especially good pet for a teenager (as a friend of mine put it, "My dog got me through my adolescence"), the well-known forgetfulness and self-preoccupation of even the best-intentioned teenagers usually make them poor candidates as the sole caretakers of living creatures.

Face it: Parents must be willing and able to assume the care of a dog themselves, or to ride shotgun on their children to see that they do it and do it right. Nothing less is humanely acceptable.

Never give a child a dog for a Christmas present—or rather, if the pet is to be a present, don't bring it into the household right at Christmas. There is too much noise, activity, and excitement. The animal won't be at its best. It will either become frightened and shy, or overstimulated and keyed up—and in either case, it will probably get an upset stomach (at both ends). A child old enough to understand can be given instead a leash, collar, and a picture of a dog with the promise that the pet is coming in, say, ten days. Or better yet, take the child to help pick out the dog, after the holidays.

While pet shops do a brisk business selling puppies at Christmas, many good shelters refuse to allow their pets to be adopted during Christmas week. They ask instead that people come back after New Year's when the holiday bustle has quieted. This greatly lowers the chances that the gift animal will be returned to the shelter by mid-January.

Many breeds and many individual dogs, while fine with older children and adults, are not suitable for families with infants, toddlers, preschoolers, or kindergartners. Some older dogs are unnerved by the unsteady gait, abrupt gestures, and seemingly strange noises very young children make, and will shy away or even bite in fear. Also, a grown dog may already have had bad experiences with children and formed a dislike for them, so it's important to find out first, at the time you adopt or buy a grown dog, how it feels about kids.

My dog Benjy was as pleasant a dog as you could possibly want with adults, but children made him nervous. He once even nipped the little girl of a visiting friend. He barely broke the skin, but scared the child, of course, and caused me intense embarrassment and concern.

Dandy, on the other hand, is sweet and patient with every child she meets, tolerating even the loudest squeals and the most inept petting (tots usually pet from back to front, against the grain).

If you have, or will have, children, look for a breed or mixture of breeds that has a reputation for being especially good with children. (For some suggestions, see "Temperament," below.)

Even so, it's well to remember that virtually all dogs will defend themselves if frightened, mauled too roughly, or actually hurt. Parents with children must be prepared to teach them firmly how to treat a dog with kindness and respect. In return, the children will be rewarded with the dog's legendary devotion.

NOBODY HOME

A sad and subdued little dog of my acquaintance is the only pet of someone who is almost literally never home, day or night. This person also travels out of town a lot, and though his neighbors tell me that someone comes in once a day to walk and feed the dog, perfunctorily, she is virtually alone for weeks at a time. That is no life for a social animal like a dog. She needs more than exercise: She is starved for companionship and affection.

Loneliness is a prime reason that some dogs bark and whine endlessly when left alone. In the city, this can be a major cause of conflict between dog owners and their neighbors or landlords. Although you can train a dog not to cry when you're out, it might be more kind to start out with two compatible dogs, perhaps siblings (though I suggest not Irish Setter puppies).

A cat can also be a good companion for a dog (see Chapter 9).

If you travel, work long hours, or are socially very active and out a good deal, you'll want to have back-up care available for your pet. A reliable live-in sitter, a really solid arrangement with a friend or neighbor, or an excellent affordable boarding kennel is needed (see Chapter 12).

An explanation frequently heard at the receiving desk at animal shelters is, "We're just not home enough to take care of him/her." Too bad that wasn't thought of before the dog was acquired in the first place.

TEMPERAMENT

The prime concern of a city person choosing a dog should be the animal's temperament. And the type of dog that will be easiest to live with in an urban environment is one that's gentle and submissive, low in dominance. This doesn't mean a dog that's a timid wimp, but an easygoing one that won't be difficult to train, that won't give you an argument every time you say "No!" or "Heel." A high-dominance dog is usually hyper, headstrong, difficult to control.

The reason dominance is important is that dogs are by nature pack animals, and you, or someone in your family, will be its pack leader. A submissive dog won't be forever challenging the pack leader and trying to get its own way. I'll talk more about dominance in later chapters such as 3, "Understanding," and 4, "Training." But because it figures in your choice of a dog for city living, it is important to mention here.

Dogs are very quick to recognize a pack leader. When I was a child, we took in a little stray dog that became my loyal playmate and companion. Laddie loved us all, but he obviously decided my father was pack leader. It wasn't that my father ever spent much time with the dog, or trained him. Dad was a very strong personality—my sister and I called him the Benevolent Despot—but that wasn't the whole reason for Laddy's respect for him. What apparently impressed Laddie was that the family treated my father as head of the household. Laddie took his cue from us and chose never to challenge the top dog.

It's easy to assume that the smaller the dog, the more suitable it is for city living. T'ain't necessarily so. Miniature Schnauzers, for instance, and some toy breeds such as Pomeranians, Pekingese,

Yorkshire Terriers, Chihuahuas, Toy Poodles, and mixtures of same are notorious yappers. They not only bark when a burglar tries to pick your lock, which is good, but they bark at neighbors, guests, the super, deliverymen, and imaginary intruders, which is not good. If you really want a dog that will fit in your pocket, choose carefully. Look for an individual animal that has an exceptionally calm temperament. If you get a real barker (and those little dogs' barks can be ear-splitting), you or your neighbors—or your landlord—may lose patience before you can train your pet to bark only selectively.

Some breeds of dogs are reputed to be higher, or lower, in dominance than others. There will always be exceptions among individual dogs, of course. But in general, the following breeds are considered to have stable temperaments and to be amenable to training, all of which make them good choices as city dogs. You might want to consider one of these purebred types or a mixed breed whose ancestry includes one or several of these.

Note that while virtually all dogs shed and require at least some grooming, and all need exercise, I have indicated those which are high in these requirements (gr., ex.). And while most dogs will be comfortable around older, considerate children, those breeds with exceptionally good reputations for tolerating young children are indicated (ch.).

Basset Hound (ch.)	Lhasa Apso (gr.)
Beagle (ex., ch.)	Miniature Poodle (gr.)
Bearded Collie (ex., ch.)	Norwegian Elkhound (gr., ch.)
Bichon Frise (gr., ch.)	Shetland Sheepdog (ch.)
Boston Terrier (ch.)	Shih Tzu (gr.)
Cairn Terrier	Siberian Husky (gr., ex., ch.)
Corgi (ex.)	Springer Spaniel (gr., ex., ch.)
Dachshund	Standard Poodle (gr., ex., ch.)
English Setter (ex., ch.)	West Highland Terrier
Golden Retriever (ex., ch.)	Wheaten Terrier (ch.)
Labrador Retriever (ex., ch.)	

You will see plenty of other types of dogs on the streets of every city in America whose owners think they're the best. There's a ninety-pound Briard in my neighborhood, a breed that few people would recommend as a city dog, but this animal is a model of excellent behavior and seems quite content.

One trendy dog is the Akita—big, handsome, alert, and strong-willed. It must be socialized very early as a puppy and trained not to attack other dogs.

"I have a lot of clients with problem Akitas," says Job Michael Evans, a dog trainer in New York City, shaking his head. "An Akita could be fine with the right type of owner in a spread-out city like, say, Los Angeles. But in a crowded city like New York, with a high density of dogs with whom an Akita has to rub shoulders every time it goes for a walk, well, it can give its owner and everybody involved a hard time."

And by the way, a city person choosing a dog should be aware that certain breeds—many hounds, for example—are known to be difficult to housebreak.

So, in selecting an urban dog, why ask for trouble? Better to take advantage of a breed or mixture of breeds with a suitable track record for city life. One person you might want to consult for advice is a dog trainer (carefully chosen, see Chapter 4) or perhaps an urban veterinarian, who certainly has a chance to observe the temperament as well as the general health of many different types of dogs.

PUREBRED VS. MIXED BREED

If what you want in a dog is affection, beauty, intelligence, fun, and perhaps some protection, a creature that will be your companion and enrich your life a million times over, then it doesn't matter whether you purchase a fancy purebred from a breeder or bail a mongrel waif out of the dog pound. Most any dog, given love, training, and proper care, can provide what you're looking for. Dogs share certain qualities of dogginess, and therein lies their wonderful gift to human beings. All domestic canids, in their marvelously infinite variety, are still dogs.

All the different breeds, from the 3-pound Pomeranian to the 175-

pound Mastiff, from the practically hairless Chihuahua to the
Komondor with its floor-length ropes of hair, were created by human
beings. From that wolflike creature that took to hanging around us so
many millenia ago, dogs have not followed an evolutionary path of
their own but have been molded by people into whatever we needed
or fancied.

It's impossible to get an accurate figure on the percentage of
purebreds among owned dogs in the United States, but a reasonable
estimate is about one-third. Some people have a strong preference
for a certain breed of dog, and for them, nothing else will do. I know
a man who simply loves English Bulldogs and has had one after
another, putting up with their wheezing and snoring and drooling
because he likes their funny faces and endearing personalities. If he
couldn't have an English Bulldog, he might pass up having a dog at
all.

There is something to be said on both sides of the purebred vs.
mixed breed debate.

With a purebred dog, you'll have some clues to the temperament
you can expect. In some mixed-breed dogs, the ancestry is quite
apparent, and you can be guided by what is known about the
personalities of the breeds they combine. Nevertheless, a dog's
environment plays a big role in its temperament. And the bottom
line is that dogs are individuals. A neighbor of mine had a Shetland
Sheepdog who was timid and snappish, but his successor, also a
male Sheltie from the same breeder, is poised and agreeable.

Purebreds and mixed breeds seem about equally liable to develop
behavior problems. Many people believe that purebreds are more
likely to be nervous and high-strung; however, if they have been
carefully bred for temperament as well as looks, this shouldn't be
true.

It's sometimes said that mixed-breed dogs are innately healthier
than purebreds. It is true that with purebred dogs there's the risk of
harmful inbreeding, especially among those from unscrupulous or
amateur breeders. Inbreeding can cause health defects to become
dominant.

Unfortunately, many purebred dogs have been bred for qualities
that appeal to the dog fancy but aren't in the best interests of the

animals. Examples of this are the Pekingese, whose pop eyes are subject to chronic lacerations; the English Bulldog, whose short snout causes severe respiratory problems; and that rare and expensive curiosity, the Shar-Pei, whose deeply wrinkled skin, not surprisingly, suffers chronic dermatological disorders. Inbreeding of some popular breeds such as German Shepherds and Golden Retrievers has caused hip dysplasia to become widespread among them.

At the peak of its popularity a few years ago, that appealing breed, the Cocker Spaniel, was ruined by inbreeding. Your average pet shop Cocker became snappish, suspicious. Fortunately, those bred by very reliable professionals remained sweet family dogs, great with children, but even today, buyers of Cockers would do well to choose carefully.

One problem with purebred dogs is that when a breed becomes popular there is a responding upsurge in the production of these dogs. Puppy mills get busy. Puppy mills, in case you aren't familiar with the term, are wholesale, factorylike places where masses of dogs are "manufactured" as fast as the bitches can give birth. The offspring, who may already be in poor health because their mothers were, are then shipped to pet shops throughout the land to meet the demands of the dog-buying public.

Transportation takes a heavy toll on these young puppies, and many sicken and die en route or arrive at the pet shops half dead. Then, the atmosphere in the average pet shop is conducive to the spread of disease, so even puppies that have survived shipment may become sickly.

Backyard breeders—enthusiastic novices who have one or a few pedigreed animals but who lack professionalism—jump on the bandwagon too, turning out pups to sell.

Both sorts of money-inspired breeding usually pass on from one generation to the next the chronic predisposition to health problems that plague so many breeds: hip dysplasia, eye defects, tumors, and bloat, among other disorders. When dogs are bred to make a buck, little or no attention is paid to genetic excellence.

Meanwhile, the truly reputable breeders try to meet the demand for a popular breed on the one hand, while also carefully trying to screen out defects and perpetuate only desirable qualities, including good temperament. That is why, if you feel you must have an adorable pedigreed Bichon Frise or a magnificent purebred Labrador Retriever, do search out the very best breeder you can. (For tips on breeders, see Chapter 2.)

Some people with allergies find that they aren't sensitive to Poodles. Apparently the dense, tightly curled coats of Poodles don't contain the allergens that other dogs' hair may have.

Show standards for some breeds—Great Danes, Dobermans, Boxers, Cocker Spaniels, Springer Spaniels, and Standard Schnauzers, for example—dictate that the animal must have cosmetic surgery: parts of their tails or ears, or both, cut off. Tail docking and ear cropping offer no health advantages to the dogs, but are supposed to effect what the dog fancy has decreed is a more aesthetically correct look.

Tail docking is usually performed on the puppies when they are only a few days old, so you won't have any say in the matter if you buy one of those breeds from a breeder. It is performed without anesthesia and is said not to hurt the animal.

Ear cropping is another matter; that is usually done when the dog is three or four months old. The operation must be performed under general anesthesia, by a veterinarian, who forces the ear cartilage into the desired shape, then tapes and binds the ears to hold the shape. The ears take about two weeks, sometimes longer, to heal. The whole thing must surely be an uncomfortable if not painful experience for a dog. Sometimes there are complications from the surgery.

Breeders who might personally harbor reservations about docking and cropping have no choice if they wish to sell their dogs. While some buyers whose dogs are going to be pets, not show competitors, would decline to have their dogs' ears cropped, others would not want to forfeit the status that presumably accrues from having a purebred dog that looks like others of its kind.

I personally find it reprehensible to mutilate a dog for such a frivolous reason. A growing number of states have followed England's example and made ear cropping illegal, but in states where it is allowed, the American Kennel Club still requires cropped ears and/or docked tails if certain breeds are to meet their show standards.

Dog shows are a pastime for people, not dogs, though harmless enough in most respects, I suppose. I'm told that some dogs actually enjoy being shown. But I'm puzzled by dog lovers who not only breed in qualities such as pop eyes and short snouts that impair dogs' comfort and health, but put dogs through cosmetic surgery for no other reason than human fancy.

Owners of fighting dogs (called Pit Bulls, in the vernacular, but American Staffordshire Terriers when purebred) often crop their dogs' ears themselves for another reason. Dogfighting, by the way, is not the occasional tomfoolery of a few backwoods rednecks, but a clandestine, illegal "sport" involving huge sums of money that goes on in all parts of the United States. In a dogfight, one dog might rip its opponent's ear, causing the other dog such pain that it retreats and loses the fight. To prevent this, many owners routinely cut off their dogs' ears. One dog that had suffered such barbarism was rescued by the Michigan Humane Society; its ears were no more than bloody stumps. "I wanted him to look mean," explained the owner, who was taken to court by the Humane Society, forced to pay a fine, and put on probation for two years, during which time he was forbidden to own a dog, any dog. (His earless dog was adopted from the Humane Society by a caring, nonviolent family.)

Mixed-breed dogs are usually the offspring of random matings by animals heeding the call of nature and without human choice in the matter. The pups may inherit all or some of the best qualities of the parents, rarely only the worst. If someone's lovable pet has mated with the dog down the block who is also a great pet, the chances are good that the puppies will have a temperament that makes them nice companion dogs.

As far as I am concerned, mixed-breed dogs have everything purebreds have except what is considered class. This matters more to some people than to others.

A friend once said to me that I should not refer to Dandy as a mixed breed, but give her a little class—make up a breed just for her.

"What would you suggest?" I asked, looking at my beautiful dog and wondering which of her ancestors contributed the dominant genes.

"Well, she probably has some Spaniel in her, and she has red hair," he observed. "Why not call her a South Irish Spaniel?"

A few days later, a man standing next to me in line at the bank was petting her. (Strangers are attracted to Dandy all the time because of her sweet expression.) "What kind of dog is this?" he asked.

Now was my chance. "She's a South Irish Spaniel," I replied, deadpan.

"Oh!" said he. "Those are marvelous dogs!"

SHELTER DOGS AND STRAYS

I have a strong bias in favor of choosing shelter dogs and strays. Of the many city dogs I know personally, well over half of the most attractive, in terms of disposition, behavior, and looks, were adopted from shelters or found. And after all, my Central Park dog, Benjy, was certainly one of the best dogs that ever lived.

Animal shelters offer a wide selection of dogs—young and not-so-young, big and little, homely and gorgeous, you name it. They often have purebreds. Usually shelter staff members can give you information on the temperament and background of a dog that interests you.

A shelter dog that has just been surrendered from a private home may be a good bet—it depends on why it was given up. A dog whose owner died, or was threatened with eviction because of a no-pet clause, or even dumped the animal for some half-baked reason can be a better pet than a dog that has come from a breeder or pet shop and never lived in a home.

True, a shelter dog may have been surrendered because of a behavior problem. Since few people will admit that the dog they are abandoning has behavior habits that they were unable, or unwilling,

"Do urban dogs suffer? Are you kidding?" *(Hope Ryden)*

Sidewalk socializing: city dogs and their owners. *(David Cupp)*

One of the best places to get a dog is in an animal shelter. Here, a puppy waits. *(Jane Sapinsky/Courtesy, Bide-a-Wee Home Association)*

A puppy, abandoned by its owner, is comforted by a shelter worker. *(Erik Friedl/From the film* Kiss The Animals Goodbye*)*

A little boy has just adopted a puppy from an animal shelter. Let anybody try to take it away from him. *(Jane Hutchison/Courtesy, Humane Society of Santa Clara Valley)*

Denning. A city pet nevertheless retains this primitive urge. *(Hope Ryden)*

Three family dogs meet the new pack member. *(Billy Powell/Courtesy, Pets Are Wonderful Council)*

to correct, they may not tell the shelter about it. Some people even lie.

"Is the dog housebroken?" the shelter worker asks.

"Oh, yes," replies the owner, who half an hour ago wiped up a puddle for the last exasperated time.

But that should not discourage you. Any dog that has lived in a cage for any length of time, whether at a breeder's, pet shop, or shelter, will almost certainly have to be housebroken by you. You might have to start from scratch, or you may only have to give the dog a refresher course, but the fact that a shelter dog is not house-trained is no reason to reject it.

An understanding person, using good sense and how-to information, can usually correct a behavior problem. Also, a dog that's a mess in one home may turn out to be perfectly well mannered in the hands of the right owner in the proper environment.

The difficulty in judging a shelter dog is complicated by the fact that a normally excellent dog may be so upset by being abandoned by its family, or may have had such terrifying experiences as a stray, that it is not itself. Some become hysterical, some depressed. I believe that if Dandy were somehow separated from her secure world and wound up in a shelter, she would simply let herself die.

Bill Berloni gets all his theatrical dogs from shelters. "I look for the dog who is not barking and carrying on, but is handling well the stress of being confined," he says. "Living in a cage is highly stressful to a dog, whether it's at a shelter, breeder's, or pet shop. If a dog in such a situation comes up to you and acts friendly, but doesn't go berserk with excitement when you speak to it, that's a good sign."

Berloni does recommend distinguishing between a dog that is quiet because it's depressed and one that's quiet but aggressive and maybe what trainers and shelter people call a fear-biter. The fear-biter may be quietly watching for a chance to get even for abuse it has suffered.

A major concern in adopting a shelter dog is its health. Animal shelters vary—I have visited nearly fifty in all parts of the United States. A few could be favorably compared to a college dormitory, not bad at all, while others are more like Auschwitz. Most fall somewhere in between. A clean, well-run shelter will probably have clean, healthy dogs. One hard fact of life is that a sickly dog at an up-to-date animal shelter is usually screened out quickly and euthanized, so the dogs up for adoption are healthy.

Obviously, it's easier to adopt the clean, healthy dog. But the other one, the poor animal in the hellhole shelter, really needs you. Know your capabilities and limits—I want adopting a dog to work for both of you.

One very good reason for adopting a shelter dog or stray is the wonderful feeling you get from knowing you have saved its life. Many people believe that animal shelters can find new homes for the pets they discard. This is magic thinking and eases any guilt the owners might feel about doing it.

The fact is that some seven million unwanted and homeless dogs wind up in shelters and pounds nationwide, each year. In spite of vigorous adoption campaigns waged by the shelters, only 20 to 30 percent of those pets ever leave. Since the shelters and pounds simply haven't the resources to care for the animals that aren't adopted, many are euthanized—nearly five million dogs a year, six hundred every hour. Those SPCAs, humane societies, and similar shelter societies that, by local contract with their communities, must accept any animal brought to them are forced to become mercy killers for people who discard or abandon their pets.

Many a dog, when it dawns on it that you're taking it home, out of the shelter or off the street, will go crazy with joy, leaping around, trying to lick your face, wagging its tail till it almost flies off. What dog lover can resist that flattering ecstasy? Often a powerful bond forms between you on the spot.

A dog that's had a hard life as a stray, or suffered abuse, may be so grateful to you for rescuing it that it remains anxious to please you for the rest of its life. Some dogs never forget that you were their savior.

A notable exception is my neighbor Paula's dog Lady. When Paula's two elderly Pekingese, Portnoy and Princess, passed on to the great plush sofa in the sky (that's what I imagine heaven is like for a Pekingese), Paula steadfastly refused my generous offers to get her another dog—or rather, she resisted my efforts to persuade her to adopt this or that dog I knew of that needed a home.

But one day Paula heard of a case she couldn't refuse: A stray who was found with its throat cut. If ever a dog had reason to be thankful for a loving home, it would be Lady, right? Not this little mutt. Lady is spirited, strong-willed, takes her great good luck for granted, and pulls Paula down the street at a run.

Paula is taking her to obedience classes and will win in the end, I'm sure. Lady will undoubtedly learn to be a good urban dog. But gratitude won't be the reason.

When you really know and love dogs, you can often simply follow your intuition. I once found a little reddish-brown dog huddled in a doorway on a busy street when I was on my way to the dentist. One look and I knew she was homeless. When my appointment was finished, I returned with food and water for her. She was still there; the doorway was set in a small recessed entry, so perhaps she felt safe there. She wouldn't allow me to touch her, but bared her teeth and growled, shrinking back if I approached too close. She gave every indication of being a fear-biter.

As I was wondering what to do with her, a man came along and got interested in the situation. He found a piece of rope, made a lasso, and cleverly got it over her neck without scaring her into flight. We didn't try to tighten the noose, but sat on a step a few feet from her and waited, with the rope lying loose.

Suddenly the little dog got up, walked over to me, and put her front paws and head in my lap! It was as simple as that—she just suddenly capitulated.

I led her away easily, took her to a veterinarian for examination and shots, and then brought her home. She behaved meekly, no problem to Dandy or my cats. She was housebroken. She wouldn't let me out of her sight, following me from room to room.

I went through all the standard procedures to locate her owner, but none materialized. I was lucky, though—I found a very nice woman whose elderly pet had recently died. She fell in love with my waif, named her Ginger, and took her home to Brooklyn. That's one city dog I am quite certain has lived happily ever after.

A final word of caution: Don't adopt a dog for somebody else. I remember watching my friend Gretchen Scanlan, who for many years was the administrative director of the fine private shelter she had helped to found, interview two people who came to adopt a dog. They had chosen a fluffy brown dog when Gretchen learned that the dog was to be a gift for the man's wife. Gretchen politely refused to let them have the dog, explaining that the person who will have the care and responsibility for the dog should be the one to select it. The man and woman pleaded; the dog was to be a surprise birthday present. Gretchen wouldn't budge. She urged them to come back with the woman for whom the dog was intended.

They did come back, a few days later, with the wife. Sure enough, she chose a dog and went home happy—but with a black-and-white, smooth-coated dog.

CHAPTER 2
PUPPIES:
The Joys and Problems

The fact that puppies are so downright adorable is a very mixed blessing for them. No animals are more cuddly, lovable, enchanting, fun to play with and watch. Yet, few can cause so much trouble and exasperation. Puppies are often adopted or purchased by inexperienced people who don't know what to expect in the behavior of a very young dog or the care and patience it requires.

As a result, puppies are punished when they shouldn't be, ruined in terms of their dispositions and behavior, and abandoned by roadsides or turned in to animal shelters by the millions each year.

Puppies are probably the greatest single victims of impulse buying. People look in the window of a pet shop, or encounter somebody in front of the supermarket with a basketful for giveaway, and they're hooked. People walk down the line of cages in an animal shelter, and this appealing little creature comes wagging at them, licking fingers, begging to be picked up. Nobody, not even a kitten, gets its message across more successfully than a puppy.

Then, the person who has succumbed to this hard sell gets the animal home and soon discovers the down side of living with a puppy. A puppy makes puddles and piles, throws up, yelps, whines, sheds, chews things up and knocks things over. Human patience quickly wears thin and out the puppy goes—frequently to the shelter or pound, which not only has to cope with the return rate of its own puppies but also those that people have acquired everywhere else— from breeders, pet stores, and private homes.

Of dogs surrendered to shelters, juvenile dogs account for a larger percentage than their numbers in the dog population as a whole. One survey of pet ownership of a few years ago revealed that 35 percent of all dogs under a year old do not last the year in the same household. Of these, at least a third are dumped on shelters. Others are placed in new homes, or abandoned.

Besides the innate charm of a puppy, one reason for its popularity is the belief that when you raise it yourself, you stand a good chance of ending up with just the pet you want. Presumably, if you get a dog accustomed very early to your habits, preferences, and so on, it will work out better in the long run than one who spent its puppyhood with someone else. Certainly with a puppy you have a golden opportunity to train it properly and establish yourself as pack leader in its eyes, right from the start.

Yet, Dandy was two years old when I got her, and she quickly became the perfect pet for me. Benjy was full grown when I found him, and he adjusted to us immediately. The experiences of many of my dog-owning friends and acquaintances are similar. Early conditioning can't be crucial.

I don't mean to suggest that city dwellers should never take on a puppy. I do urge you, though, to do a lot of serious thinking.

SPACE AND TIME

Your house or apartment should be considered in the light of the amount of time you have to give to the dog your puppy will grow up to be. A puppy that will become a distance runner will do okay in almost any size space, as long as you have time to exercise it enough.

However, bear in mind that you'll have to spend an inordinate amount of time on your puppy, much more than on an adult dog, socializing it and training it to do well in a city environment. Since a dog doesn't reach adulthood until it is ten to twelve months old, maybe longer, it may take as long as eight or ten months of effort on your part to train it well. You'll want to not only house-train it but teach it not to mouth or chew on people or things, not to get into the garbage, not to wail when left alone, not to pull when walked on the leash, and not to jump up on people. Takes time!

Ideally, a puppy should only be brought into a household where someone is home most of the time. It needs a great deal of love and attention, for the best city dogs—or any dogs, for that matter—are those that feel wanted and secure.

A puppy needs frequent feedings. (For what, how much, and how often to feed, see Chapter 5.) You can expect to be cleaning up after it for quite a while. A pup can't achieve good bladder and bowel control before it is at least four months old, and besides that, many veterinarians recommend that you not take it out on the street anyway until it has had its last shots (between twelve and sixteen weeks). Once you begin house-training it, that means frequent excursions to the street to teach it to relieve itself there.

A pup may be lonely and howl if left alone for long hours, disturbing the neighbors. Working people who are away from the house for nine to ten hours at a time can't give an infant dog the companionship it needs.

If you're sure you want a puppy but can't provide all this patient care during its first few months, you must make arrangements in advance with a reliable person to come in a couple of times a day.

Plan ahead to devote your full attention to your puppy for the first few days it's in your home. This is not as much work as it sounds, by the way, because the pup will sleep a lot, giving you at least some time to yourself. For those few days, it's sort of like caring for a human infant. When my children were babies, I used to flop down for a nap the minute they closed their little eyelids—I needed it!

As for the size of the dog, how can you tell how big a little handful of a pup will grow up to be? With a purebred dog, that's fairly easy, because its eventual size will be within a predictable range. Also, it's known that females tend to be somewhat smaller than males.

The full-grown size of mixed-breed pups is harder to estimate, unless the parents, at least the mother, are known. Often the coat can give you a clue to a pup's parentage. A popular belief is that you can judge a puppy's eventual size by the proportions of its feet. But sometimes a mixed-breed pup with huge paws becomes only a medium-size dog with big feet. Or vice versa—once in a while a pup with paws that aren't anything much to speak of grows up into a rather big dog with comparatively little feet.

JUDGING TEMPERAMENT

You'll want a dog that is between eight and twelve weeks of age—old enough to be taken from its mother without undue trauma, young enough to adjust well to people.

Puppies that have lived too long—say, over twelve weeks—almost exclusively with their mother and littermates have a harder time when brought into a human home. Also, a pup that has lived in a cage for its first twelve weeks will be shy and withdrawn in a strange environment. For this reason, good breeders, and the staffs of good animal shelters, try to handle their puppies frequently, to help socialize them.

If the mother dog is present when you go to choose a puppy, observe her to see if she is friendly. Normal protectiveness of her babies is one thing; severe anxiety or hostility is another. If the mother is unduly suspicious, she may have passed on this trait to her pups.

Spend some time alone with the puppy you like. Even a very young dog will exhibit definite personality traits.

One personality test you can give is to cradle the dog on its back in your arms like a baby. A trusting dog will just lie there, and if you put your face down close, it will try to lick you. Then slowly tilt the dog's body so the head is slightly downward. If the pup whines, struggles, tries to jump out of your arms, or if it becomes so terrified that it goes rigid with fear, this animal will be harder to socialize.

A puppy that lies down and presents its stomach, however, is showing submissiveness and may be a lot easier to live with in the city than a swaggering extrovert will be. Submissiveness is not to be confused with timidity; it simply signifies low dominance. A submissive dog is just not into power.

Bill Berloni of Berloni Theatrical Animals, who is experienced in gauging the temperament of dogs, recommends the runt of the litter as a good city dog. "The runt will be easier to train," says Berloni. "It has already accepted its low status and will not be competing to be boss in your household."

A pup that's excessively fearful, or highly excitable, isn't hopeless, but will need more attention and probably longer training than a friendly, calmer dog. A busy urban person might find it hard to devote whatever time it takes to help a puppy overcome extreme characteristics that can present problems in city living.

Female pups are usually gentler, easier to train than males.

A puppy that has been abused may be withdrawn and shy, even snappish, with strangers, but can become trusting and affectionate in the hands of a kind and patient person. If it has been seriously traumatized, it may always be shy with people it doesn't know, but even more devoted to you and your family.

A family I know adopted a ten-week-old puppy that had been abused. The previous owner, a man, had punished her until she was covered with bruises and cuts from his beatings and could do little more than cower in a corner of her cage at the animal shelter.

The family spent a long time rehabilitating her, and she became a happy, loving dog, but she has never forgotten her early mistreatment. She is now four years old, but if a man she doesn't know enters the house, terror strikes her heart and she is off like a shot to hide, trembling. She will probably carry this fear all her life. This is an example of what physical punishment can do to a dog's spirit.

JUDGING HEALTH

Hardest to resist sometimes is the sickly puppy. Symptoms such as a potbelly (which usually means worms), a cough, a discharge from the eyes or nose, and evidence of diarrhea can be found in dogs in pet shops, shelters and pounds, and even breeding kennels. If there's ever an animal that can awaken compassion and the nurturing instinct in all but the hardest of hearts, it's a pitiful pup.

It is very rewarding to take a poor little sick pup home and, with love, care, and good veterinary advice, restore it to health. But if you have other dogs, you must protect them from whatever the puppy has. And it can be devastating if, after you've invested a lot of emotion, time, energy, and money in the puppy, it dies anyway.

I know a number of healthy, beautiful dogs that were near death when rescued by sympathetic, capable people. But the cure may be difficult, and you may be risking disappointment, so be sure you're up to it.

A healthy puppy will have a firm, rounded body, clear eyes, and white teeth in pink, healthy-looking gums. Its ears will be clean, with no foul odor of infection or parasites. Its coat will be free of patches that can indicate skin disorders or parasites, and the skin under the fur will be white and healthy-looking. If the pup has a little bump in the middle of its stomach or its groin, by the way, that could be a hernia.

The pup will respond when you call it and snap your fingers, and will be able to follow a movement of your hand.

You will definitely want to make an appointment to take any dog you choose to a veterinarian immediately for a checkup. Also, the pup will need a series of vaccinations. If the person from whom you obtain a young puppy tells you it has had all its shots, be suspicious, because the final immunizations are usually not given before fourteen to sixteen weeks.

PET SHOPS

To obtain a puppy, the most rewarding and responsible thing you can do is to head for the animal shelter and bail out one that needs a home. However, if you have your heart set on a particular breed and no shelter in your vicinity has one at the moment, you may be debating between a breeder and a pet shop.

While there may be some good pet shops, most of them are purely commercial establishments that acquire their animals from puppy and kitten mills, or disreputable breeders, and sell them like merchandise. Often, the blasé attitude of people who work in these shops tells you a lot. The owners and employees are probably not intentionally cruel, but they regard the shops as businesses, and if the inventory is miserable, they may not even notice, and if it sickens and dies, that's written off as a business loss.

An ordinary pet shop has a pronounced smell, unless it has glass-enclosed cages which hide the smell. Overcrowding is obvious, with cages too small for the animals to lie down or move about comfortably. The cages may have openwork metal floors, with trays underneath to make cleaning easy. Such floors mean less work for the employees but are uncomfortable for the animals. If a dog or cat is kept more than a few weeks in this type of cage, its legs and feet can be damaged.

A gaily decorated, well-stocked pet shop in a famous department store in New York City has glass-enclosed cages with openwork metal floors, and some of the cages are so small that the dogs can scarcely turn around and the cats have no place to stretch out except in their litterboxes. A pet shop should be judged from the point of view of the animals in it, no matter how attractive the place looks to people.

A decent pet shop will tell you where it gets its dogs, but most buy them from puppy mills, rarely from breeders. A puppy mill dog has never lived in a home or had human companionship. It will probably have inherited health defects because it was produced on a wholesale basis with no genetic screening.

The breeding females in a puppy mill are forced to produce offspring like machines and may well be malnourished, even sick. Though state and interstate laws regulate the age at which pups can be taken from their mothers and shipped, too often underage animals are crated and freighted, often over great distances, to wholesale dealers and then to pet shops. Some die on the way; a large percentage arrives sick; others are so weakened and stressed that they become ill after they arrive at the dealers' or pet shops. Many pet shop animals appear lethargic and sick.

If you buy a dog at a pet shop, you're paying the retail price, which includes the puppy mill's price, plus the shipper's, the dealer's, and the pet shop's markup. If you buy directly from a breeder, you will almost always get a far superior dog for the same price or less.

I'm not the only person who badmouths pet shops. Many books and information pamphlets about dogs will tell you the same thing, with good reason. Consider yourself well warned.

BREEDERS

I know it's asking a lot of you, as a city dweller, to buy a purebred dog from a breeder instead of a pet shop. Dog breeders don't live in cities—they're in the suburbs, small towns, or country. To locate a good breeder, you have to do some research. Pet shops are all over town; you have only to look in the Yellow Pages. It's a lot more trouble to buy your purebred puppy from a reputable breeder, but believe me, it will be worth it to you.

There are national breed clubs consisting of breeders, owners, and aficionados of many specific kinds of dogs, and a good way to locate a breeder of the dog you're interested in is through its national breed club. You can get the addresses of breed clubs from the American Kennel Club, 51 Madison Avenue, New York, NY 10010. Dog magazines and some Sunday newspapers also carry ads of breeders of various kinds of dogs.

But once you have the names of some breeders, how do you judge a good one?

A good breeder has a clean, humane kennel—or may even keep the dogs in the house as pets, so they are well socialized from the start of their lives. He or she usually breeds only one type of dog, not several, and gives a lot of personal attention to each animal. Some of the best breeders are purely hobbyists, not commercially motivated.

He or she will encourage you to take the dog you select to a veterinarian for a health checkup within forty-eight hours and will offer to take the pup back and refund your money if it is found to be unhealthy.

A good breeder breeds for temperament as well as for points in the show ring, and as I have said, for city people temperament is of paramount importance. Such a breeder will furnish you with references—people to whom he or she has sold dogs. This breeder does *not* sell to pet shops.

If the dog's parents are registered with the American Kennel Club or other registry, the breeder should have registered the litter and therefore will be able to provide you—*at the time of purchase, not later*—with a partially filled out application form for registering your individual dog. The registration form is for you to complete and send, with the fee, to the registry. The AKC cautions against buying from a breeder who can't provide you with registration application papers, partly filled out, at the time you buy the pup.

The fact that it is registered, in itself, says nothing about the quality of the dog you are buying. It only means that the pup is the offspring of registered parents.

You might, by the way, be able to buy a puppy at a discount if the breeder believes it is not of show quality. That doesn't mean you're getting a less desirable dog. It just means you wouldn't have a champion in the show ring. If what you want is a pet, what do you care if it has white paws, for instance, or a curly tail?

CHILDREN AND PUPPIES

People sometimes ask me if a dog already established in a household will be jealous of a new baby. I'll talk about that later, in Chapter 3. However, for parents who already have small children and are acquiring a new dog, a puppy could be an excellent choice.

Whereas an adult dog may or may not like little kids, a puppy has an open mind. When carefully supervised, a child and a puppy can be great playmates, and very strong bonds often form between children and dogs that are raised together.

I want to stress, however, that a mother who's the sole caretaker of a baby or young child should not have the responsibility of a puppy laid on her—she has her hands full enough as it is. This is especially pertinent advice for a city mother because of the activity necessary in house-training a puppy where the outdoors is not easily accessible. Walking a puppy the required six or seven times a day would certainly be a burden on her. Some of my urban friends have raised puppies by paper-training them, but this setup, with soiled newspapers around, might be undesirable with a baby or toddler in the house—and sometimes it's harder to curb-train a dog that has already been paper-trained.

A child must be carefully watched to be sure it doesn't hurt a puppy. Children can unintentionally literally maul a puppy to death. A pup, like a kitten, is very vulnerable, with soft, fragile bones. Children must be taught from the very beginning that a puppy is not a toy.

Dr. Mark Lerman, a veterinarian friend of mine, described a recent scene in his clinic.

"A mother came in with three little girls and a sick puppy," he said. "Each child was trying to carry the puppy, and they were pulling and snatching at it between them. They couldn't even keep their hands off it while I was examining it. I soon realized that the only thing wrong with this dog was that it was being handled to death. I kept it in my hospital overnight, just to give it a much-needed rest, and when I returned it, I had a long talk with the children and especially with the mother, explaining that the puppy needs a lot of rest and mustn't be handled all the time. I could see my advice had absolutely no impact. What I suspect will happen is that sooner or later the pup will bite in self-defense, and then the family will get rid of it, saying it has a bad disposition.''

Another reason supervision is needed is that an exuberant puppy can unintentionally knock down a small child.

A very young child should not try to pick up or carry a puppy at all. Instead, have the child sit down on the floor or in a low chair and place the puppy in his or her lap. That way, the child can have the pleasure of cuddling the dog but can't hurt it by dropping it.

Here is a list of important rules for anyone—including children—raising a puppy:

Never pick up a puppy by the scruff of the neck.
Never pick up a puppy by the legs, head, ears, or tail.
Never drag a puppy by the legs, head, ears, or tail.
Never tease or frustrate a puppy.
Never disturb a puppy while it's sleeping.
Never strike, shake, or spank a puppy.

The fact that mother dogs sometimes carry their pups in their mouths by the skin of their neck doesn't mean we should pick them up that way. The proper way to pick up and carry a puppy is with one hand under the chest, the other hand supporting the hind quarters.

Let a puppy sleep as much as it wants—it needs the rest.

A pup should very definitely be trained, but never physically punished. Hitting or spanking it will only make it afraid. It can't get the connection between the spanking and the act you're punishing it for. That's like hitting a tiny baby for soiling its diaper. Physical punishment will not teach a dog anything but will make it fear and hate you.

Children especially must be firmly taught never to punish a dog. Very young children should not try to train or discipline a dog; that's the pack leader's job. A child and a puppy should be pal and playmate, fellow comforter and companion, not master and slave.

Children are the ones most likely to engage in rough play with a puppy, and it's important that they be taught better, for everyone's sake.

TOYS AND PLAY

The time when you will probably be spending the most time playing with your dog, and providing it with toys, is during its puppyhood. Also, puppies will make up their own games with whatever attracts them—your shoes, for instance—and must learn what items are off limits.

Some people give their dogs old socks or shoes to play with and chew on. This might be fine with some older dogs, but most, especially puppies, will have trouble distinguishing between theirs and yours, since theirs were yours in the first place. Your average pup won't understand why it's okay to chew on a discarded loafer but not one of your new Ferragamos, or what's different between the worn-out sweatsock you gave it and the good pair you left on the bathroom floor. My advice is to not give your dog anything at all of yours to play with. Let it have its own toys.

The best dog toys are made of rawhide, hard nylon, or hard rubber, *unpainted*. Soft rubber toys are not good because they are too easy to chew up. When bits of the rubber are swallowed, they can play havoc with the dog's insides and even cause death. Painted toys can cause lead poisoning. And wooden toys are dangerous, too—they can splinter.

Enjoying a puppy's capacity for play, and its comical antics, are among the reasons for having it in the first place. By all means, play with a puppy, and encourage children to do so—but with these caveats in mind:

Don't play just before or after feeding.
Don't play on a slippery floor such as wood, vinyl, or tile: The

puppy needs secure footing or it can tear a muscle or dislocate a joint.

Don't play with a puppy on the stairs—and in fact, it needs help just going up and down, especially down. Uncarpeted stairs are especially dangerous to a pup. Wait until it is grown and can navigate stairs easily before allowing it to go up and down unaided. If you have stairs, better install a gate at the top for the duration.

Don't tease or frustrate a puppy or do anything to provoke aggression, even in play.

Don't play tug-of-war with a puppy.

Don't encourage or permit a puppy to bite anything but its own toys.

Don't play with a puppy more than a few minutes at a time because it will become overstimulated and exhausted—or aggressive.

Of all these warnings, probably the hardest to heed is the one about playing tug-of-war, because the pup itself will initiate this game. Don't accept the challenge. It's amusing to see a young dog grapple with a rag or piece of rope, shaking its head and even hanging on so hard with its jaws that it can be lifted into the air. The trouble is that the pup never learns that its jaws can hurt.

A veterinary researcher at Purdue University, Dr. John Stump, has cautioned against this. "When two puppies play together, the one that gets bitten will squeal or yelp. That's the signal meaning, 'That's enough,' so the biter learns something about the strength of its jaws," he says. "But when the dog bites a piece of rope that someone is pulling, it gets no sense of how hard to bite before letting go, since it hasn't learned that shut-off signal."

It may be cute when a little puppy play-bites your hand, sleeve, or pants leg, or chews on your shoelaces, but this very definitely should be gently but firmly discouraged. Otherwise, before you know it, the dog grows up and, meaning no harm, sinks its teeth into someone's hand, or rips a sofa pillow. Then the confused dog finds itself in big trouble—for using its jaws in a way that you encouraged or permitted in the first place.

A dog should never get the idea that its teeth are to be used on any part of the human body, clothing, or household object. You will just be setting it and everyone else up for a bad incident.

If a puppy bites in the course of play, quickly tell it "No!" sharply, and stop the play. In fact, it might be a good idea to let out a yelp, even if it hasn't hurt you, and then stop the play for a while. The dog should get the message that it has done something wrong. For more information on training a puppy, see Chapter 4.

It's great fun for a puppy to chase and retrieve a ball. Just don't let it scamper across a slippery floor or it can wind up at the vet's with a dislocated hip or shoulder. Be sure the ball is small enough for the dog to grasp in its mouth but not swallow.

After a puppy has had all its shots, it can be taken outdoors. If you have access to a well-protected yard, dog run, or other confined area that permits dogs, that's a good place for vigorous play. Just make sure the fencing doesn't have spaces big enough for a little body to squeeze through. And don't make the mistake of letting the dog off the leash unless you are in an enclosed area. You'd be surprised how fast a pup can run. Many a misguided owner has assumed he or she could catch a fleeing puppy and discovered that the only thing that stopped it was the wheels of a passing car.

PROTECTING A PUP

You want to protect not only your possessions from the pup, but your animal from household items that can hurt or kill it. It's best to put away anything valuable for the duration of its puppyhood. Keep all closet and cupboard doors tightly closed; cover the garbage securely; put books, plants, and other tasty valuables out of reach; and disconnect lamps and other electric appliances except when you are home and supervising the puppy. Better yet, when you're out, confine the pup in a large wire cage, the type called a kennel crate. (More on kennel crates in Chapter 4.)

Dr. Audrey Hayes of the Animal Medical Center, in New York City, one of the largest animal hospitals in the United States, mentioned the following items as among those that have been removed by surgery from the stomachs of dogs: chicken bones, nylon stockings, Brillo pads, string, pillow stuffing, splinters of wood, pieces of wicker.

Dr. Hayes tells of one puppy owner who took off her earrings and placed them on her night table while she took a nap. When she woke up, she couldn't find one of her earrings. After searching everywhere, she gave it up for lost. A few days later, her pup became ill. At the Animal Medical Center, X-rays revealed the earring lodged in the animal's stomach. It was an earring for pierced ears, so the point was stuck neatly in the stomach wall. After it was removed surgically, the puppy recovered, and the poorer but wiser owner got her earring back.

However, no matter what mischief a puppy gets into, never try to train it not to play with things, or punish it, by hitting it. First of all, hitting is counterproductive and won't accomplish your goal. Second, the puppy won't understand and you'll ruin its disposition. Third, it's mean to hit a puppy, as cruel as it is to strike a human baby.

N.B. Don't forget to enlarge a puppy's collar as it grows. It sounds incredible, but some idiot owners have forgotten to do this, allowing the collars gradually to choke their poor dogs. I have heard several shelter workers speak of having to euthanize dogs that were found sick and deformed from just this oversight. The collar should be just loose enough for you to slip a finger between it and the animal's neck.

As to where a puppy should sleep, you're not going to get an argument out of me if you feel it should be in your or your child's bed. But when the pup is very small, it might get hurt if it falls out of a bed that is several feet off the floor. So it might be best to get it its own cozy bed, placed away from drafts.

If the puppy misses its mother and siblings and cries the first few nights, you might try putting a softly playing radio near its bed, or wrapping a ticking clock in a towel and placing it in the pup's bed; these have been known to lull and soothe a homesick little animal.

Housebreaking and obedience-training a puppy are much the

same as for an older dog. You'll find suggestions for these in Chapter 4.

One thing about an urban puppy: While you are socializing it to be friendly with people and other dogs on the street, you'll have a chance to meet a lot of new people, because eight out of ten will want to stop and pet your puppy.

CHAPTER 3

UNDERSTANDING:
How Your Dog Thinks and Feels

How often have you heard someone say, "I would love to have a dog, but I think it's cruel to keep one in the city"? Such a person sincerely believes that in order to lead a happy life, a dog must be free to run all day in the wide-open spaces. This notion is firmly held in spite of the evidence that dogs who are free to run all day outdoors actually spend the greater part of their time sleeping or lounging around. Well-cared-for city dogs might get even more exercise than country dogs who are left to their own devices.

The central thesis of this book is that a properly cared-for urban dog can be perfectly content, and that in fact, city life is not unnatural for it, as long as it is in the stewardship of a loving and enlightened owner. The domestic dog seems perfectly programmed to adapt to living with its master in a house or apartment.

City dogs probably have a much closer relationship with their owners than do country or suburban dogs. Dogs and owners are likely to spend a lot of time indoors together and to sleep in the same room. The very act of going for walks together strengthens the bond. Backyard or rural dogs may get to interact with their owners only at feeding time.

It's important, however, to have at least a working knowledge of how your animal views you and the world, especially before you attempt to give it any sort of training. Even though the evolution of the domestic dog as a species or subspecies parallels that of human beings, and it has lived with us almost forever, it brought with it into the cave certain primitive traits that it still shares with its wild relatives. This chapter will give you some background on the nature of dogs in order to help you get the most out of Chapter 4, which will deal with behavior training.

There are two basic instincts that today's domestic dog has preserved in its race memory: its pack instinct and its denning instinct. Both of these influence its behavior, whether it is a huge, lumbering mixed breed or a three-pound pedigreed toy whatchamacallit.

THE PACK

Most primitive and contemporary wild canids are social animals, living in packs with well-defined hierarchies and carefully observed rules. That's why feral dogs form packs whenever possible and stick together. There is usually a pack leader, often an alpha female as well (top female dog, mate of the leader). Each dog is aware of its rank in the pack, but looks to the leader for direction, protection, and maintaining order. Members of a pack observe rituals, display greeting behavior to each other, and are sensitive to one another's emotional states. Being a pack member makes a dog feel comfortable; nothing is worse for it than not belonging or being driven out.

To the domestic dog, its human family is its pack, and the family home is its den or territory. You, or someone in your family, are your dog's pack leader. Often the leader is the person who feeds and walks the dog, though sometimes it's the head of the household by sheer force of personality, as my childhood dog Laddie recognized my father to be. If you live alone with your dog, you're unquestionably It, unless you abdicate the role.

In the wild, canid pack leaders are usually male, for the simple reason that a female is often pregnant or nursing and therefore not in a position to be in charge of the pack, settling arguments, keeping out intruders, and the like. This distinction about the gender of the leader is apparently lost on domestic dogs, however, for they will accept a woman as pack leader as readily as a man.

If a dog has been pack leader itself, perhaps in the litter, or aspires to be one, it may not automatically relinquish that position to you. You will have to assume it yourself and convince the dog that you are in charge, or you may wind up in second-rank position to your dog—at least, in its mind. Unless you are some kind of masochist, that defeats much of the pleasure of owning a dog. It's as unbecoming and unwholesome for a dog owner to be a slave to his or her tyrant of a pet, for that's what the animal will become, as it is for a parent to relinquish leadership to a spoiled brat of a child. With a dog, it can even be risky, both for the dog's safety and everyone else's.

You must be able to brush and bathe your dog, give it medicine, take stuff out of its mouth when it has picked up something it shouldn't have, and obedience-train it. If your dog dominates you, you'll find it difficult if not impossible to do any of these things.

You enter the relationship with your dog with a built-in advantage, since you provide the shelter and control the feeding, walking, games, and protection. So, if you play your cards right, it shouldn't be hard to assume leadership over even a canine born leader. The dog will become a fine companion as a result, and the bond between you strengthened.

Because a dog intuitively expects and even welcomes directions from its pack leader, it isn't cruel to train it to do what you want, as long as the training is done humanely, with love and understanding, and working with rather than against the animal's instincts. You want to communicate, clearly and firmly, in language the dog can understand.

Every dog owner can cite instances of his dog reading his mind. I remember I used to be astonished at my dog Benjy in this regard. All I had to do was think, "When I finish what I'm doing, I'm going to take Benjy out," and he would instantly get up and walk to the door, looking back at me expectantly. I swear to you I made no motion that could have tipped him off. I don't make any claim that dogs can actually read minds, but they do seem to pick up messages that we communicate unwittingly.

Ann Ottney Cain, a family therapist and university professor, tells a story about one of her students who was interviewing a family that had applied for therapy. The student got the impression that the grandmother of the family disapproved of the whole idea of therapy and had no intention of cooperating, even though she was outwardly polite. Suddenly the dog, who had been sitting next to the grandmother, walked across the room, jumped up on the couch beside the student, and bit her!

Now for an example of a communications gap between a dog and its owner. There's a Yorkie in my neighborhood who is aggressive toward other dogs—she barks and snarls and carries on at the sight of everyone she meets. She can't do much actual harm, but she makes every encounter unnerving and unpleasant. Unfortunately, she encounters Dandy every so often, and even though Dandy is five times bigger and the world's gentlest and most submissive dog, this Yorkie acts as if she were going to eat Dandy alive.

The Yorkie's owner, instead of reproaching her disagreeable pet, bends down, caresses her, and says soothingly, "There, there. Good girl, good girl." She thinks that by doing this, she will reassure the dog and thereby stop her objectionable behavior. But the message the Yorkie gets is, I did my job well and now she is rewarding me. The pattern is set: See another dog, bark and snap ferociously, and get rewarded with petting and compliments. The owner, unable or unwilling to communicate disapproval to her Yorkie as a pack leader would, simply doesn't see the situation from the dog's point of view.

It is perhaps primarily the pack instinct that accounts for the dog's legendary loyalty and also its protectiveness. Remember that nature programs a species for survival—either survival of the individual or, in the case of social animals, survival of the group. The primitive dog looked to the pack leader for guidance and approval because that meant its survival. It instinctively defended the pack and the pack's territory because that helped the group as a whole to survive. Each member of the pack was loyal and protective, whatever its rank within the group.

This does not mean that a dog reacts only to instinctual stimuli. I think today's domestic dog is not only able to reason but is also capable of profound devotion and loyalty to its owner, especially if the owner is a kind and benevolent pack leader. Sadly, it will also remain loyal to an owner who is indifferent, even somewhat abusive, unless it is pushed beyond endurance. Then a dog will defend itself and turn on its attacker, even if he or she is the pack leader.

Certain species of social animals—mammals, birds, and insects—are known to risk and even sacrifice their individual lives for the protection of their particular groups. We know, for instance, of birds that hobble along the ground and feign injury to lead predators away from the nest or even the colony, and of certain primates that, when attacked, will help protect the offspring of other members of their colony. Stories abound of dogs who have saved members of their families from harm, at great risk to their own lives. The modern dog has simply substituted its human family for its own canine pack.

THE DEN

The domestic dog seems to be a descendant of denning canids, and just as it regards its owner or one family member as pack leader, it considers its family's home as its den. Therein lies its value as a watchdog and defender of the property. A subordinate dog will be as protective as a dominant dog.

The denning instinct may also be the reason it is possible to house-train dogs. A basic tenet of all den dwellers is that you do not soil your den. Come to think ot it, perhaps that's the reason we can housebreak our children. Human beings, unlike many other primates, have been denning animals ever since we began to live in caves, wigwams, huts, igloos, and the like. Nondenning animals, such as horses and cows, are virtually impossible to house-train—it's not in their instinctual makeup.

The pack and denning instincts manifest themselves differently in the personalities of cats and dogs. Some wild felines, like dogs, are denning animals—but most species of cat are not pack animals and don't recognize the authority of a pack leader. That's why cats have the reputation for being independent, even aloof, and why people who demand absolute subservience in their pets can't stand cats.

A well-treated domestic cat will be loving and companionable, and you can of course train it to a certain extent—that is, you can modify its behavior so that it will observe reasonable house rules. And anyone who has ever watched a cat drive an intruding cat out of its backyard can see the territorial instinct at work. Some cats have even been known to warn their owners when strangers were sneaking around the property. But you can't teach a cat to lead the blind or to round up sheep, and the only way you can get one of its captive wild cousins to jump through a flaming hoop in a circus is to brutalize it. The dog, however, can learn to do what its pack leader asks because compliance is built into its makeup and because being obedient to an owner it loves makes it feel comfortable and happy.

Training is crucial to successful urban dog ownership but can be a frustrating experience for owner and dog if the owner repeatedly tries to teach in a way that works against, rather than with, the dog's nature. Using the dog's denning instinct in house-training it is a lot more successful than punishing the animal for making mistakes. And knowing how to assess a dog's behavior correctly not only smooths your relationship with your own pet but is extremely helpful in handling its encounters with people and other dogs on the street.

BODY LANGUAGE

It's certainly not hard to figure out what your dog is telling you when it meets you at the door after you've been out for a while—the joyful grin and madly wagging tail say it all. Most of us quickly learn our pet's basic repertoire of overt language. But some of the signals dogs give are subtle or confusing. Being able to read a dog's body language and to understand how the animal thinks and feels is especially necessary for urban dwellers. You not only want to be able to interpret your own pet correctly but, on the street, you want to be able to tell friend from foe.

Let's say your dog meets a strange dog off the leash. The other dog approaches with great interest, ears alert and tail wagging. Doesn't a wagging tail mean friendliness? Not necessarily.

This dog is giving out other signals that spell hostility. Its tail is wagging, but stiff and held high. The eyes have a hard expression and stare into your dog's eyes. The dog's hackles (the fur along its shoulders and back) are raised. The animal's whole posture signifies aggression. Even without growling or showing its teeth, a dog behaving like this has a chip on its shoulder. Unless your dog immediately shows submission and placates the aggressor, you should remove it from the scene quietly and quickly.

On the other hand, a friendly—or merely curious—dog's tail will most likely be wagging, but in wide sweeps, hanging down. Ears are down and fur is smooth along the shoulders and back. The dog will not attempt to look you or your dog in the eye. It will go through the typical sniffing pattern with your dog—first nose to nose, then the genitals. Offer this dog the back of your fist to smell, and then you can probably pet it if you wish.

In another situation, let's say your dog meets another and, after the usual preliminary sniffs, suddenly bounces down on its chest and elbows with its ears flattened and its rear end in the air. Unless the other dog's owner recognizes your dog's body language, he or she may snatch the animal away protectively, misinterpreting your dog's behavior as aggression. Your dog was giving off perfectly clear signals—"Let's play"—yet was misunderstood.

A dog that merely wants to play may also jump excitedly and bark, grin and wag its tail, run around in circles, and roll over. Even at her advanced age, Dandy often greets another dog with this behavior.

But when Dandy meets the Yorkie who raises such a row when we pass on the street, Dandy acts as if she doesn't even see her. She looks right through her. It is not uncommon for dogs to pretend not to see people or other animals they dislike. They may also keep their distance while watching out of the corner of their eye.

Sometimes a dog meeting another dog, or a person, lies on its belly with its ears flattened and the fur along its back flat and smooth. It looks away and may roll over onto its back. Is it afraid? Is it a coward and a wimp if it does this with another dog? In most cases not—it may well only be showing submission. It is probably saying, "I am recognizing that you are the boss (pack leader)." Or it could be telling the other dog, "I'm not into power—I don't want to fight." Low-dominance dogs often display this behavior. This style usually makes a good city dog who can be easily trained and will avoid confrontations.

Fear is a more obvious signal. A frightened dog crouches, with its tail hanging low or tucked between its legs. Its head is down, ears are laid back though perhaps not flattened, and hackles are usually raised. The dog may instinctively crouch close to the ground to protect its belly, and it may tremble and approach you and your dog in circles. Because a scared dog can quickly become a fear-biter, the best course is to stand still with your hands by your sides and above all don't look the animal in the eye—that's a real challenge. Don't corner it or turn your back on it, but speak to it in a soothing voice. Unless it gets over its fear, relaxes, and shows friendliness or submission, it's best to move away quietly.

Correctly interpreting a hostile dog's body language may not only help you protect your dog but may save you from getting bitten yourself. If a strange dog approaches you giving off signals of aggression when your dog is not with you, behave as you would with a frightened dog, especially by not looking it in the eye and not extending your hands. If the dog is barking, that's all the more reason to be cautious, because however often you've heard that a barking dog doesn't bite, it isn't true. Speak to the dog in a normal voice until it walks away or stops giving off the unfriendly signals. Then back away calmly yourself.

A dog's mouth can tell you a lot. Dogs do grin by pulling the corners of their mouth back and baring their teeth. Sometimes a blissfully relaxed dog will close its eyes and actually smile. But when a dog wrinkles its nose, raises its upper lip, and shows its incisors and canine teeth, that's a snarl.

Children should be taught to interpret a dog's body language, as well as other safety measures concerning dogs (see "Aggression," below). Approximately one million dog bites are reported in the

United States each year, and the majority of victims are children under ten.

Every observant dog owner learns to recognize the body language of his or her pet when it's sick. Refusal to eat is of course a primary one, yet there are many illnesses of which loss of appetite is not a symptom. A dog walking with its head somewhat down and its back arched, for example, could have an orthopedic problem, or stomach pain. Unexplained and atypical crankiness can mean illness, or anxiety. Such subtle signals should not go uninvestigated.

A dog's range of vocalizations is another meaningful form of body language. Every dog owner can tell from the pitch of his or her pet's bark the mood or even the content that the animal is communicating. (An experienced dog lover may even interpret fairly accurately the message a perfectly strange dog two blocks away is putting out.) A bark can be welcoming or playful, or can signify loneliness, fear, or anger.

In the city, much of a dog's natural inclination to bark must be discouraged. It's asking a lot of a dog to learn to differentiate between the whish of the handyman mopping the hall of your apartment building and the quiet scrape of a burglar picking the lock on a neighbor's door. Teaching a dog to bark only selectively requires a difficult manipulation of the animal's instincts, but in town, it's often necessary, for everyone's sanity.

Dog owners who are close to their pets will swear that their dogs often imitate their own moods—mirroring their excitement, joy, depression, anxiety. I believe this is true. Dogs certainly become greatly upset when their owners are in a rage about something, or quarreling, or weeping. Some very definitely react to hearty laughter—they'll grin and wag their tails and try to take part in the fun. Dogs pick up on our body language and usually read it more correctly than we do theirs.

They do sometimes misinterpret situations. But irrational fears in dogs can be understood if you look at a situation from their point of view. Holidays are a case in point. Halloween, for example, can be heaps of fun for us, and we may enjoy the little kids in costume trick-or-treating. Your dog, however, may think the world has gone mad. It will most likely get upset at the masks and funny clothes and the constantly ringing doorbell and can even become aggressive because it is scared. Keep the animal away from the front door, confine it in a comfortable place in the house, and keep a firm grip on the leash when you're on the street. Even Dandy, that most serene of dogs, barks at costumed people on the street on Halloween.

And I have never known a dog who enjoyed the Fourth of July.

As for Christmas, all your pet senses is a lot of excitement, new objects in the house, and probably strange people coming and going. Help your pet remain as calm as possible, let it hide in a quiet place if it wants. Some dogs retreat to the back of the closet on December 24 and don't voluntarily emerge for more than a few minutes until January 2.

AGGRESSION

The vast majority of dogs never bite and in fact live their entire lives without ever so much as growling at a person; however, aggressiveness is a major behavior problem that causes millions of dogs to be abandoned or surrendered to animal shelters every year. If a dog is surrendered to a shelter for a behavior problem, there's a chance it will display the same problem in its next home unless the problem can be eliminated by appropriate training. For the fortunate few dogs whose owners have patience and will spend the money, aggression is also a primary factor that keeps dog trainers in business.

What causes a dog to be aggressive? There are several possibilities. Illness could be one; even a normally sweet-tempered dog may growl or snap if you attempt to handle it when it's in pain or if it feels so wretched that it wants to be left alone. Stress can make a good-natured dog turn snappish. Fear of a real or imagined threat to itself or to a member of its pack can of course cause a dog to attack. A traumatic experience it had as a young dog can turn the animal aggressive if the same situation recurs, or the dog imagines it. Jealousy can bring on aggressive behavior, especially if the dog is insecure or overly protective in the first place.

Aggressiveness can be inherited; some breeds have a greater tendency to aggression than others, and among purebred dogs, careless breeding can pass on this trait. Then there are the trained attackers—guard dogs, security dogs, sentry dogs, and the like.

Of the million reported instances of dog bite reported each year, virtually all of them result from owned, not stray, animals. And while deliverymen and meter readers suffer their share of attacks from dogs, a 1982 university study revealed that most of the victims are owners, family members, or neighbors of the aggressive dogs. Children under ten are bitten most frequently, and according to the study some 45 percent of all children between ages four and eighteen suffer dog bite at some point. In high population areas—cities—dog bite can be a concern to everyone, dog owners in particular.

The fact that most dog bite victims are children raises the question of whether the children may have unwittingly provoked the incidents. It's important to teach children not only to be gentle with their own dogs but to treat all dogs with proper respect. Some parents unfortunately instill fear of dogs: "Watch out, that dog will bite you!" they say, automatically pulling their child away from every dog they meet. This may prevent the child from ever being able to appreciate and enjoy dogs or to be comfortable around them. It might even help establish a phobia that could haunt the child all his or her life.

Children should be taught a few basic cautionary rules. They should learn, for instance, always to ask the owner before petting a dog and always to be gentle. They should be taught very early never to swoop down on any dog from behind, never to grab it around the neck, never to take a bone or toy away from it, and never to put their hand through a fence to pet it. Children seem to be born with an interest in dogs, but I think a civilized quality such as empathy with animals has to be taught.

On the street, a dog tied up or on the leash may be more likely to act aggressive because it feels cornered. Before I knew this, I had a curious experience with a dog I found running loose, no collar, no owner in sight, on a block near my house. It was a handsome, well-fed, well-groomed young Shepherd, and he came up to me acting friendly enough. I couldn't leave him, for fear that he'd run out in traffic and get hurt or killed, as so many unleashed dogs in the city do, so I put my scarf around his neck to lead him to my house and take him from there to the ASPCA, which would give the owner a chance to retrieve him.

The minute I collared the animal with my scarf, he turned into an attack dog who took it upon himself to defend me against everyone on the street. He caused a commotion in the lobby of my building, holding all comers and goers at bay. Fortunately someone drove us up to the ASPCA shelter, the dog and I in the back seat, where he lunged and snarled and barked out the car window at passersby every foot of the way. Once we arrived at the building, the dog intimidated the security guard and everyone entering and leaving. I was at the point of despair when a young kennelman came to my aid, approaching us nonchalantly and quietly, communicating nonthreatening authority. True to form, this quixotic dog stopped his menacing behavior and trotted off meekly with the kennelman.

Through several ASPCA staff members whom I know, I kept tabs on the dog and heard that no owner ever materialized to claim him, but he was later adopted. I hope he went to someone who was good to him and calmed him down.

I think this young Shepherd had been trained as an attack dog, and badly trained at that, since he obviously couldn't distinguish a real enemy from a bystander. Thank goodness he apparently thought of me as his friend.

What if an aggressive dog actually attacks you or your dog? There are no good answers to this question. All I can suggest is that if the attacker is coming at you, fend it off not with your hands but with whatever arm you don't use for writing, cover your face, and yell "No!" with all the authority you can summon. Try not to get hysterical or to take the offensive because that will only excite the dog more (though if it's a small dog, kicking it might drive it away).

If the aggressive dog attacks your dog, the recommended solution is to turn a hose on it or pour a bucket of water over it, but how often do you have a bucket of water with you on a city street? All you can do is try to hit the attacking dog with a stick, umbrella, or any similar object you can seize, but don't get your hands in the way—even your own dog might bite you by mistake in trying to defend itself. Whether the aggressive dog is attacking you or your dog, it's a terrifying scene, and it's the reason nobody should have an aggressive dog in the city, or *any* dog off the leash.

You have probably heard it said that dogs often look like their owners, and you may even know amusing examples of it. A notion that makes more sense is that dogs will take after their owners in temperament—nice people will have friendly dogs, hostile people will have aggressive dogs, and so on. Since dogs appear to have an uncanny ability to read our thoughts, or at least our body language, it's tempting to accept this supposition as fact.

However, in my own experience I know of many exceptions that make me wonder about this theory. For instance, the woman who owns the aggressive Yorkie is a very sweet person. And another neighbor of mine, very macho with the sensibility of a Neanderthal, has a gentle, appealing little dog.

Human beings have a lot of ambivalence about submissiveness. On the one hand, we love dogs for their loyalty, for their obedience, for the unconditional friendship they give us. On the other hand, we scorn these very subservient qualities, and the word "dog" in our language (or bitch, cur, and the like) is perjorative. In many parts of the world today, dogs are still universally treated with horrible cruelty—and we ourselves are far from being the nation of dog lovers that we often mistakenly assume we are.

We train the dog to do our bidding and take pride in its accomplishments—but secretly, unconsciously, we may look down on an animal that is so obedient. The dog is in a no-win position, damned if it *is* totally devoted and damned if it *isn't*.

These contradictory feelings about dogs may be deeply embedded in our collective unconscious. When an individual dog owner regards aggression as a quality to be admired, his or her dog could very possibly respond accordingly. The owner might unconsciously encourage belligerent behavior in the pet.

A hostile dog has no place in a city, where it is in constant contact with people and other dogs. Such an animal is a danger to itself and others. The only situation in which a dog should be appropriately aggressive is one in which there is a very real, immediate threat to it or to a member of its human family. Otherwise, something is very wrong.

Firm, patient training can sometimes change a dog with this type of personality—see Chapter 4—unless the cause is biological. There are those rare dogs with innate streaks of violence that cannot be corrected. If patient effort does not succeed in making the dog's disposition reliable, then other arrangements must be made for the dog. Harsh as it sounds, humane euthanasia may be the best answer for these poor beasts.

PROTECTIVENESS AND JEALOUSY

A dog cannot be relied upon always to interpret correctly the behavior of strangers. A perfectly friendly person with a loud voice and hearty manners who comes up to you on the street, or enters your home, can be perceived by your dog as an enemy, at least until it reads your reaction to the person and realizes that everything's okay. You don't want a pet that bites first and figures out afterward.

A dog who has lived with a single owner can feel very threatened when the owners marries or acquires a roommate and will try to "protect" its owner. If the dog knows that aggressive behavior won't be tolerated, it may resort to other means of expressing its anxiety—breaking house-training, chewing up things around the house, or barking when left alone. A wise owner will understand the dog's point of view and realize that sympathy and patience are in order. The behavior can be prevented or stopped, or the dog may discontinue it of its own accord as soon as it feels reassured.

A dog will sometimes misbehave just to get attention. Within the pack, negative attention is better than none, and thus a pet dog who feels ignored and rejected may prefer even to be scolded by its owner than snubbed completely—at least then the owner is focusing on the dog. Apparently the worst thing you can do to a dog is ignore it.

A dog can get carried away with its sense of protectiveness. I once knew a dog so protective of the children in her family that she misinterpreted the intentions of a neighbor who came to the door and bit the woman in the ankle. A dog with its instinct as highly tuned as that can be dangerous. Not only can the animal hurt someone, perhaps seriously, but it might get you a lawsuit.

Because dogs have such a close relationship with people, they have picked up certain primarily human emotions, of which jealousy is a notable one. Jealousy is touching to see in a dog because it reveals its dependency and love. But this emotion can also cause aggression, and for that reason, if your dog has any possible reason to be jealous of someone, you will want to pay attention and help your dog overcome it.

The arrival of a new baby in your household is a case in point, particularly if the infant is a first. To your dog, this small creature is an intruder, especially because it makes strange noises and gets an enormous amount of your attention—attention that perhaps used to be lavished on the dog. The dog's feelings are the canine equivalent of sibling rivalry and can be dealt with in much the same manner, by giving the dog extra affection. When the dog tries to inspect the baby, let the dog approach, don't push it away. Keep control of the encounter, but let the dog smell the baby. Give the pet every reason to feel it has not been replaced, while making sure it understands that the baby is a pack member.

As often as possible, take the dog with you when you go out with the baby, and try to include it when guests make a fuss over the new family member. When you bring the baby a new toy, bring the pet one also, or at least give it a treat. Whenever you return home after being out, don't rush to the baby immediately and ignore the dog. A working couple I know noticed their dog becoming somewhat cross over their new baby but found that if they gave the dog a big warm greeting, even for just a few minutes, when they came home at the end of the day, the dog was content.

I *do* suggest not leaving the dog alone in the room with the baby, not until you can be absolutely sure that the dog is relaxed, takes the child for granted, and isn't harboring a grudge. Be aware that a dog may seem to accept the newcomer at first but then build up a resentment gradually. I don't mean to make the dog sound sinister—in the overwhelming majority of instances, people introduce new babies into their households with no problems whatsoever from their dogs. I'm just suggesting keeping the dog's point of view in mind. Some dogs accept any and all new family members right away; other dogs' noses may be out of joint for a while. Know your dog, be aware of how it might think and feel, and don't take chances.

Some dogs are simply one-person or one-family dogs and that's it. This may endear them to their owners, and there's nothing wrong with it as long as the dog isn't actually hostile to other people. My neighbor Bill Hickey has a big woolly dog named Bucky that he bailed out of the ASPCA several years ago. Bucky had been abused by his previous owner and was quite shy with strangers at first. He's pretty agreeable now, but he has never forgotten that Bill was the one who rescued him, and he idolizes Bill. But Bill says Bucky won't let anyone else in their apartment. I've suggested (nagged is more the way Bill might phrase it) that he teach Bucky to accept at least one or two other persons, in case he ever has to go to the hospital or if some other emergency arises, so someone can go in and care for Bucky.

The Humane Society of New York took in a stray German Shepherd that had been captured one bitter winter day in a graveyard where she was guarding her puppies. The pups had frozen to death and the mother was half dead from hunger and exposure. After a long rehabilitation at the Humane Society, the dog became physically healthy but remained so timid she was almost autistic.

She was adopted by a sympathetic and understanding woman who named her Jenny and spent months trying to reassure and socialize her. The result: a passionately adoring one-woman dog. Jenny isn't hostile to other people—she's still shy. But no one will ever hold a candle to her owner.

Dandy loves me but also almost everybody else. I have a dear friend, Anna, who stays in my apartment and looks after Dandy and the cats when I travel, and they are devoted to her. The first time I left them in her care, I telephoned long distance after a few days to see how things were going. Anna reported what they were all doing and how they were acting. Apparently they were not only bearing up well—it sounded as if they didn't even miss me. I remember my mixed feelings. I was glad that they were happy, of course, but gee, did they have to be *that* happy?

Chapter 4

TRAINING:

The Well-Behaved Urban Dog

I believe the future of dogs in cities depends a great deal on how well they behave. They are already a threatened species, and the trend in housing rules and city ordinances could soon place them on the endangered list. The best hope for those of us who wish to keep these marvelous animals with us in our urban homes is to see to it that they are perfect canine citizens.

Your urban dog must be far better behaved than its suburban or country counterpart. This sounds unfair, but actually, having your dog under control not only enhances your own peace of mind and respects your neighbors' rights—it also helps assure your dog's comfort and safety. A dog that barks and whines when left alone is not only a pain in the neck to all within earshot but is itself miserable, suffering from separation anxiety. A dog that picks fights with others on the street is not a comfortable dog and can get into serious trouble, hurt or even killed.

It seems to me that the behavior training priorities for the owner of a city dog are house-training and socializing. House-training covers not just learning to control body functions but being quiet when left alone and not damaging household property. Under socializing, I would include helping a dog to become gentle and friendly, teaching it proper street behavior, and training it to obey basic obedience commands (come, sit, down, stay, heel, and no).

TOUCHING

It is no accident that an animal that's kept as a companion and object of affection is called a "pet." This word reveals the importance of the touching, fondling, caressing, and nurturing that are summoned forth in the relationship between ourselves and our companion animals. And petting is a two-way street, because it involves not only the pleasure of stroking, on our part, but encourages affectionate responses in the animal.

A well-socialized cat when petted will arch its back, purr, rub against you; even a horse that is treated much like a pet will bow its head and nuzzle. And a dog will express its pleasure in many ways—tail wagging, "smiling," dancing about or rolling on its back, perhaps even leaning against you with a dreamy expression on its face. When its beloved owner's hand drops affectionately on its head, a dog will almost certainly acknowledge the gesture with some happy response.

In fact, one of the major pleasures in having a dog in the first place is touching it—hugging it, playfully scratching its ears, running a hand soothingly down its warm head and shoulders. But these acts go beyond the enjoyment they bring to us—they are a way of strengthening the bond between pet and owner, of making the dog feel loved, and of socializing the animal to human beings.

If you are entering dog ownership with a puppy, now is a good time to start it out on the right paw, so to speak. It is probably unnecessary to advise that you pet your puppy a lot, because how can you resist? Encourage other people to do the same. Every hug and cuddle goes into the pup's little bank of experience and helps inculcate in it the belief that human beings are just swell and can be trusted. That's the right attitude for a dog to have, especially in the city. Your job is to provide a life for it in which nothing serious happens to destroy this belief in the goodness of humankind.

Dandy seems to believe that this is the best of all possible worlds and that most people and other animals are nice, except when I double-cross her by taking her to the veterinarian, an ordeal for which she eventually forgives me. But I can't take much credit for her sunny attitude because she was already that way when I got her. I think she must have been treated very well when she was a puppy.

Get your puppy accustomed to being manipulated, as if it was being given a thorough physical examination. Look in its ears and under its tail; open its mouth and put your fingers in. (I wish I had thought of doing this to Dandy when she was young; now, if I have to give her a pill that I can't hide in her food, I practically have to use a crowbar to open her clenched teeth.) Examine your puppy's toes. Start brushing and combing and grooming the pup very early. Do all this frequently while it is growing up, and keep doing it even after it's grown.

Stroke your puppy even when it is eating, and take its food bowl away for a moment, then give it back. You don't want a dog that will bite your hand off if you touch it or its bowl while it's eating—a common reaction of a dog that hasn't been properly socialized. I remember once a new kitten ran over and, before I could intervene, stuck its head in Dandy's bowl while she was eating—a potentially dangerous act, since many dogs would have growled, snapped, or bitten. Dandy's reaction was simply to eat faster.

It's good to cradle a puppy on its back as you would a baby. Get it used to being carried about, by you and by other people. But please don't forget the advice I gave you in Chapter 2 about the right ways to hold and play with a puppy, because they are important also in the socializing process.

I don't mean to suggest that you handle a young dog nonstop, never giving it a moment to rest or just be quiet by itself. As Dr. Lerman pointed out in Chapter 2, children especially should learn to respect an animal's right to be left alone when it's tired or has had enough. For this early touching to socialize your puppy and defuse any possible aggressive tendencies, it must be pleasurable to the dog—otherwise it will have the opposite effect. If the puppy is pestered and mauled, rather than handled in a loving and under-standing way, the opportunity for it to develop an angelic disposition will be ruined.

An adult dog can be socialized in much the same way as a puppy, except that you may have to go slowly if it has been abused, neglected, or mishandled in any way. Be especially careful, for example, about touching its food bowl when it is eating. If the dog has ever gone hungry, it may have developed an anxious attitude toward food and might react instantly to what it perceives as a threat to filling its belly. But with continued reassurance and good treatment, the dog will eventually learn to trust you and other people.

Most dogs hate to have their feet touched or handled, and it's a good idea for city people especially to get their pets used to this. Not only will you probably need to clip your dog's toenails occasionally, but you'll want to wipe its feet when it comes in with wet or muddy paws, and it's no fun to have to cope with a struggling animal in order to do it.

HOUSEBREAKING

Two important pieces of advice, before we get down to the nitty-gritty of housebreaking: Don't even attempt to house-train a puppy until it is between three and four months old, because that's as hopeless as trying to toilet-train an infant. The dog simply hasn't developed reliable bladder and bowel control. And secondly, if anyone tells you to punish a dog for its mistakes in the house by rubbing its nose in the mess, forget it. That is dumb, ineffective, and cruel.

Be especially patient with a dog that has lived in a cage, as in a shelter or pet shop or even at a breeder's. Being caged in that way suppresses the dog's natural instinct not to soil its den, because the animal has no choice. However, if a shelter dog has been a housebroken pet and hasn't been caged too long, it may quickly remember its training when you get it home.

Begin housebreaking a dog, including a puppy when it's old enough, by taking it to the street at regular times—upon waking in the morning, after each meal, after play, when it gets up from a nap, and the last thing at night. Keep a regular schedule, and also take the dog to the same place on the street each time. Whenever it performs at the curb, pet and praise it extravagantly. (And don't forget to clean up any fecal matter.)

When you're with your dog in the house, keep an eye open for signals that it might have to go out. (Use a baby gate if necessary to prevent it from going to a room where you can't watch it.) The animal will start sniffing in corners or on the rugs, often turning in circles and acting agitated. That's your cue to spring to your feet and whisk your pet outdoors—and this will reinforce the learning process.

When you're not home, the best plan is to confine the dog to a place where it can't hurt the floor—the bathroom or kitchen—or in one of those folding, heavy wire cages called kennel crates or safari cages, lined with newspapers. The confinement space should be big enough for the animal to lie stretched out and should contain newspapers, its water bowl, and some toys. The dog will instinctively adopt the crate or confinement area as its den, and because dogs are loath to soil their den, the animal will try to hold its elimination needs until it is taken out. As the dog begins to relieve itself on schedule and only outdoors, then you can gradually let it have the run of the house when you're out.

Bill Berloni recommends establishing a time limit within which a dog must learn to relieve itself at the curb. If the animal hasn't done its business within, say, half of a city block, bring it back in and make it wait until next time. The dog's discomfort may inspire it to react more quickly when taken out. Otherwise, especially with a male dog, you may find yourself pacing up and down at the curb some winter night waiting and waiting for your pet to perform. When it gets the idea and urinates or defecates at the curb within a reasonable time, reward it, of course, until it gets the habit.

Some city dwellers prefer to paper-train their dogs. Follow the same general procedure as if you were taking it to the curb, but instead, take it regularly to a place where you have spread newspapers thickly. When it relieves itself at the right place, pet and praise it.

There will be accidents. These can be exasperating, but try not to get mad at your pet. One way to clean up a puddle on a carpet or upholstery, by the way, is to blot it first with paper toweling, if possible putting several thicknesses of paper towel under the spot as well. Then wash the spot with a solution of one part vinegar to two parts water. Let the vinegar solution sit on the spot for a little while, then blot with more paper towels.

My friend Miriam, an experienced dog and cat owner, swears by the use of rubbing alcohol to remove all types of pet-related soiled spots. Be generous with the alcohol, wiping vigorously on both sides of the rug or fabric, she says. Then prop something under the wet spot, or put thick layers of paper toweling under it, while it dries.

A dog may break house-training when it is anxious about some change in the household—a death in the family, the arrival of a baby, a new person living in the house, a move, or the acquisition of a new pet, for example. Dogs are creatures of routine and habit and can feel very threatened even when they merely sense a change coming, which they may perceive as impending doom. But a previously housebroken dog doesn't start soiling in the house out of spite— instead, it is upset. The way to deal with that is to figure out what's bothering the animal and take steps to reassure it.

On the occasions when Dandy gets desperate, especially now that she's old, she tries to use the cats' litterbox. How's that for brains? I anticipate that this might happen by spreading a lot of newspapers on the floor right next to the litterbox, and she uses them.

A dog that has just moved from the country or suburbs to the city may have a hard time at first, especially with house-training. It may refuse to relieve itself in the street; the pavement doesn't feel right to a dog that is used to grass under its feet. Also, it may be unable to relieve itself if it is nervous and afraid of the traffic.

Be very patient with the animal and give it lots of encouragement and reassurance, keeping the same schedule for walks that it had before. Take it out frequently and be sure it gets enough exercise. You might have to confine it when you're not home and watch it closely for signals when you're there, just as if you were starting housebreaking from scratch. Don't worry, it will learn, probably in just a few days.

PROBLEM BARKING

One of the most important things you will ever teach your dog is not to bark, howl, or whine when you're out. Not all dogs vocalize when left alone, but if you hear yours making a ruckus as you approach your door, or if a neighbor has complained, you must deal with this problem immediately and successfully—for your animal's sake, for your neighbors', and for your own if you wish to keep your pet.

Very few people would place a year-old baby in a playpen, give it some toys, put in a bottle of milk in case it got hungry, and go off and leave it for eight or ten hours without expecting the baby to display signs of severe anxiety during this lengthy social isolation. Human beings are innately social creatures, and most of us suffer greatly if separated for very long from our fellows.

Dogs, almost without exception, are also social beings (remember the pack behavior described in Chapter 3). Laboratory dogs that are kept in isolation for experimental reasons suffer even more than human prisoners that are sentenced to solitary confinement, for the dogs have no understanding and no hope. And a pet, especially a puppy, deprived of companionship for many hours experiences the same feelings of abandonment that the human baby would feel. Both express separation anxiety.

According to Dr. Peter Borchelt, consultant at the Animal Behavior Clinic of the Animal Medical Center in New York City, the first reactions to being left alone, in both babies and dogs, are crying, elimination, and destructive behavior. Many dog owners misunderstand these actions on the part of their pets—they interpret the dog's "naughtiness" as an effort to punish them for leaving.

"Dogs don't have the complicated thought processes that would be required for them to punish their owners for doing something they didn't like, such as leaving them alone," says Borchelt. "When the dog vocalizes, it is simply expressing anxiety. Young animals in the wild, when separated from their mothers, will call and call, an instinctual reaction that helps their mothers locate them. Possibly the dog's reaction is similar—it may be signaling its location to its absent owner. When the dog eliminates, it is leaving its scent. And when it totals the house, it is trying to escape, trying to get out so it can reattach to its owner.''

Other, more subtle signs of separation anxiety are moping, failing to eat or play, psychosomatic responses such as imaginary illnesses or injuries, and hyperactivity, attention-getting behavior when the owner returns home.

Puppies, separated first from their mothers and littermates, then from their owners when the owners go out and leave them alone, will instinctively begin to cry. Borchelt also points out that an animal that has been passed around to successive owners, attaching itself to someone only to be permanently separated from him or her, is more likely to suffer from separation anxiety than a dog that has lived for a long time with a dependable owner and feels secure.

But the important thing to remember is that a dog that cries or shows other signs of anxiety when left alone is not a bad dog, is not misbehaving, but is reacting to normal insecurity. What you want to do is to reassure the dog that you'll be back and to convince it that it must wait for you quietly.

To train a dog not to bark, you must catch it in the act. Pretend to leave your house, but wait outside the door until the animal starts up, then dash in and reprimand it. Most dogs begin to wail within fifteen minutes, so you won't have to hang around your hall for hours.

On the other hand, just as often, come back in *before* it starts to bark and pet and praise it. It's important that the dog learn to distinguish between the behavior that elicits a strongly disapproving ''No!'' and the behavior that gets enthusiastic hugs and kisses. In the beginning, you may have to go in and out at ten-second intervals, but you'll find you can gradually extend the time. Keep up this training for fifteen-minute sessions, several times a day. Don't give up.

If you are friendly with your immediate neighbors, you might solicit their cooperation. Ask them to let you know whether your pet has complained or been quiet when you were out. That way, they will know you are concerned and actively working on the problem, and their feedback can help you to ascertain how quickly your dog is learning.

Some dogs are helped by the sound of a radio playing quietly. Others are comforted by the presence of another pet. But the main thing is that your dog gets the message about how you expect it to behave when you're not home.

You don't want to teach your dog never to bark—that would be like expecting a child not to speak or a bird not to sing. Also, if you reprimand your pet every time it makes a sound, it might keep quiet when there's a prowler outside, or when there's a fire. True stories abound of instances in which the barking of a pet has saved lives by attracting help when needed. Also, it is natural for a dog to bark for joy when playing or greeting its owner, and that should be allowed. What you want is for your pet to bark selectively, so it only has to remember the few instances when barking is forbidden.

If your dog barks every time a neighbor passes the door of your apartment, you might open the door and let the dog see who it is, reassuring it at the same time. If the dog learns to recognize the sounds that are regular and normal, not suspicious, it will know not to sound the alarm.

Many dogs will bark because of irrational fears. Once, to my intense embarrassment, my dog Benjy set up a ferocious barking when a disabled guest arrived at my house using a walker. The guest handled it beautifully, spoke calmly to the dog and encouraged him to approach her and be petted. After Benjy had examined the walker closely, all the while listening to my guest's soothing tones and my reassurances, he decided the thing was okay and forgot about it.

But if a dog always barks nonstop at some feared object that it encounters with some regularity—a vacuum cleaner, for instance— then it's necessary to desensitize the animal so it won't drive you and the neighbors crazy every time you clean the house. Start by having someone else use the cleaner at some distance from the dog, and only for a few minutes. Reassure the dog continually when the motor is on. Reward it as soon as it can tolerate the cleaner without barking. Then gradually step up the time the cleaner is on and slowly decrease its distance from the dog. Be patient—remember the animal is not trying to bug you, but trying to warn you about a fearsome object.

In 1984, a town on Long Island passed a "noise ordinance" that would impose a fine on anyone whose dog barked continuously for longer than fifteen minutes. News of this law struck a responsive chord with some people and had some national reverberations. However, as one dog owner pointed out, such a law puts legal weapons in the hands of dog haters. In cities that fail to enforce laws against such widespread nuisances as the earsplitting din of rock music on portable radios, such laws do indeed seem discriminatory. I definitely think people should train their dogs not to bark when left alone, but the laws already in place that cover nuisances, including noise, are sufficient. What our cities need is enforcement of existing laws, not further legislation against dog owners.

OTHER BEHAVIOR PROBLEMS

One of the first things your dog will do, especially if it's a puppy, is jump up on you and on everyone who gives it attention. The animal is only trying to get close and establish eye contact, but it's best to discourage this behavior. You don't want it jumping up when it has muddy feet, for instance, but you can't expect the animal to understand what's wrong with muddy feet. A big dog jumping up on an elderly or frail person, or a child, even in the friendliest way imaginable, can hurt. So what you want to do is teach your pet to keep all four feet on the ground when interacting with you or other people, period.

There are several recommended ways to teach a dog not to jump up: You can step lightly on its hind toes, you can bump it in the chest with your knee, or you can grasp its front paws and push it backward so it is off balance. Any of these should be accompanied by the command, "No!" Then, after the dog gets down, ignore it for a few minutes. Bill Berloni says the worst thing you can do to a dog, humanely, is to ignore it. Dogs are so anxious for approval and acceptance by their owners that they'll do most anything to get noticed.

After a moment, when you're sure your pet has got the message and has stayed down, pat and praise it. Remember, be consistent. Don't confuse the dog by letting it jump up just this once, and then pushing it down and saying "No!" the next time. And don't give up.

Jumping on the furniture when left alone—any dog with sense will try it at least once. There's an old joke about a dog that had a habit of sneaking up on the sofa or a chair for a nap when its owners were out. Though the dog was always at the door to greet them when they came home, the owners would go around the room feeling the seats of all the furniture, searching for telltale warmth. Whenever they discovered the dog had been naughty, they'd punish it. So one day they came home and found the dog blowing on the sofa cushion to cool it off.

Seriously, if you don't wish your pet to lie on the furniture, you must catch it in the act of jumping up, or actually there. Scolding the dog after it has already gotten down won't do it. To catch the animal, you have to outsmart it, using the same method as teaching it not to bark, by going out and waiting in the hall till you think it's had time to settle on the sofa or wherever, then returning unexpectedly. Burst into the house and if the dog has indeed sacked out on the cushions, yell "No!" The dog will probably jump down and run, but if it stays where it is, push it down to the floor and say "No!" Do this several times a day.

And equally important—go out and come back in before the dog has had a chance to get up on the furniture, and then reward it. Keep extending the time you wait before coming back in.

When you have to go out for other than training reasons, by the way, don't reward the dog unless there's some way you can be sure it hasn't been lying on the furniture and jumped down the minute it heard your key in the lock. It may have blown on the cushion to cool it off!

A puppy is going to want to sleep in your bed with you, and this is a matter of choice on your part. Lots of dog owners let their pets sleep with them, and I certainly don't see anything wrong with that.

But if you prefer that your pet sleep in its own bed, at least keep the bed in the room where you sleep. Remember that your dog loves you, and its idea of where it should always be is at your side—especially in the dark of night.

To help a little puppy get used to sleeping alone in its own bed, try putting a warm hot water bottle (wrapped in a towel) and a clock with a tick loud enough to hear (also wrapped in a towel) in the bed with it, to approximate the warm bodies and heartbeats of the mother and siblings it misses.

Just like babies who go through a stage of putting everything in their mouth, puppies tend to chew on anything they find that looks tasty—sox and shoes, handbags and books, electric light cords, you name it. They do this especially when they're teething, of course.

The way to deal with this is to confine the pup when you're not around to keep an eye on it. Shut it in the bathroom or kitchen, or invest in a kennel crate as I suggested for use during housebreaking, and settle the pup there whenever you go out.

Adult dogs also sometimes chew up household objects or their owners' possessions when they're left alone. According to Borchelt, this is another expression of separation anxiety. This redirected behavior is similar to the way some of us bite our fingernails or drum our fingers when we're nervous. A dog that's ordinarily a paragon of perfect house behavior can resort to destructive chewing when left alone at times of dramatic change in household routine. Seeing packing cartons around before moving, or suitcases before a trip, for example, can trigger it. A kennel crate is also useful at such times. A normally well-behaved dog will stop of its own accord as soon as the household settles down again and familiar routine is restored.

Remember the dog's denning instinct; putting it in a small room or kennel crate for part of the time is not cruel but protects both the dog and your possessions. Put its bed, a towel, anything cozy and comfortable for it to lie on in the room or at one end of the crate, spread newspapers as far from the bed as possible, in case of accidents, and give it some safe toys to chew on. Chew toys are an important part of a dog's accoutrements anyway—hard nylon bones, hard rubber toys, objects that can't splinter or break up if chewed (for example, not plastic, wood, or soft rubber).

If you confine a dog in the kitchen or bathroom, by the way, be sure to put poisons, garbage, and the like—anything the animal might get into—out of its way.

It will be easier for your dog to distinguish its own toys from other objects if you limit the number of toys to just a few. If a dog has too many playthings scattered about, it can get confused about which are its own.

As I've said, I think it is a bad idea to give a dog something of its owner's to chew, like an old shoe or sock, because the dog can't tell a worn-out sneaker from a brand-new Gucci loafer. When I put that in a magazine article, a reader wrote and told me that her dog had one of her old shoes as a chew toy and never bothered her good shoes— and she sent me a cute snapshot of her dog biting its very own, old shoe. Obviously, I was wrong as far as her dog is concerned, but I pass this advice on to you anyway.

Job Michael Evans recommends leaving a personally scented dog toy (a hard nylon or rawhide chew bone, for instance) with your pet when you leave it alone. You scent the object by rubbing it firmly on your palm. Make eye contact with the dog and then offer it the scented toy. Evans discourages overemotional goodbyes and hellos—he says they keep some dogs on edge and more prone to chewing when left alone.

Some dogs, especially puppies, have a tendency to mouth you— take your hand or arm in their mouth and gnaw on you, not enough to hurt, usually, but just enough to be annoying. When a dog does that, don't snatch your hand away, or push the dog away. Instead, say "No!" loud and firm, remove the dog's mouth, hold it closed for a moment, and then ignore the animal. You might even get up and walk away, get involved in something else for a while, to make your point.

DEALING WITH AGGRESSION

Mouthing is not an aggressive act, but growling and showing teeth definitely are. A growl, snarl, or warning bark is the prelude to a bite. City dog owners cannot afford to have aggressive dogs. Even if your dog is gentle with you and your family and only hostile to others, this just won't do in the city, where the animal is constantly exposed .to other people and other dogs.

First of all, I can't imagine that it would be pleasant to have a dog you had to watch constantly, worrying about what it might do. Second and most important, an undependable dog might hurt someone. That would leave you responsible for the suffering your dog has caused, and also open to a lawsuit, to say nothing of the fact that your dog might be destroyed by the authorities of your city.

Be aware that aggressive dogs can also turn on their owners. It is known that not only do the vast majority of dog bites occur from owned dogs, but a sizable proportion of them are instances of dogs attacking their owners. Certainly something is very wrong when this tragedy occurs—the dog may have had irreparable harm done to it in the past, or its owner might abuse it, or it might be sick. But if you take on a dog with an unstable disposition, even if it seems perfectly loyal to you, you can't trust it.

Also, dogs can make mistakes, just as we do. We had a bad experience with this involving Dandy and a guard dog. My son was walking Dandy peacefully on her leash on the sidewalk past a garage. Suddenly a huge German Shepherd came roaring out of the garage and attacked Dandy. He bowled her over and bit her in the chest—a bad puncture wound that narrowly missed her lung—before the garage owner and my son could pull the dog off her. This idiot dog made two mistakes: First of all, he perceived the public sidewalk as a part of the territory he was supposed to guard; secondly, he attacked before he discovered Dandy was a female. (Normally, male dogs do not attack female dogs, and vice versa.)

The Shepherd's owner apologized all over the place and paid Dandy's veterinary bill. But this is an example of why guard dogs, and attack dogs, are a bad idea. I think it is wrong to turn dogs into weapons: It perverts their nature and distorts the loving and loyal relationship between them and human beings. The episode also indicates how a presumably well-trained dog can get confused at times. And if a befuddled dog happens to be aggressive, it can be dangerous.

Physical punishment increases, not decreases, aggression. As I pointed out earlier, the vast majority of reputable dog trainers consider hitting a dog counterproductive, and this goes especially for aggressive dogs. The owner's attitude plays a prime role: If the owner becomes angry and impatient, in any type of training, it will confuse the animal and make the problems worse.

Don't worry that if you have a submissive dog it won't try to protect your home in a threatening situation—in all likelihood it will. Its readiness to do this stems from the pack and den instincts I discussed earlier. Your dog will defend home and loved ones not out of aggression but because it is programmed by its heritage to do so.

In all honesty, I have to say some dogs are more likely to remember and act on those instincts than others. While I think my former dog Benjy might have gone for the jugular of a mugger, I doubt very much that Dandy would. People have told me, Oh yes, she would be a different dog if an ugly situation arose and you were in danger—but I have never believed it, even when she was young. However, her job is just to be a pet and a companion, not to guard me or mine.

The first thing to do, at the first sign of an aggressive tendency in a dog, is to have the animal spayed or castrated. Neutering will calm the dog and make it much more trainable.

Next, obedience training. Many urban SPCAs or humane societies, as well as private trainers, offer dog-training classes. Or better yet, if your dog is especially difficult, hire a professional trainer to work just with you and your pet. Otherwise, the animal's bad habits will just get worse, and then you will truly have a serious problem.

It goes almost without saying that you should also give the dog a great deal of affection and patient but firm leadership. In addition, help it to get used to other people in nonthreatening situations (on the street is a good place to start, as opposed to the dog's own home). Careful, regular, and casual contact with friends who like dogs will go a long way toward reassuring and socializing an aggressive dog. I can't stress it too much—city dogs must be well socialized.

If you do hire a private trainer to help you, be very selective. There are a lot of nuts out there in the dog-training business. There seems to be an especially high proportion of authoritarian men who use this profession as a means of getting rid of their own hostility and frustrations by brutalizing dogs into submission.

One type you should particularly look out for are those who use electric shock collars on the dogs during training. Even if your idea of the dog for you is a high-strung Doberman or a Shepherd with a big chip on its shoulder, the worst thing you can do is subject it to this kind of torture. You want a kind, firm, knowledgeable person who really likes dogs and has trained the pets of people you know personally whose judgment you trust.

SIMPLE OBEDIENCE TRAINING

Fundamental in having a city dog that's a joy to you, to itself, and to everybody else is teaching it to obey a repertoire of simple commands. This won't be hard to do if you have reasonable expectations of your pet and approach the training in a positive way. Ask not, How can I *stop* my dog from doing thus-and-such? Ask, rather: How can I get my dog to *do* thus-and-such? For example, instead of thinking, How can I stop my dog from pulling on the leash when I walk him/her? concentrate on teaching your dog to walk properly at your side.

Simple obedience training consists of teaching a dog to come when called, to sit and stay, to lie down, to heel (walk at your side), and to respond correctly to the word "no." Stick to one-word commands and be consistent—come, sit, stay, down, heel, and no.

Don't say, "Cut it out," or "Stop that, sweetheart, I don't like it when you do that," when what you mean is "No!"

Don't feel apologetic about training your dog, as if you were being mean to it or taking away its rights. Remember that the animal will feel better when it knows that you're in charge, that you know what you're doing, and that it will get love and approval from you when it does what you want it to. Be clear and firm in giving commands, and reward the dog lavishly for good behavior.

Betsey Sesler, a young woman I know in Dallas, adopted an Irish Setter named Katy who had been turned in to the SPCA because she was "bad with kids." Katy was a cowering, shy, slinking dog who did not know her name, was not housebroken, and was afraid of everyone and everything.

The first thing Betsey did was take Katy to obedience classes. "I can honestly say that obedience training made Katy blossom," she reports. "It gave her a sense of purpose and accomplishment, developed her self-confidence. She has served as my teaching dog in SPCA humane education programs and is wonderful with children. And in fact, she has won first place in obedience classes at many dog shows, including the American Kennel Club's most advanced title." Betsey believes her work in training Katy has put her relationship with her pet on the highest level possible between a human and an animal.

Bill Berloni, of theatrical performing dog fame, points out that there's a difference between teaching and correcting. "People are too quick to reprimand a dog," he says. "If your dog persists in doing something, in spite of your efforts to the contrary, ask yourself if you simply haven't gotten the message across—maybe the dog just needs more teaching, or a different method of teaching, instead of correcting. If the dog really knows what you want it to do, and has been doing it for some time, but for some reason suddenly does something else instead, then and only then can you assume it needs correcting."

There are two schools of thought about using food as a reward when training a dog. The only trouble with the food reward is that sometimes you'll be giving lessons out on the street so you'll have to carry dog treats with you. Also, the dog will learn to expect a treat and will be disappointed if that reward is not forthcoming every time it does what you want. For that reason, I'd suggest giving praise and a pat or hug along with a little treat such as a bit of cheese or dog tidbit in the beginning when your dog masters a simple obedience lesson, and then phasing out the food reward gradually while stepping up the praise and petting. Eventually your dog will be just as ecstatic about "Good boy!" or "Good girl!" as it was initially over a food treat.

Use "No!" sparingly, but in a way that communicates firm disapproval, making sure the animal knows exactly what it is you object to. Adjust the severity of your tone to the dog's temperament—some dogs will cringe pathetically at a reprimand, while others won't pay any attention at all unless you raise your voice. Berloni claims that all he has to do with Sandy, the dog that he trained to celebrity status in the musical *Annie*, is raise his eyebrows and Sandy knows he should stop whatever it is he's doing.

Berloni suggests that your tone of voice should definitely be different for the word "no" than for the other commands. If you lose your temper and yell "Come!" in an angry voice, what dog is going to want to respond? Give the obedience commands in a friendly voice, and express annoyance only with "No!"

Frequently precede or follow a command word with the dog's name. Dog trainer Job Michael Evans recommends eye contact for three or four seconds whenever you give your dog a command. He feels this helps let the animal know that you are pack leader.

Some trainers recommend corporal punishment—a rap on the nose or swat on the behind—when a dog misbehaves. You may have heard the folded newspaper theory—that you should smack a dog with a rolled-up newspaper when it has been "bad." I wouldn't use any hitting at all, and the best dog trainers I know are also vehemently against it. If you are patient and persistent, you should be able to teach your dog by making clear what you want and then rewarding it with displays of your love and approval.

Before you start obedience lessons, two important pieces of advice: Don't try to obedience-train a puppy before it is three to four months old, or you will just confuse it and frustrate yourself. (You can start training it yourself or with a private trainer after that age, but wait till it's older—five to six months—before you take it to an obedience class with other dogs.) And don't try to train a dog for longer than ten to fifteen minutes at a time, or it will become tired or bored and will grow to hate rather than enjoy the lessons. Two sessions a day should be about right.

Also, be sure that every member of the family agrees on what and how the dog should be trained. If the animal gets conflicting messages on its do's and don'ts, it will be confused and training will break down completely.

Come, Sit, Down, and Stay

"Come" is probably the easiest command to teach, especially when followed by the dog's name, because it indicates to the animal that you are calling it to you to give it affection. But you must insist that it respond every time, even when it has an interest elsewhere. If the dog doesn't come when you call it, go and lead it by the collar to where you were standing. Some dog trainers recommend using the leash, even indoors, to draw the dog to you when you say "Come!"

The importance of teaching your dog to come when called shouldn't be underestimated by city dog owners. Even though your dog will always be leashed on the street (I hope), there may be places such as fenced dog runs where it will be running loose, and you may want to get it away from troublesome dogs or people. Or on the street, you may accidentally lose hold of the leash for some reason. I know a beautiful Golden Retriever that was startled by a sound on the street just at a moment when his owner, her arms full of packages, had unknowingly dropped his leash for a few seconds. The dog bolted, ignored her call, dashed into the street, and was hit by a truck. So you want to be sure your pet's response to the "Come!" command is as reliable as possible.

Also, there will be plenty of occasions indoors when you want to call your dog to you and have it respond. You want to groom it, take it out, have it meet company. Or say you want to give it a bath, and you have a nice tubful of warm water all ready—you don't want to have to search for your pet and drag it out of hiding.

One rule on which all dog trainers agree: Never, never call your dog to you and then punish or scold it. This will only make the dog hate and fear you and will more likely ensure that it will ignore you or run in the opposite direction when you call it. You can hardly blame it for that. Try to get the dog to associate "come" with pleasure and rewards.

"Sit," "Down," and "Stay" should be taught together, since there's no point in teaching your pet to sit or lie down if it gets up and walks away two seconds later. You teach a dog to sit, obviously, by giving the verbal command and by pushing its rear end so that it sits down. If it stands up immediately, say "Sit!" again and push it into the sitting position. Keep this up until the dog remains seated long enough for you to say "Good dog" and stroke it.

You might want to use the leash for this exercise, so that you can pull your dog's head up while you push its rear end down.

Use the leash for teaching "Down" also. Have your pet sit, and face it with your foot on the leash. Raise your hand, palm toward the animal, and when you say "Down," make a downward sweep with your hand and get the dog into a lying position. With a little dog, you can pull it down by the collar; a big dog may require a push at the shoulders or a gentle pull forward of the front feet. However you do it, get the dog into a lying position and praise it. Give it a food reward until it learns to obey the command automatically, then gradually phase out the food but keep up the praise. Keep practicing, making sure the animal associates "Down" and the hand signal with the prone position.

There probably won't be many occasions outdoors when you'll be telling your dog "Down," but indoors, a well-mannered dog might be told to lie down if, for instance, you are serving guests and your pet is getting under foot, or if you are visiting with it in someone else's house.

"Stay" is a little harder, because when you walk away the dog will naturally get up to follow you or stroll away. Put the palm of your hand in front of the dog's nose while the animal is seated or lying down, and say "Stay." Then, bending over and keeping your hand in the same position, slowly walk around it. If it gets up, say "No!" make it sit again, and repeat the exercise. When the dog remains seated, reward it. Once it has mastered staying still while you walk around it, try backing away, holding your hand palm forward, toward the dog. If the dog gets up, say "No!" and go and make the dog sit or lie down again. Repeat the exercise, for ten-to-fifteen minute sessions, several times a day, until it gets the idea.

Job Michael Evans suggests that city dog owners teach their dogs always to sit, even without the command, at the door when they return from a walk, so they can get out their keys and unlock the door easily without having the dogs milling around waiting to be let in. This makes sense.

Heel

Few experiences with a dog are more aggravating than trying to walk one that is all over the place, straining and lunging forward on the leash, or dragging behind. You'd be surprised how strong even little dogs can be when they are not properly leash-trained. But what a pleasure it is to walk down the street with your dog trotting nicely at your side.

Ideally, walking your dog should be a matter of give and take. The dog has a right to find just the perfect spot at the curb to relieve itself, and sometimes this takes a little circling and pacing back and forth. Let your pet fool around a bit, as long as it doesn't become preoccupied with another animal's droppings.

On the other hand, once it has relieved itself, you have a right to insist that it come along with you if you are in a hurry or have errands to do. When I walk Dandy, I let her do her business and give her some time to dawdle and sniff because she enjoys that. Then I tighten the leash and make her come along with me. Often I take her with me to the copy center, to the cleaner, to the newsstand, or wherever, even to the bank. If I stop to talk with a neighbor, she waits patiently.

Here's a tip for good street manners with a dog: Naturally you can't take your pet into a grocery store, restaurant, deli, or the like, because that would violate local health laws, but if you enter a non-food type of store, always ask the proprietor, or the first person you see who works there, if it's okay to bring your dog in. Even though it's probably not illegal for an animal to be there, it's a nice policy to respect the preferences of the store owner or manager. You'd be surprised how welcome you may be if you ask first. Not only that, but you help improve the image of city dog owners generally.

In teaching your dog "Heel," the consensus among dog trainers is that you walk with your dog on your left, holding the leash closely with your left hand and the end of the leash with your right. Don't ask me why the dog must be on the left—my feeling is your pet should learn to walk at your heel on either side. But to go with the experts, at least start out teaching it to walk on your left. Start walking forward. If the dog pulls ahead, give a quick, short tug on the leash with your left hand and say "Heel, boy" (or girl, or use the dog's name). Don't yank the animal off its feet, but give a tug firm enough to be felt.

Your instinct might be to keep the leash so tight that the dog can't pull forward. This may prevent it from ranging ahead, but it doesn't teach it to walk at your heel. The dog must walk there on its own, not because it's held so tightly it can't run ahead. Keep up working on the "Heel" command until the animal finally walks beside you, then give it a lot of praise and petting. Ten minutes of lessons at a time are enough, several times a day.

The same technique applies to a dog that's hanging behind. A puppy especially may do this when you first take it out on the leash. Don't drag the animal along, but coax it in a friendly voice, giving short tugs at the leash (again with your left hand) until it decides to come along, then praise it. It should get the idea that what you want is for it to walk along with you.

Job Evans suggests that a puppy be carried for its first few excursions on the street. Hug the dog close to you at about shoulder level and let it take in the strange sights, noises, and smells from the protection of your arms. This makes the puppy feel secure, and it will be less likely to be afraid when you eventually put it down and start to teach it to walk on the leash.

Some dogs catch on quickly and in a few days are walking at your side very nicely. Other dogs—many strong-willed little terriers, for instance—require an inordinate amount of training and patience. Hang in there.

I've seen dogs that have been trained not to look to the right or the left and to ignore other dogs on the street. This is a good idea for people who have dogs that tend to be quarrelsome with other dogs and who haven't socialized their pets. But with a friendly city dog, I personally think it's nice to let it have plenty of social intercourse with other friendly dogs. Dogs on the same block get to know one another and form friendships. Dandy has several friends of her own species—Melissa, Bucky, Brandy, Fritz, Katy, Ludvig, Willie, Ruffian, and Brando, among others—and is a great admirer of a German Shepherd named Jasper even though he tends to ignore her.

Bill Berloni cautions, however, not to push dogs on each other. Even if you have a friend with a dog and you think it would be ever so nice if your dog and your friend's pet were pals, the dogs are entitled to their preferences. They must not fight—that's against the rules—but they should be permitted to ignore each other if they want.

Incidentally, it's well to be cautious about children with dogs on the leash, unless you know them. You can't trust a child to have control of his or her dog on the street.

In the process of modifying your dog's behavior, to turn it into a perfect house pet and urban dweller, the key words to remember are patience and perseverance. Training a dog can be boring, discouraging, and exasperating. Some owners give up and either learn to live with their pets' bad habits or get rid of the animals. Neither course is good.

A dog can be such a pleasure and give such rewards in terms of love, companionship, and loyalty, it is well worth your while to invest the time and energy required to help it become a well-behaved city pet.

CHAPTER 5

DIET:

Keeping Your Dog Well Nourished

Food is more than just fuel for our bodies. It comforts us, nourishes our souls, and gives sensory pleasure. The preparation and dispensing of food is an expression of love and hospitality. Food has much emotional baggage and enters into the relationship between owner and dog in ways that go beyond merely providing sustenance.

Few dog owners just fill the feeding bowl and set it before the animal in a perfunctory way. Feeding is a social event for us and our pets, an important element in the bond between us. It's usually accompanied by an interplay of communication. Many of us, as we prepare each meal, talk what psychologists have termed "motherese"—nonsense chatter in soothing tones. Meanwhile, the dog plays its part in the little ceremony, gazing at us bright-eyed and eager, dancing about, tail awag. Chow time is frankly a trip for both dog and owner!

It must be relatively easy to sustain a dog, considering the bizarre dog diets I've heard of. I once knew a hound that subsisted for years on raw carrots, cottage cheese, and rawhide chips. But I've also known a Toy Poodle that was fed the same macrobiotic diet its owner ate; not surprisingly, the animal deteriorated and became ill. The owner took it to a veterinarian, who fortunately persuaded her to feed her pet appropriately.

When I was a child, our dog was fed leftovers from our table, with dog biscuits as bedtime snacks. Our food was simple down-home fare—well-balanced meat and vegetables, nothing spicy, pickled, or exotic. Apparently our diet gave Laddie enough nourishment, for he lived a long, healthy life. Today, however, our own food habits have changed—many of us eat less meat, for instance—and our diets might not give our pets the balance of nutrients they need for optimal health. Furthermore, we know a lot more about dog nutrition now. Food from our tables is fine as supplement, but shouldn't comprise a dog's total diet.

I no longer eat meat, for philosophical reasons, but my dog and cats eat dog and cat food. A dog can apparently be healthy on a vegetarian—or at least meatless—diet, but you have to know a lot about canine nutrition to make sure the animal gets all the protein, fat, and nutrients it needs.

Properly fed dogs live longer, happier lives and are sick less often than those on poor diets. And city dog owners have a strong personal motivation, second only to our concern for our pets' well-being, to keep our animals' GI systems in top working order. Any apartment dweller who has had to cope with a dog with an upset digestion will know what I mean.

COMMERCIAL DOG FOOD

Just because a dog is considered a carnivore, that doesn't mean it should eat nothing but meat. Even carnivores in the wild don't eat meat exclusively. Like their primitive ancestors, contemporary wild canids—coyotes, wolves, and other cousins of our pet dogs—consume the vegetable matter in the stomachs of the herbivores they kill. Also, since the dog moved into the cave and began to cohabit with us, it has become more of an omnivore, like us. An all-meat diet could cause serious nutritional deficiencies. The well-cared-for dog today is fed a balanced diet and is better off for it. The balance depends on several factors, including the animal's age and lifestyle.

Few of us are going to make our own dog food, which is certainly possible but a lot of work—not only preparing it but studying up on canine nutrition to be sure we put in the right ingredients in the correct amounts for our individual dogs. Fortunately, we don't have to, for most commercial foods not only spare us the cooking but provide good nutrition.

The problem is that there are so many commercial dog foods to choose from. Supermarket shelves offer an overwhelming abundance of cans, boxes, packages, and bags, all purporting to contain total nutrition, the best diet we could possibly feed our pets. If you have picked more or less blindly, you might have hit on what's best for your dog—or perhaps you could make better choices.

Dog food comes in several general forms: dry, canned, and semi-moist. Dry dog food is meal, kibble, or little uniform hard nuggets, packaged in boxes or bags. Canned dog food falls into two types: ration, which is very dense and may look like cooked cereal; and meat, which looks rather like stew. Semi-moist dog food is usually formed and colored to look like hamburger, chunks of raw meat, or meat patties, and is sold in individual packets in boxes. All contain both animal and vegetable protein, fat, fiber, and the vitamins and minerals dogs need, plus moisture. They differ in composition and methods of processing. Also in price. The dry dog foods are the least expensive; the meat-type canned foods are the highest priced.

A major difference is the amount of water each type contains. Dry dog foods generally contain 10 to 12 percent moisture; canned, 70 to 78 percent; and semi-moist, 30 to 35 percent. The water is necessary in processing the food and makes it edible and palatable.

The dry dog foods are cereal-based, containing mostly vegetable protein, with meat meal and bone meal. Most of the ration-type canned foods and the semi-moist foods contain mainly vegetable protein with meat by-products.

Semi-moist dog foods also contain salt and a small amount of corn syrup sweetener. The main attractions of semi-moist foods are for dog owners: eye appeal and convenience. They have no special advantages for dogs.

There are commercial dog foods for dogs with medical problems—bladder stones, kidney or heart disorders, or sensitive digestive systems—that require special diets. These foods, available through veterinarians, have helped extend the lives of many pets.

Special commercial foods for puppies, fat dogs, older dogs, and dogs doing high-stress work have percentages of ingredients to meet the needs of these groups. Some are sold in supermarkets, some through veterinarians.

You shouldn't have any problem selecting the right commercial food for your particular dog once you have the information you need to make a wise choice.

Dog food manufacturers go to a lot of trouble to make their products look (and smell) good to us, the dog owners. A dog doesn't care if its food looks like hamburger or cereal, yet somehow we feel we're giving our pets better stuff if it looks rather like something we wouldn't mind eating ourselves. However, what really matters is whether a food has the right proportion of ingredients for an individual dog, and whether the dog likes it, not how appetizing it looks by our standards.

One school of thought holds that dogs don't care about variety and are perfectly happy eating the same food day after day. Maybe so. But I personally think they do enjoy different-tasting food now and then. I vary Dandy's diet in terms of flavors. It is true, however, that an abrupt and extreme change in diet can upset a dog's stomach.

Also, each dog is an individual, and what one dog thrives on may not be easily digested by another. Dry dog foods, for example, give some dogs gas, and semi-moist foods give others diarrhea.

Then there are the finicky eaters, who have decided preferences and will turn up their noses at food that most dogs lick their chops over. I think it's best not to let a dog be too fussy. The little tyrant gets the idea that if it holds out for something it particularly loves, you'll cave in and serve that. I've heard people say their dogs absolutely refuse to eat anything but thus-and-such. If thus-and-such happens to be the nutritious food the dog should eat anyway, fine, but sometimes what a dog gets hooked on is the canine equivalent of junk food, or a single food like liver, which can cause a toxic buildup of vitamin A.

This dog is a great family pet, but might take exception if a stranger tried to pick up the baby. *(Patricia Seilheimer/Courtesy, Pets Are Wonderful Council)*

A well-behaved dog amuses itself watching out the window while waiting for its family to return. *(Hope Ryden)*

Three city dogs learning basic obedience: Heel, Sit, and Down.
(Jane Sapinsky/Courtesy, People Training for Dogs)

A healthy puppy waits to be adopted from a shelter. Note the alert expression, clear eyes and nose, good coat. *(Kathy Chochrun/Courtesy, Humane Society of New York)*

The face of stress: "Somebody's leaving. Where do I fit into the plans?" *(Courtesy, The Alpo Pet Center)*

Unsafe: This dog is vulnerable to being stolen. *(David Cupp)*

Unsafe: This dog could fall out and be killed, or be thrown about and be injured. *(Animal Protection Institute of America)*

If your dog is already a fussy eater, refusing anything but its one or two favorite foods, I suggest phasing other foods gradually into its diet—mixing small amounts in each meal, with whatever the animal is hung up on, and increasing the amounts of the new food gradually. Also, be strong. It's very hard to hold out against the reproachful looks and hurt attitude you'll get from your pet, but remember, no dog is suicidal over food. It will eat eventually.

Dogs enjoy dog biscuits and other commercial dog snacks and treats, and owners enjoy feeding them. Though they aren't intended to be a dog's sole diet, many are nutritious. They're certainly better for dogs than the sweets we eat. I bet it would be hard to find a dog owner who doesn't give his or her pet a bite of cookie, a piece of cake, or a little ice cream now and then. This sharing is part of the pleasure of the bond between pet and owner. Unless what you're eating is chocolate, which is harmful to dogs, giving your pet a taste won't hurt it if done in moderation.

Just remember that sugar is no better for dogs than it is for us. There's a nice old lady in my building who likes to give Dandy sugar doughnuts, of all things. Naturally, Dandy likes the lady very much as a result, and the lady gets a big kick out of this. I am reluctant to be a kill-joy, but I wish she'd settle for giving Dandy dog treats or something like pieces of hard cheese or raw vegetables instead.

By the way, if someone tells you that sugar gives dogs worms, that is silly. Worms are living parasites that a dog can acquire from various means of contact with the organisms or their eggs. But not from sugar.

Health food stores sometimes sell commercial "natural" pet foods. If the ingredients and guaranteed analysis are within the range that's right for your dog, there's no reason not to buy them if you like.

But there's every reason not to give your dog real bones.

Bones are widely believed to be normal fare for a dog, and this notion keeps many veterinarians busy—and causes dogs that aren't lucky enough to get quick veterinary care to suffer and die. Steak, chop, pork, rabbit, chicken, and other fowl bones should *never* be fed to a dog under any circumstances. They splinter and can cause mouth and throat injuries and bowel impaction.

Some dog experts give their blessing to knuckle bones. My feeling is, why ask for trouble? If there's any risk to your pet, it's better to give the animal something else to chew on—a commercial dog food bone or a hard nylon toy bone—that can't hurt it.

When you have bones in the garbage, by the way, get rid of them immediately, because even a well-trained, well-behaved dog won't be able to resist the temptation to pull them out and eat them.

Reading the Labels

The labels on dog foods display a list of ingredients, in the order of the amount they occur in the product, plus a guaranteed analysis that tells you the percentage of the main components—protein, fat, fiber, and moisture. The only way for a layperson to judge a dog food is to know something about what the ingredients and analysis mean. Otherwise, you can go crazy reading and comparing labels.

Much of the following information comes from a book called *Canine Nutrition and Feeding Management*, written for veterinarians by a panel of veterinarians and other scientists, and published by Alpo. (Much independent research into animal nutrition is funded by pet food companies.)

If the name of a canned dog food product includes the word "dinner" or "platter" or some such, after the meat, poultry, or fish named (for example, "beef dinner"), the product must contain 25 percent of the named ingredient. If the meat, poultry, or fish named is not modified, the product must contain 95 percent of the named ingredient or ingredients (for example, "beef & chicken"). Meat is a source of high-quality protein for a dog.

Soybean meal, soy flour, and soy grits are good sources of vegetable protein, as well as of vitamins and minerals. Egg, wheat germ, and cornmeal also supply supplemental protein and other nutrients.

Meat and poultry "by-products" mean lungs, spleen, kidneys, liver, brain, stomach, and intestines and add supplemental protein. Meat meal and bone meal are the dry rendered product from animal tissue. They contain supplemental protein and minerals such as calcium and phosphorous.

As for the "guaranteed analysis," the percentages of the contents vary among commercial dog foods. The amounts that are right for your city dog depend on whether it's a puppy, adult, or older dog, and whether it's thin, average, or overweight, as well as on its general health.

The need for protein—that is, amino acids—is basic, and dogs need it especially in puppyhood, old age, and in high-stress lifestyles such as rounding up cows, performing on the stage or in dog shows, or leading blind persons. Adult city dogs who live as pets need only moderate amounts of protein—18 to 20 percent in dry food, 8 to 10 percent in canned meat, and 16 to 18 percent in semi-moist.

Fat is especially important in helping a dog maintain a good coat. In fact, if there's too little fat in a dog's diet, its coat can become rough and dry, its skin scaly. Sometimes a dog with dry skin will scratch so insistently, you can mistake the cause for fleas.

On the other hand, too much fat can cause digestive problems and weight gain. And if you add too much fat to a dog's diet without also increasing iodine and thiamine proportionately, you can throw off the balance of nutrients and cause nutritional deficiency.

Most dry foods contain 8 to 10 percent fat; canned meats, 4 to 8 percent; and semi-moist, 6 or 7 percent. These amounts should be plenty for healthy adult city dogs.

Fiber is not digested by dogs but is simply bulk and helps intestinal motility. High fiber content (above 5 percent) in a food will cause an increased amount of stool.

I've heard that some people add ascorbic acid to their dogs' food. Commercial dog foods don't supply it directly, so these dog owners assume their pets need it. But according to *Canine Nutrition and Feeding Management*, a dog's need for vitamin C has never been established, and adding it could disturb digestion and suppress immunity.

It's best not to fool around adding vitamins, minerals, or whatever to your dog's diet unless your veterinarian specifically suggests it. Very tiny dogs might need extra nutrients because their stomachs won't hold enough at a meal to give them the daily quota they need.

If yours is a pint-sized dog, ask your veterinarian about this. But in general, dog foods are quite carefully balanced, and gratuitously adding certain nutrients could move the concentration of them up above optimum levels. It's not true that if a particular amount of a vitamin is good, more is automatically better.

The calorie requirements of dogs differ according to the stages of their lives and their lifestyles. Obviously, growing dogs and working dogs need more, urban pets and old dogs need fewer. But most pet food products do not list the calories on the labels. It seems to me it would be a good idea to do so and that dog owners should learn what the amounts mean in terms of their own dogs.

MAINTENANCE DIET

Leaving aside those dogs that can't digest dry food easily and those that must be on special diets, generally the best diet for a healthy adult city dog is dry food supplemented with a small amount of additional protein and fat. Because dry food contains comparatively little water, a dog gets more nutrients per cupful than from the same amount of canned or moist dog food. It may also be good for the teeth.

Canned meat dog food is a convenient and nourishing supplement. One to two tablespoonfuls of canned meat are enough supplement for a half-pound of dry food (just under three cups). Moisten the dry food a little first to make mixing easier.

Ration-type canned dog food does not improve the protein quality of dry food. It's adding cereal to cereal.

An excellent supplement is egg—one whole egg per half-pound of dry food. If the dog is on antibiotics, you should cook the egg first. But otherwise, you don't have to cook the egg as long as you are sure to mix in the whole egg. According to Dr. Ben E. Sheffy of the James A. Baker Institute for Animal Health, at Cornell University, raw egg white is harmful only if fed alone without the yolk, or if the dog is taking antibiotics.

Milk, one part to four parts dry food, adds both moisture and protein. However, if your dog hasn't been drinking milk since puppyhood, phase it into the diet gradually to be sure it doesn't cause diarrhea. Don't use skim or low-fat milk. Use whole or evaporated milk, which is far less likely to cause diarrhea. Cottage cheese, one tablespoon per half-pound of dry food, is also good.

To bring the fat content in a dry food up a bit, you can mix in a little meat drippings, chicken fat, or corn oil—but sparingly. Only one teaspoon per half-pound of dry food. That small amount will help without upsetting the balance of nutrients.

Be sure to refrigerate any food your dog leaves after a meal. While dry food alone has an exceedingly low spoilage rate, adding supplement—even water—makes it spoil in just a few hours.

One good meal a day seems to be right for most adult dogs, though toy breeds might need two—they may not be able to consume enough at one feeding to get all the daily nutrients they need. Old dogs also may do better if their total food amount is divided into two small meals a day, to avoid overload on the digestive system.

Some city dogs owners prefer to give their dogs their meal in the morning. Since it takes twelve hours for food to pass through its system, the animal will have its major bowel movement on the evening walk, and that's usually it until the next evening. However, if you eat dinner at home, it's very hard not to feed your dog, too. It will beg and look appealing, and if you give it snacks, you not only risk making it gain unwanted weight, but lose the point of the morning feed. Therefore you might find it easiest to feed your pet at the same time that you have your own dinner.

Also, cats normally eat twice a day, and if you have a cat as well as a dog, how can you feed one and not the other? That not only hurts the dog's feelings but may set up an unnecessary competition and jealousy in the dog toward the cat. Dandy has always had at least a snack when my cats have breakfast; it's only fair.

Cats need more protein than dogs, by the way, and commercial food for them is balanced accordingly. Cats should not be fed dog food. However, it won't hurt your dog to eat cat food once in a while.

HOW MUCH IS ENOUGH?

Since a dog is an adult for most of its lifetime, I'll discuss the food requirements of adult city dogs first, then puppies, and finally older dogs. And since obesity is a condition of many city dogs, I'll address fat dogs separately.

A well-treated adult city dog in comfortable surroundings lives an undemanding, generally nonstressful lifestyle, unlike that of, say, a working ranch dog, a guide dog, or a dog that has to live outdoors year-round. Therefore, its food energy needs are relatively low.

But there is apparently as much individual variation in the food energy requirements of dogs as there is among human beings. We all know people who can pack away prodigious amounts of food and remain slim, while others of the same height and build have to count calories. It's the same with dogs. Dog nutritionists estimate that one in every twenty dogs will vary significantly from the average energy needs on which the commercial dog foods are based. That one dog will need more, or less, food than is recommended on the can or package for dogs the same weight. The variation can be as much as 20 percent.

In order to ensure that dogs fed a commercial diet will get all the nutrients they need, the manufacturers tend to recommend amounts at the high end of the scale. City dogs generally need less. Dandy, for instance, weighs around thirty pounds and, as I mentioned, is fourteen years old. For dogs her weight, the National Research Council's "Nutrient Requirements of Dogs," which was published in 1974, recommends a daily diet of either three and one-quarter cups of dry food, two and one-quarter fourteen-ounce cans of ration-type canned food, or two fourteen-ounce cans of meat-type canned food. These amounts seem insane to me. Dandy gets a mixture of these types of food, but the total amount she consumes each day is about half these quantities—and she is well padded and healthy. Unless your city dog gets an unusual amount of exercise and is very young, you will probably feed it considerably less than what's suggested by the National Research Council or on the packages and cans.

If caring dog owners err on how much to feed their pets, it's usually on the side of too much. City dog owners especially tend to feed more than their dogs need for the lifestyle they lead. That's not good; not only is it unhealthy for the dog, but once the pet gets used to receiving a certain amount of food, it feels deprived if it gets less. The animal complains and looks at you reproachfully, and it's a hard-hearted owner indeed who can hold out against this pressure. That's why it's best not to let your dog become overweight in the first place.

With some dogs, you can judge whether or not they're the right size just by looking at them. But with long-haired or fluffy dogs, it's not so easy. *Canine Nutrition and Feeding Management* suggests a good method for gauging whether a dog is carrying too much or too little fat. Try it with your own dog:

Stand behind the dog, place your hands over its ribs with your thumbs meeting at about the middle of its back. Spread your fingers on the ribs and press down a little on the vertebrae with your thumbs. Now slide your hands gently forward and backward—you should be able to feel a thin layer of fat over the ribs. If you feel the rib bone ends too easily, the dog is thin. If the ribs feel smooth and wavy and you can scarcely feel the rib bone ends, the dog is fat.

Free-choice feeding, by the way—leaving food out for the dog to eat at will—is not a good idea for city dogs. Don't count on your dog to control its own food intake to maintain a desirable weight. It will surely stuff itself and get sick or fat, or both. Also, you want to get your dog into the habit of eating at more or less the same time so you can predict when it will have to relieve itself.

Most dogs will quickly gobble up all that's in their bowls and look around for more. Some dogs will eat a little more leisurely. But if a dog doesn't eat all of its meal at a feeding, the food may spoil. And apartment dwellers should be especially cautioned against leaving food around because it can attract bugs.

So pick up the bowl as soon as the dog walks away. If there's food left, put it in the refrigerator and add it to the next meal. Wash the bowl clean after every feeding.

Feeding a Puppy

A puppy grows rapidly for its first six months, and during this time good nutrients are more important than ever. Puppies need more protein and fat than adult dogs of the same weight. But their food should have less fiber.

Protein needs vary among puppies. According to the James A. Baker Institute for Animal Health at Cornell University, puppies of toy breeds need more protein and fat than larger-breed puppies of the same age. An eight-week-old Toy Poodle, for example, needs more than 24 percent (dry food) protein and more than 14 percent fat, but an eight-week-old Great Dane should get only 22 percent protein and 10 percent fat. If you can't find exactly what's right for your puppy on the supermarket shelves, find a dry food that has the right amount of fat and increase the protein content with canned meat dog food.

Commercial dry *puppy* food has high-quality ingredients but is rather expensive. You can feed a pup equally well with regular dry dog food supplemented with canned meat (not ration-type) dog food, or with cooked ground beef—one part meat to ten parts dry food. Add enough water to make the food edible and palatable to the pup. Milk (whole or evaporated) is also good—one part milk to four parts dry food. In addition, mix in one egg yolk every few days.

Semi-moist food may act as a laxative with a puppy. If you introduce it into the diet, do so a very little at a time.

Let refrigerated food come to room temperature before feeding it to a puppy.

The amount to feed varies of course with the pup's weight—you wouldn't give a little Yorkie the same amount you'd feed a young Golden Retriever. Keep track of a puppy's weight and be guided by the label on the package of dry food—but feed less than the label recommends because, as I pointed out earlier, those suggested amounts are generally more than a city dog needs.

One important caveat: A rolypoly puppy is cute, but for its future health, keep it on the lean side. This goes especially for a middle-size or large breed, or a mixed breed of that size. According to Dr. Audrey Hayes of the Animal Medical Center in New York City, letting a pup become fat is setting it up for serious skeletal disorders later on—hip dysplasia, swollen joints, and other orthopedic problems. This is because the bones of a growing dog can't remodel fast enough to support excess weight. Not that your puppy should look skinny and malnourished—just slim.

It's hard not to feed a puppy all it wants. For one thing, you'll feel guilty when it wolfs down its food and begs for more. In addition, city dog owners are in continual contact with other dog walkers and dog lovers. You'll have to endure the gratuitous comments and advice of people who think you're starving your dog. The remarks will range from a polite, "Isn't he/she a little thin?" to a glaring, "How come you don't feed him/her?" You can explain or not, but don't apologize—you're protecting your dog's health.

A puppy eight to twelve weeks old needs four evenly spaced meals a day. At three to six months, three meals a day. Giant-breed pups may need three meals a day beyond six months because they mature later than smaller dogs. Great Danes and other dogs of that size don't reach full growth until they're one and a half, even two.

From age six to eight months or so, most dogs need to eat twice a day—morning and night. By eight months, they generally do well on one good meal a day.

A puppy of about six months old may go somewhat off its feed because it is teething and its gums are sore. Soften its food and give it something to gnaw on—a hard nylon bone is good. Otherwise, however, if a puppy refuses two meals in succession, and you are certain it isn't teething, it's a danger signal and you should consult your veterinarian quickly.

Remember, no romping with a pup just before or after a meal.

Feeding an Old Dog

Old dogs digest and utilize nutrients as well as or better than young dogs. It's in the kidneys that old age takes a toll—and this has given rise to a controversy among authorities in canine nutrition, and among dog food manufacturers, about the amount of protein an old dog should be fed.

One argument holds that since the kidneys are vulnerable, the dog should be fed a low-protein diet to reduce the workload on the kidneys and slow the deterioration of kidney function.

However, studies have shown that because the utilization of protein declines in older dogs, they therefore need *more* than they formerly got, and of a high quality. Unless a dog has been diagnosed as having chronic renal failure, in which case it needs a special diet, its protein should not be automatically reduced as it advances in age. And in general, animal protein is of a better quality than plant protein.

Another reason against reducing protein is that old age can be stressful for a dog, and all dogs need more protein when stressed. The old dog doesn't understand why it can't hear or see so well, why its limbs are stiff and weak. If it becomes incontinent, it feels humiliated. It is easily upset by changes in the household routine. The owner of an old dog should not only pay close attention to its diet, but give it lots of extra affection and reassurance.

A good diet for an older dog with good teeth could be moistened dry food mixed with canned meat dog food in equal amounts. Ideally, the dry food should be low in fiber—not over 5 percent. Or, you could feed an old dog canned ration-type food mixed equally with canned meat dog food.

In addition to the special commercial diet for dogs with kidney failure, there are foods for dogs with other disorders of aging. Heart disease, another killer of old dogs, can be helped with a special low-sodium diet. These foods are not sold in supermarkets but through veterinarians.

Any change in diet should be phased in gradually, to avoid upsetting the animal's digestion and habits. Be sure to stick to the dog's regular feeding schedule. According to Dr. Ben E. Sheffy, two considerations should be paramount in the feeding of any animals: moderation and regularity, and this maxim is especially important for aging animals. He suggests that two small meals daily, nine to ten hours apart, might be best for an aging dog, to help digestion and utilization of nutrients.

You'll find yourself filling the water bowl more often for your old dog. Not to worry if it drinks somewhat more, but if it's at the water bowl every little while and can't seem to get enough, a prompt visit to your veterinarian is indicated. Excessive thirst can be a sign of kidney problems.

Feeding the Obese Dog

Obesity is a real health hazard for a dog, and one to which city dogs are especially prone. One obvious cause, of course, is lack of exercise. Another may be that for the dog of an extremely busy owner, mealtime may be the time when the dog gets the most attention, and so food takes on an exaggerated importance for the animal. The dog craves more and more food, and the owner responds because that's his or her way of showing the pet affection. Food may also mean more than it should to a dog that isn't walked enough and allowed to interact with other dogs and people, or that has to spend many long hours at home alone.

The best way to deal with obesity of course is not to let your pet become fat in the first place. Losing fat once it's on is as hard for a dog as trying to lose excess pounds is for most of us. However, if you can stand the begging and the reproachful looks, the simplest way to help a dog lose weight is just to feed it less and cut out snacks. I know this is easier said than done, especially if your pet is accustomed to getting a bite of almost everything you eat and is rewarded with treats for good behavior, but it is in the animal's best interest.

You might try feeding your pet very small meals more often. This will keep it from getting ravenous between meals and convince it that it's getting more food than it really is. Just be sure the dog's total daily intake is less. Adding lettuce to its food is another way of filling the animal up without increasing calories.

There are commercial dog foods for obesity that contain plenty of nutrition but also a lot of fiber. You can feed a dog its usual amount of these foods and they'll satisfy its craving because they are filling. City dog owners should be aware, however, that these foods create more stool, so be prepared.

Increased exercise will of course help a dog to lose weight. But don't suddenly subject a fat dog to vigorous exercise. Work up to it very gradually.

There's another good way to help an overweight dog slim down: acquire another dog, an active, younger dog. In all probability, they'll become friends and play together. But even if the older dog only grudgingly accepts the other, the stepped-up walks and change of pace around the house will keep it more active. For suggestions on the smoothest way to introduce a new pet, see Chapter 9.

I'm a strong believer, by the way, that each pet should have its very own feeding bowl. Food being as important as it is to an animal, having to share can set up an unnecessary anxiety. Also, animals vary in the rates at which they eat. If more than one dog eats from the same bowl, the speedy eater will get more than its share, and the slower may go hungry. My cat Tommy, for example, inhales his meal in a few seconds; Gina and Joey eat at a normal, businesslike rate; but Olivia eats slowly and fastidiously, stopping now and then to gaze into space before resuming eating. If Olivia had to share with any of the others, she'd never get enough to eat.

Dandy, being much bigger than any of the cats, could easily thrust her face into one of their bowls and steal their food, and because they like her they probably wouldn't scratch her. But the rules are that she must wait until each cat walks away from its bowl—then, if she can beat Tommy to it, she can check it out for crumbs.

Owners of multiple pets must supervise meals to be sure justice is served.

WATER

It's not a good idea for city dogs to have food left out for them to eat at will, but they should be able to drink water whenever they want. Fresh water in a clean bowl should be available at all times.

Some city people might be tempted to withhold water from a dog to prevent elimination accidents, especially when they're trying to house-train it. But that's deleterious to the animal's health, as well as mean.

By the way, allowing a dog to lap water out of the toilet is not only tacky-looking, it's unhealthy for the dog.

Excessive drinking can be a danger signal. It might be that the dog is merely thirsty from exercise or an overly warm house, but as we have noted, it could also mean kidney problems, especially in an older dog. Normal daily intake of water is approximately one pint for each ten pounds of the dog's weight.

CHAPTER 6

HEALTH:

Keeping Your Urban Dog Fit

Despite the belief that city living is unhealthy, I strongly suspect that well-kept urban dogs are healthier than suburban or country dogs. Dogs that live as our close companions are probably more carefully looked after, and any illnesses they do get are more quickly noticed and treated. In general, veterinary care is easily available and immunizations are routine among urban pets.

Nevertheless, because your pet is likely to be in contact with many other dogs, it is important that you keep its vaccinations up to date and that you recognize early signs of sickness so you can provide prompt medical care when your dog needs it. Also, not all illnesses are preventable by immunization, and no matter what good care you give it, your dog will almost certainly get sick at some time or other—especially as it gets old.

As a city dweller, you will probably have your choice of several veterinarians and be influenced by the advice of your friends, just as we all are in selecting our own medical doctors. Listen to dog-owner friends whose judgment you trust.

In picking a veterinarian, you'll want to balance the wisdom and experience of an older professional against the sophisticated training of a more recent vet school graduate. Naturally, you'll want him or her to have a clean and tidy clinic, with no overwhelming smell of either animals or disinfectant. Notice how he or she handles your particular pet. Can you sense a genuine liking for animals?

If your pet must be hospitalized, ask to see behind the scenes first. Will it be kept in a clean and comfortable cage?

I tend to like a vet who explains everything thoroughly, who spells out technical matters and gives me credit for normal ability to understand them. I also appreciate an easy, unpretentious manner.

One veterinarian, Dr. Jay Kuhlman, endeared himself to me not long ago over what I thought was a problem with Dandy. Last year, he had operated on her to remove a basal cell tumor, a small nodular growth not uncommon in older dogs which in her case had appeared on a hind leg. Months later, I found what seemed to be the same thing on one of her front legs and rushed her to him for examination.

Attentively, he took a look at the spot I indicated. "That's one of her footpads," he said matter-of-factly.

In my own defense, I must point out that the spot I had discovered was not one of the pads of the foot that the dog walks on, but the curious pad on the leg back of the wrist. Still, it was nothing more than a normally calloused footpad.

I bet a lot of veterinarians would have snickered, maybe even sneered, and made me feel like more of a fool than I already did. Jay Kuhlman didn't bat an eye. This incident doesn't prove his professional skill, which is considerable, but it's an example of his nice, noncondescending manner with clients. I wouldn't put up with being treated in a pompous or brusque way, and in a city with plenty of veterinarians, nobody has to.

If you don't have a car, one factor you might want to take into consideration is a veterinarian's distance from your home. If your dog is too big to fit into a carrier, you'll have a problem getting a taxi to pick you up, unless you have the great good luck to hail a cab driver who likes dogs. Your city might have an animal ambulance service: check the Yellow Pages. But otherwise, bear in mind that in very hot, bitter cold, or rainy weather, a sick, injured, or elderly dog will have a hard time walking many blocks to the doctor.

Today there are many veterinary specialties—ophthalmology, cardiology, oncology, and neurology, to name just a few—each of which requires several years of extra training, board examinations, and certification. If your dog should develop a problem that you want to consult a specialist about, your city or state veterinary medical association could refer you to one. Also, these specialists are generally available at veterinary colleges or at large animal hospitals such as the Animal Medical Center, in New York, or Angell Memorial, in Boston.

VACCINATIONS

Immunization against the big five canine diseases—distemper, hepatitis, leptospirosis, parainfluenza, and parvovirus—can be given in a single vaccine. A puppy should receive its DHLPP inoculations in a series: the first at six to eight weeks of age, the second at nine to eleven weeks, and the final between twelve and sixteen weeks. Don't expose the urban puppy to other dogs on the street until after the last shot.

Parainfluenza, by the way, is one of the complex of canine respiratory diseases known as kennel cough. While the vaccine is not effective against all of the infections included under the umbrella term "kennel cough," it offers at least partial protection.

Every dog should be given a booster of DHLPP vaccine annually. There is a vaccine for distemper, hepatitis, parainfluenza, and parvo that does not include leptospirosis. It is less expensive than the DHLPP, and some veterinarians feel that vaccinating against leptospirosis is unnecessary for well-kept city dogs.

Rabies is another matter. In some states, all dogs are legally required to receive rabies vaccine; in other states, it's optional. You might think, rightly, that the chances of an urban pet coming into contact with rabies are slim. Rabies is rarely transmitted from dog to dog; generally, an animal has to be bitten by a rabid wild animal—usually a skunk, bat, raccoon, or fox—in order to become infected. The image of rabid stray dogs roaming neighborhoods threatening pets and people is unfounded, according to the U.S. Center for Disease Control. Though nearly all the rabid dogs examined in one study were unvaccinated, 87 percent of them were owned.

Even though your pet is unlikely to meet a rabid skunk while walking down the street on a leash with you, I think regular rabies shots are a good idea. For one thing, you might want to take your dog with you to the country for a picnic, or vacation. Secondly, in the event that something should happen to make your dog bite someone, you will most certainly want to be able to prove that it has been vaccinated against rabies. You could be sued, and even if you weren't, your dog—if unvaccinated—would be quarantined.

A puppy should have its rabies shot at about six months of age, Inoculation lasts from one to three years, depending on the type of vaccine used.

ILLNESS SYMPTOMS

You don't need me to tell you that obvious problems such as severe coughing; inflammation of or discharge from the eyes, ears, nose, or throat; discharge from the vagina, penis, or anus; bleeding from any of the above; a lump under the skin; or evidence of continuing pain or tenderness in your dog require veterinary attention. In fact, any deviation from normal behavior and appearance should be regarded as significant, worthy of your attention, especially in a very young or old dog.

Some symptoms are subtle or confusing, however. A dog that hunches up its back and walks strangely may be suffering from back trouble, abdominal pain, or a problem in the anal region. Dandy once had such symptoms, and I thought she had developed an orthopedic problem until the vet diagnosed it as an abdominal infection.

Here are symptoms that could indicate your dog is sick:

Loss of appetite is an early warning signal. Healthy dogs generally devour their meals with gusto. One theory about this is that in the wild a dog must grab its share of the kill in a hurry, before other pack members or other predators muscle in, and that modern dogs retain this instinctual sense of urgency. It's the only explanation I've heard that accounts for a dog's atrocious table manners.

Therefore, loss of appetite is probably one of the first things a dog owner notices when the pet becomes ill. Certainly not all disorders cause loss of appetite, and it can be brought on simply by hot weather, change of diet, or some change in household routine; however, it is a symptom not to be ignored if it continues. Not to worry if your pet walks away leaving its food untouched once, but you should be concerned if it refuses a second meal, especially if it's an old dog or a puppy. Dr. Audrey Hayes says that if you have a pup of one of the very small breeds, missing even one meal could be harmful, for the puppy might become hypoglycemic (low in blood sugar).

Evaluating loss of appetite in a puppy is tricky, however. It can be a sign of serious illness—but on the other hand, a pup four to six months of age may simply go off its food or slow down because it's teething. It may even cause you further anxiety by running a low fever and having slight diarrhea and enlarged lymph nodes or tonsils. If teething is truly the problem, soften the puppy's food so it can eat comfortably. Also, give it a harmless hard toy such as a hard nylon bone, hard rubber ball, or rawhide bone to gnaw on.

If a dog is really ill, loss of appetite is rarely the only symptom it will display. Keep your eyes open for others as well.

Weight loss is something you may not notice all at once. Usually, in fact, someone else who knows your dog will mention it, especially if the person doesn't see the dog every day. Then you'll take a hard look at your pet and see, yes, it does seem thinner than usual. Unless your dog is too big for you to lift, weigh it on the bathroom scales. (Do this the way veterinarians do: Weigh yourself, then weigh yourself with your dog in your arms; the difference is the dog's weight.)

You'll want to consult your veterinarian if your dog loses weight without an obvious reason such as increased exercise or a change of diet. Remember, even three or four pounds can mean something, depending on the size of your dog. A loss of four pounds in a twenty-pound dog is one-fifth of its total body weight. Obviously, in order to gauge weight loss, you'll need to know your dog's normal weight, so be sure to keep track of that.

Vomiting and diarrhea, however, are two symptoms that city dog owners can't miss. They too can mean everything or nothing. Dogs tend to vomit from time to time quite normally. Sometimes a dog will vomit a frothy light yellow liquid. This is probably just gastric fluid, caused by an empty stomach. If the dog vomits food right after eating, it may have eaten too much too fast, or eaten something undigestible. That's usually when the vomitus looks elongated and ropelike: The food came from the esophagus.

If the animal seems well otherwise, a single bout of vomiting or diarrhea doesn't mean you must rush it to the vet. But do watch it closely for additional symptoms and to see whether the vomiting or diarrhea continue. (For home treatment for occasional vomiting and diarrhea, see "Borderline Health Problems," below.)

But frequent and violent retching, frequent and forceful diarrhea, or evidence of blood in either or both means trouble. What sort? The dog could have any of several illnesses (especially if unvaccinated), it could be eating spoiled food (garbage, for example), it could be poisoned, or it could be suffering from extreme stress. Vomiting and diarrhea are characteristic of a whole range of disorders, mild or serious. With experience, you'll be able to recognize the difference in your own dog. All I can say is don't panic every time your dog throws up or has a single case of the runs. But if either persists, you should take the animal to your vet, even if you don't notice other symptoms.

Fever is hard to detect: A dog is covered with hair, so you can't feel its cheek or chest to see if it's unusually warm. Don't go by the nose; it's not true that a dry warm nose indicates sickness. You might be able to tell a little bit by feeling the inside of a dog's ear, but really, the only accurate way to find out if a dog is running a fever is by taking its temperature.

A dog's normal temperature is between 100 and 102 degrees. Above that means fever. Below that could also be a sign that something's wrong. A temperature under 99 degrees is one of the symptoms of shock, which is very serious indeed. I'll tell you how to take a dog's temperature (below).

Fever is usually accompanied by increased water consumption, decreased appetite, lethargy, and depression, but these symptoms can also occur without fever. A dog that's dragging around and depressed for more than a couple of days should see a veterinarian, whether it's running a fever or not.

So, then, here is a list of the symptoms to watch out for. If your dog has any one of these persistently, or displays a combination of several, it should be seen by a veterinarian.

Persistent cough

Inflammation (for example, of the skin, ears, eyes)

Discharge (from any body opening)

External bleeding

Lump under skin

Continuing pain or tenderness

Loss of appetite (partial or complete)

Weight loss

Persistent vomiting

Persistent diarrhea

Fever

Lethargy, depression

BASIC HOME CARE

Here are tips on the ways and means of determining the state of your pet's health and rendering simple home care.

To take a dog's temperature, shake down a rectal thermometer and grease it well with petroleum jelly or KY jelly (or if you don't have either of those, use face cream). Your dog is not going to stand still and let you insert the thermometer into its rectum, so you'll have to have somebody else restrain it, or else make it lie down on its side and hold it down the best you can, all the while talking quietly and soothingly.

Lift the dog's tail and gently push the thermometer in one or two inches, about half the length of the thermometer, rotating it as you insert it. *Don't let go of the dog or the thermometer*, cautions Dr. Hayes. If the dog takes off with the thermometer still in it, you might have to give it an enema to get the instrument out! Leave the thermometer in at least two minutes.

Remember, 100 to 102 degrees is normal. A temperature much above or below that is a matter of concern.

To get a urine sample, use a disposable aluminum pie tin or other good-sized disposable container to capture the urine in. Wait until the dog starts urinating, then slide the container into position. Then transfer the urine into a smaller disposable container with a tight lid. You can keep it in the refrigerator for a few hours, or overnight if necessary, before delivering it to the veterinarian.

To get a fecal sample, slip a plastic bag over your hand, pick up the feces, dispose of all but the sample, turn the bag inside out, and fasten it securely. If you have to keep the sample in the refrigerator for any length of time (overnight, say) before delivering it to the vet, put the plastic bag into a disposable plastic container with a tight lid.

To give a dog a pill, first try to disguise the pill in food. If the medication is in a capsule and isn't too bitter, you can open the capsule and mix the contents in your pet's dinner. Try just a sample first, to see if the dog will eat it. You don't want to waste medicine if the animal is going to refuse its medicated food.

A pill can be wrapped in a piece of meat or cheese. I always give Dandy a plain piece first, to lure her into thinking she's just getting a treat, and then I put the pill in a second piece. Then I give a third piece as a reward.

However, if you have no alternative but to get the pill or capsule into your dog without food, put the animal in a corner so it can't back away. Or, work from the side, facing the same way the dog is. Speak gently and reassuringly. Use one hand to grasp the dog's upper jaw and press the lips against the teeth back of the fangs. The pressure will cause the animal to open its mouth, and now you want to act quickly because it will probably be struggling. Don't throw the pill down the dog's throat, but place it on the tongue and then hold the mouth shut. Hang on and stroke the dog's throat until you're sure the pill is safely on its way. When the dog licks its lips, it has swallowed. Follow with praise and petting.

To give liquid medicine, use a plastic syringe or eye dropper. Raise the dog's head a little, pull the cheek out to form a pouch with the side of the mouth, and squirt the medicine in. If you have to administer more than a few drops, give a little at a time; otherwise, the dog will spit it out—all over itself, you, and the room. When the dog has swallowed it all, follow with praise and petting.

To test for dehydration, pull the dog's skin up a little at the back of the neck. When you let go, the skin should immediately settle back into place. If the skin remains standing up when you let go, the animal is dehydrated. By the way, it's a good idea to try this first on your pet when it is healthy, so you'll be able to recognize the difference should it ever become dehydrated.

CANINE DISORDERS

Here are brief descriptions of some of the more common canine disorders that an urban dog might be subject to. When you see how serious the first six are, you'll understand why it is essential to have your pet vaccinated against them.

Distemper

This deadly viral disease attacks the dog's respiratory, gastrointestinal, and nervous systems. It is characterized by weakness, lethargy, dehydration, lack of appetite, fever of 103 to 105 degrees, cough, discharge from eyes and nose, vomiting, and diarrhea. It is highly contagious, spread in the air or from direct contact with an infected animal; it can even be brought in on people's clothing. There is no cure for distemper. In the event that an animal receiving supportive care recovers, it may have residual neurological damage for the rest of its life.

Dr. Hayes points out that occasionally veterinarians see puppies of about four months old who, despite a good vaccination history, show mild symptoms of distemper, including the neurological signs. Those cases suggest that the pups are the offspring of mothers who had the distemper virus and passed it to their pups in utero.

Hepatitis

Infectious canine hepatitis is a viral disease that particularly affects a dog's liver. Symptoms include lethargy, abdominal tenderness, fever of 103 to 105 degrees, cloudiness in the cornea of the eyes, possible discharge from eyes and nose, and an orange cast to the inside of the mouth (jaundice). It is spread from the urine, stool, or saliva of an infected animal. *(It is not the same virus as the human hepatitis virus, so is not contagious to people.)* There is no cure for infectious canine hepatitis, though an animal receiving supportive care and antibiotics sometimes recovers.

Leptospirosis

This bacterial disease attacks the kidneys. A dog with leptospirosis is weak and lethargic, with appetite loss and stiff muscles. It vomits, has diarrhea, fever, often a discharge from eyes and nose and red patches on tongue and gums. The leptospirosis organism is spread from contact with the urine of an infected animal (rats may have it). Antibiotics may perhaps pull a dog through.

Kennel Cough

This term covers a number of viral and bacterial respiratory diseases, including parainfluenza and tracheobronchitis. A dog with kennel cough can have one or several of the diseases. While not particularly serious, it is highly contagious (the organisms are carried in the air). If one dog in a pet shop has it, you can be pretty sure the rest do too.

Kennel cough is characterized by a hacking cough that is worse at night. This cough is dry, as distinguished from the productive cough of pneumonia. The dog may even gag and develop a watery discharge from eyes and nose. With rest, warmth, cough suppressants, and antibiotics to prevent pneumonia, a dog can recover from kennel cough. But while it's sick, it should be isolated from all other dogs, even those that have received DHLPP vaccine, because the vaccine does not give complete protection from all the possible varieties of kennel cough.

Parvovirus

A relatively recent and particularly virulent disease, parvo is especially lethal to puppies. Symptoms include lethargy, depression, fever, extreme dehydration, and especially severe vomiting and watery diarrhea that is highly odious and occasionally bloody. Pups with parvo can die suddenly, and those that survive may have heart damage. It is spread in stool but can also be brought in by people who have walked where diseased dogs have been. While there is no cure for parvovirus, dogs may recover after long, expensive, supportive care.

Rabies

There are two types of this killer. In the dumb type, the animal is stuporous, drools, can't swallow. Its jaw drops open and paralysis follows. A dog with the furious type goes crazy, attacks anything that moves. In the last stage, the dog is paralyzed. Rabies is spread through the saliva of an infected animal. A rabid dog dies after great suffering.

Intestinal Parasites (Worms)

Puppies quite commonly have worms; if the mother has them, the pups contract them through her milk. Even healthy adult urban dogs can get them just from greeting other dogs or sniffing in the gutter. City parks are common sites of reinfestation. Before describing the different types of worms that dogs are subject to, a few words on worms in general:

Intestinal parasites will cause weight loss, dull coat, possibly diarrhea. Some types of worms can cause a dog to have an itchy rectum, and the animal will drag its bottom along the ground, sidewalk, or floor in a scooting manner, trying to ease the itch. But bear in mind that the dog could instead be trying to ease the discomfort of blocked anal glands (see "Professional Groomers" in Chapter 8).

If you suspect your dog has worms, be sure to have a stool sample checked by your veterinarian, because the medication to get rid of them must be specific for the type of worm. Never dose your pet with one of those commercial over-the-counter worm medicines. Worms must be destroyed by carefully regulated doses of poison, and the goal is to kill the worms, not the dog.

Mild cases of intestinal parasites do not make a dog seriously sick in the initial stage and are easily gotten rid of with proper medical treatment. But if allowed to persist and multiply, worms can kill a dog, especially a puppy.

Home remedies such as garlic will not prevent or kill worms. And as I mentioned in Chapter 5 there's a fairly common myth that sugar gives a dog worms, which isn't true either.

It's not a bad idea to have your urban dog's stool checked fairly regularly for worms, even if there are no obvious symptoms. You might not know your dog has them until the infection is bad enough to damage its health.

Roundworms (ascarids) are common in puppies. They're called roundworms because their bodies are round like spaghetti, not flat like tape. In fact, when you see roundworms in a dog's stool or vomit, they look like spaghetti. They can give a dog a bloated stomach, poor coat, and diarrhea and cause weight loss.

Tapeworms are long flat worms (when I say long, I mean they can actually grow to several feet in length in the poor dog's intestines). But what you see in the animal's stool or perhaps around its anus is tiny segments, like grains of rice. Tapeworm may be asymptomatic, but if a dog has a big one it can cause mild diarrhea, weight loss, a dull coat, and an itchy rectum.

An important thing to know is that fleas are the host of the most common type of tapeworm, and if your dog has fleas, it will almost certainly also have tapeworm, and you must get rid of *both*.

Hookworms and *whipworms*, which have similar symptoms, may be far more serious than tapeworm. In addition to making a dog thin with a dull coat, they can cause bloody diarrhea and anemia. An anemic dog's gums are very pale.

Coccidia is usually found among pups raised in unsanitary conditions. A puppy with coccidia will not thrive but will have a cough, low fever, chronic diarrhea, and an emaciated appearance.

Giardia, a protozoan parasite, is difficult to diagnose and according to Dr. Hayes should be suspected when other types of worms have been ruled out. Urban dogs rarely have giardia, but a dog bought from a pet shop or brought in from the country could suffer from it.

Urinary Disorders

Cystitis, a bacterial infection of the bladder, is the most common of these. The dog strains to urinate, and there may be blood in the urine. A urinalysis and a culture and sensitivity test must be made for diagnosis and to determine the organism that is causing the infection. Then an appropriate antibiotic will usually clear it up.

Bladder stones, caused by chronic infection or metabolic problems, can be serious and painful. Dogs of all ages can be afflicted, females more than males, and small dogs somewhat more than large.

Some types of bladder stones can be dissolved by prescription diet, but if the urethra becomes blocked, the dog will be unable to urinate and may die without immediate medical attention, usually surgery. Once a dog has had bladder stones, they can recur, so the animal should remain on a prescription diet and medication to help prevent the stones from forming. Hill's, makers of Science Diet foods, has developed three prescription foods specially formulated for dogs that have a tendency to form bladder stones; these foods are available through veterinarians.

Heartworm

This is an insidious and very dangerous parasite that is transmitted from dog to dog by mosquitoes. It can be prevented by a daily pill taken during the mosquito season, or possibly year-round in warm climates near water. Cure is possible only if the parasite is discovered before symptoms appear.

Heartworms, which can be twelve to fourteen inches long, live in a dog's heart and surrounding blood vessels. When an adult female heartworm produces larvae, these circulate in the bloodstream. A mosquito sucks the infected dog's blood, and the larvae incubate in the mosquito for a couple of months. Then the mosquito bites another dog and transmits the larvae. It takes a few more months for the larvae to reach the second dog's heart and another couple of months before the larvae become adult worms and produce their own larvae. I tell you these details to make the point that it can be six months between the time a dog is bitten by an infected mosquito and the time the larvae can be detected in the dog's blood by a specific heartworm test.

If detected early, the adult worms can be killed with carefully regulated injections of arsenic. If undetected, heartworms will eventually cause heart disease, with symptoms such as a cough, breathing difficulties, weakness, and fatigue. You can prolong the dog's life somewhat by treating it for heart disease, but eventually the heartworms will cause fatal congestive heart failure.

Heartworm used to be a danger only to dogs in the country and suburbs, especially in the South, but it is now found in virtually all parts of the United States and Canada. So if you live where mosquitoes are plentiful or take your dog with you to vacation areas with water, you should have it tested yearly and *if it is uninfected*, give it heartworm pills as directed. The pills are reliable in preventing heartworm, but the reason the dog should always be tested before they are given is that if somehow there has been a slip-up in administering the medication faithfully and the dog has become infected with heartworm, the preventive medicine can kill the dog.

External Parasites

A discussion of fleas and ticks belongs here because they can become a health problem; a severe infestation can weaken a dog and in fact can make a small dog or puppy anemic and vulnerable to other disorders.

Fleas not only may cause weakness and anemia but can make a dog scratch and bite itself to the point of badly irritated skin and open wounds.

Even city dogs can get fleas. They can hop from one dog to another, they can hide in bushes, they can be lurking in carpets and upholstery where an infested dog has been. One likely place to find fleas on a dog is on its back at the base of the tail. They are also commonly visible around the head and neck, and in the "armpits" and inner thighs. You can see the tiny parasites scuttling through the hair. Or, if you don't see the actual creatures, a telltale sign is black specks like pepper—those are flea droppings.

Some dogs are allergic to flea bites, and it can take only one flea to send the animal into paroxysms of furious scratching, without the baffled owner detecting a single parasite in the pet's fur.

Fleas require immediate action, before they infest your house. Most people look to flea collars as the solution, but I have found them to be of limited value. But if you do resort to a flea collar for your dog, here are some words of caution:

Never put a flea collar on a puppy.

Never ever use a flea collar in combination with other remedies such as a spray, powder, or dip.

Don't put the collar on too tightly—you should be able to slip your finger easily between the collar and the dog's neck.

Don't put a flea collar on too loosely either, because the dog might try to chew on the collar, get its lower jaw under it, and become poisoned by the substance in the collar. For this reason you should always cut off any excess (and throw it away where your pet won't find it and think it's something to chew on).

Examine your dog's neck regularly for any sign of redness or irritation and remove the collar at once if this occurs. Don't replace the collar when the redness clears up. Some dogs are unusually sensitive to the chemicals in flea collars.

Remove the collar whenever you bathe the dog, and don't replace it until the animal is completely dry.

Those medallions that are supposed to kill fleas when attached to a dog's regular collar are totally ineffective, in my experience. I think you really have to use powder, spray, dip, or special flea shampoo. (Follow the directions on the labels faithfully, and never use a dip on a puppy.)

I've gotten rid of fleas on Dandy by standing her on newspaper and dusting her thoroughly with flea powder. It's no good just to sprinkle the powder on: You have to push the fur against the grain and powder the skin. Then brush and comb the dog thoroughly, and fleas will drop off on the newspaper. (Be sure to roll up the newspaper tightly and burn it afterward.) Repeat this procedure periodically, according to directions on the can. In fact, just regular combing and brushing alone will help, but if you suspect your pet has a flea or two, be sure to do it over a newspaper and burn that immediately, and dip the comb and brush in alcohol.

Some people swear that giving a dog a little powdered, debittered brewer's yeast in its food every day will keep fleas off the animal; presumably brewer's yeast leaves a scent in the skin that fleas don't like. I don't know if this is true, but brewer's yeast is nutritious and can't hurt. There are two new commercial products, Proban and Spot-On, the former to be taken internally, the latter to be applied to the dog's skin; you might consult your veterinarian about using one or the other. They don't prevent fleas from infesting your dog, but they do kill them once they bite.

But there's no point in getting the fleas off your dog if they are already in its bed and in your rugs and upholstery. You have to wash the dog's bedding and vacuum clean your house from top to bottom. If your dog becomes reinfected regularly, you might have to vacuum daily during flea season. Put flea powder in the vacuum cleaner bag to kill fleas as you clean, and be sure to burn the bag as soon as you're finished. For a really serious infestation, it might be wise to call in an exterminator.

Ticks, though they're a problem mainly to dogs that live in or visit the country or suburbs, can sometimes be found on dogs that are walked in city parks, or even just around the block.

These bloodsucking parasites bury their heads in a dog's skin. To get rid of one, dab it first with a cotton swab dipped in linseed oil, nail polish remover, or alcohol (whiskey will do). Then use tweezers to pull the tick off, taking care not to get any of its blood on your hands. Destroy it immediately by flushing it down the toilet or burning it in an ashtray.

If you get only the tick's body but not the head, the dog's skin will be mildy irritated for a while, but in all likelihood there's no real harm done.

The reason for being cautious with a tick is that if it is infected with a certain organism, it can cause Rocky Mountain spotted fever in humans, and even in dogs—surprisingly, it has recently been diagnosed in a few dogs. Also, some rare dogs get tick paralysis, which disappears when the tick is removed.

Ticks are hard to spot on long-haired dogs. Also, they don't drive dogs crazy with itching the way fleas do. Flea collars may give some protection, but the best way to deal with them is to give your dog a once-over examination after each walk in grass or shubbery, looking particularly between the toes and inside the ears.

Ear Infections

According to Dr. Hayes, these are common, especially in long-eared dogs. The reason flop-eared dogs are more susceptible to them is that a dog's ears need air circulation in order to stay healthy. The symptoms include tenderness, redness, a brown discharge or wax, and an unpleasant odor, but unless you examine your dog's ears daily, the first sign you may notice is that the dog is carrying its head to one side, shaking its head, or pawing at its ear. Ear infections require veterinary attention and medication.

Strays and other dogs that have had to live in unsanitary conditions, especially puppies, may have *ear mites*—microscopic organisms that cause itching, redness, and extreme discomfort. They are contagious to other animals. Ear mites can be got rid of by persistent use of prescription eardrops that contain an insecticide.

Tooth Problems

Dogs normally have forty-two teeth—twenty in the upper jaw and twenty-two in the lower. They're lucky in one respect: They rarely get cavities. But they can get abscesses, periodontal disease, gingivitis, and other tooth and gum problems just as we can.

A dog with a toothache will obviously have difficulty eating and may also shake its head and paw at its mouth. Its breath will usually be odoriferous, and there may be facial swelling and irritated gums. Loose teeth will bleed. A dog with any of these symptoms should have veterinary attention.

The most common disorder of a dog's teeth is the buildup of tartar, which is a brownish stain just below the gumline. Excessive tartar can cause gum infection. It's usually more of a problem with older dogs, although some dogs seem to form tartar on their teeth more than others.

A good diet that includes crunchy food and hard toys of nylon or rawhide to chew on will help prevent tartar formation. And some dog owners wipe their dogs' teeth and gums daily with a cloth or a toothbrush dipped in baking soda, salt, or regular people toothpaste. It's good to accustom a dog to this from puppyhood; otherwise, you'll have to have a very passive dog, at least till the dog learns to tolerate it. It will help prevent tarter from forming. If the tarter gets really bad, the veterinarian should scrape it off with an instrument.

Puppies cut their permanent teeth between the ages of three and six months, often with some discomfort. They need hard objects to chew on—nylon, rawhide, or leather toys. Be sure to check a puppy's mouth daily to be sure no new teeth are emerging in spots still occupied by baby teeth that haven't come out yet. In this case, it's best to have the baby teeth pulled so the permanent teeth can come in straight.

Skin Disorders

When a dog has a dull, dry coat and suffers from persistent itching, the cause may be insufficient fat in the diet or, more likely, an infestation of fleas, or—even more likely in city dogs—the dry heat or air conditioning of an apartment. However, itching can also be a symptom of allergy, so you'll want to check with your veterinarian before the poor animal gets an infected spot from biting and scratching itself.

Stray dogs or dogs that have been kept in unsanitary homes, kennels, pet shops, and shelters and exposed to a lot of other animals may have caught *ringworm* or *sarcoptic mange*, both of which manifest themselves on the skin. Ringworm, which is not a worm but a fungus, is characterized by small, scaly circles from which the hair has fallen out, usually on the head, neck, and legs. The lesions enlarge and spread over the body, causing mild itching. Ringworm is contagious to humans and other animals. Prompt treatment is essential, but fortunately ringworm isn't as hard to get rid of as it once was.

Sarcoptic mange is a parasitic mite that burrows under the skin, especially on the head, ears, chest, abdomen, and back by the tail. Symptoms are hair loss and little red blisters that itch the dog and have a musty smell. It is also contagious, including to people, and once your veterinarian diagnoses it, you'll want to treat it immediately. It's not hard to cure.

There's another kind of mange called *demodectic* or *follicular* ("red mange") characterized by bald patches, typically beginning on the head and legs, that become raw and red. The patches may spread and cause the dog to lick and scratch itself constantly. Demodectic mange is not contagious to people or normally healthy dogs and cats. It can be controlled and treated, but once it becomes generalized, getting rid of it is a full-time job.

Orthopedic Problems

One of the most common of these is *hip dysplasia*, a painful arthritic condition often seen in big dogs. There may be a hereditary factor, or the animal may have been overweight while growing. Hip dysplasia can show up in dogs as young as four or five months of age, but it usually comes on between nine or ten months and up to two years. It affects the hind legs, causing the dog to limp or have an odd gait and to have difficulty getting up and lying down. Another fairly common disorder is *elbow dysplasia*, characterized by front-leg lameness and often seen in young German Shepherds.

Patellar luxation is a problem of the kneecap of small breeds such as Toy Poodles and Yorkshire Terriers, which may cause the dog to run on three legs.

Dachshunds, Cocker Spaniels, Pekingese, Miniature Poodles, Dobermans, and Great Danes seem to be particularly susceptible to *disc disease*, which puts pressure on the spinal cord and causes back or neck pain. A dog with disc disease has difficulty walking, even temporary paralysis.

All of these orthopedic problems can be treated with medication or surgery.

Heart Disease

A young dog can have heart disease from a congenital defect or from residual damage caused by a disease such as parvo. Old dogs may develop an insufficiency in the heart valves or degeneration of the heart muscle. Symptoms are a persistent cough, easy fatigue, sometimes an enlarged belly. In some cases, congenital disorders of the heart can be repaired surgically. The life of an old dog with heart disease can be prolonged with rest, medication, and special diet.

Diabetes Mellitus

Much like diabetes in people, this disorder is first suspected when a dog eats more but loses weight, drinks excessive amounts of water, and urinates more frequently. If unrecognized and untreated, diabetes mellitis also causes depression and eventually vomiting and diarrhea. The animal must receive insulin by injection, which the owner can learn to give routinely, and its diet must be regulated.

Stress

If an urban household pet dog suffers from clinical stress, it is usually the result of severe anxiety, triggered by such events as moving; the arrival in the household of a new baby, spouse, or pet; the death of another pet or of a beloved person; being left alone too much and for too long periods; boarding; or showing. In some cases, aging, trauma, or illness can cause stress.

Prolonged stress can bring on symptoms much like those of other disorders: loss of appetite, vomiting, diarrhea, listlessness, depression, in addition to behavior changes such as irritability, barking, or breaking house-training.

Whatever the cause, sustained stress can exhaust a dog. Its fight-or-flight response is kept in a continual state of alert, and this emotional wear and tear can adversely affect the immune system.

The first order is to rule out any physical causes of the dog's symptoms. Then, the best treatment for stress would be changing the situation that produces it, if possible, or at least helping the animal adjust to it. A high-protein diet might help.

The temporary use of tranquilizers can help a dog through a severely stressful period, but you should never give it your own tranquilizers. These drugs should be only of a type and dosage prescribed by a veterinarian for your specfic dog in specific circumstances.

BORDERLINE HEALTH PROBLEMS

Occasional constipation, diarrhea, and vomiting could be called borderline because they can often be quite temporary, isolated disorders in an otherwise healthy pet. As long as other symptoms are not present, they will respond to simple home treatment.

Constipation is relatively rare in dogs, so if your pet is constipated, be sure nothing has happened that could cause an intestinal obstruction. If your dog has been into the garbage and eating bones, for example, or if you have reason to believe it has swallowed some hard object, be on the alert for straining and obvious discomfort when it tries to defecate. An intestinal obstruction can be serious and requires veterinary attention.

However, a dog can become constipated from a diet lacking in fiber, from insufficient exercise, or from not drinking enough water. Old dogs sometimes become constipated if they're arthritic and don't move around enough.

A laxative such as mineral oil (one or two teaspoons, depending on the size of the dog, sprinkled in its food), a little milk, or a teaspoon of milk of magnesia should give relief. But if the constipation persists or recurs frequently, your veterinarian should prescribe for your individual dog.

Diarrhea, as noted earlier, can be brought on by a whole host of physical and psychological causes, just as it is with us. If your dog's diarrhea has blood in it, or persists for longer than a day, your vet should examine the animal, even if nothing else seems to be wrong.

For a single bout of diarrhea with no other symptoms, give the dog Kaopectate or Pectolin every four hours—one teaspoon for a toy breed, one and one-half teaspoons for a small, two teaspoons for a medium-size, one tablespoon for a large, and two tablespoons for a giant breed. Withhold food for twenty-four hours, then give a bland diet—cooked chicken, cooked egg, cottage cheese, rice, that sort of thing. Make sure the dog has plenty of fresh water available, and keep it warm and quiet.

As for *vomiting*, if you have stayed with me through this chapter, you know by now that vomiting can be a symptom of many different conditions. So the first thing you want to do is determine the cause. Spoiled food? Heatstroke? Worms? Anxiety? Poison? Or is the dog merely throwing up light yellow gastric fluid because its stomach is empty, or getting rid of food that didn't agree with it?

If there is blood in the vomitus, or if the dog seems ill, then of course you should take it to your veterinarian. In fact, a second or third bout of vomiting should also be called to the attention of your vet. But if the dog seems otherwise normal, you can treat it yourself and watch it carefully.

Home treatment is simply to withhold food and water for about twenty-four hours, but offer the dog ice cubes to lick because the vomiting may make it thirsty. (The reason for withholding water is that drinking may start up the vomiting again.) If the dog hasn't vomited during the twenty-four-hour fast, feed it a bland diet— cooked chicken, rice, cottage cheese, and the like—for a few days.

NEUTERING

For many years, before I knew better, I avoided having Dandy spayed. I had no intention of breeding her, and she was never off the leash, so she couldn't get pregnant accidentally. So why put her through surgery? I asked myself. Well, I learned why the hard way. She had a couple of false pregnancies and then developed pyometra (an extremely serious uterine infection), and I almost lost her. The surgical and anesthetic risks involved in removing an infected uterus are far greater than those of a simple spay. There's no comparison in expense, either.

Also, because she had not been spayed earlier, Dandy developed mammary tumors in middle age that had to be surgically removed. I wouldn't want your dog to go through these life-threatening problems, and I hope to spare you the worry, guilt, and expense.

At first thought, it seems extreme to interfere surgically with an animal's natural urges to mate, but there are good reasons—medical, behavioral, and social—for doing it.

Domestication has changed the sexual habits of dogs. Wild canids have quite limited sexual activity—they reach sexual maturity later than domestic dogs, females are in estrus only once a year, males produce sperm only then, and mating within the pack is restricted and often monogamous.

By contrast, today's small and medium-size pet dogs are sexually mature before they are a year old, males are always able and eager to mate with any receptive female, and females, except very large breeds, usually have two heat periods every twelve to eighteen months.

If two modern dogs were to mate twice a year for six years, producing an average number of pups, who in turn had an average number of offspring, at the end of six years, 73,000 dogs would have been born! This is one reason why some *five million* unwanted dogs must be euthanized every year in animal shelters—there aren't enough homes to go around.

This unhappy situation is commonly referred to as the "pet overpopulation problem," which somehow seems to imply that it's the pets' fault. Until some progress is made in adjusting the number of dogs that are born to the numbers of people who want to give them homes, until there is some sensible regulation that balances supply and demand, it is irresponsible for pet owners to neglect neutering their animals.

There is ample evidence that neutering—that is, castration of males and spaying of females—not only makes dogs better pets, especially in the city, but very definitely protects their comfort and health. It also adds to the comfort of urban dog owners, and any city dweller who even considers breeding his or her pet should be dissuaded. Here's why:

The Female Dog

An unspayed female dog goes into heat every six, eight, or nine months, depending on her breed and individual body rhythm. This is a stressful time for her, lasting three to four weeks. She is nervous and often breaks house-training, her disposition suffers, her vulva swells uncomfortably, and for nine or ten days of the heat period she has a discharge which may be slight or copious and bloody. When she is walked on the street, she is often snappish with people and with other dogs, especially with males, who will pester her unmercifully.

If she is not bred, she will most likely eventually suffer false pregnancies—extremely stressful hormonal disturbances during which the dog is convinced she is pregnant. She makes a nest, is reluctant to leave the house. Her appetite increases, she puts on weight, and her breasts swell and produce milk.

When she is in estrus, the cervix (passage leading to the womb) is open. If an infectious organism gets in, it can flourish when the cervix closes at the end of estrus. She is also susceptible to pyometra, an endocrine disorder that can lead to a serious bacterial infection of the uterus.

On the other hand, mating is not always simple, not for her or for her partner, and should not be attempted by well-meaning amateur owners, only by professionals, for strange as it seems, the dogs often need help. Otherwise they can injure themselves or each other. Also, the female, in spite of being in heat, may hate the male dog on sight, panic, and attack him viciously. You can't always simply let nature take its course.

Whelping is difficult for many dogs. Many require Caesarians, some die, and in that case the puppies must be hand-fed around the clock and may die anyway. If you have an especially superior purebred dog and are motivated by thoughts of making money selling the pups, you might instead wind up with staggering veterinary bills, no puppies, and possibly no mother dog.

If your idea was to breed your female pet dog to give her the pleasure of motherhood, be assured that she couldn't care less whether she ever becomes a mother or not. Dogs don't look at motherhood the way we do. Mating is simply an urge, and even if all has gone well, motherhood is an obligation that a pregnant female dog may fulfill only grudgingly. Many females that have been great household pets resent their puppies, won't even nurse or clean them.

You have probably heard parents say they plan to breed their female dog so that the children can learn biology or experience the "miracle of birth." I have a hard time being patient with that myopic and irresponsible point of view. It causes the animal welfare and animal control workers to despair, for they are the people who must euthanize the millions of pets that don't get adopted into homes.

Uninformed and uncaring dog owners dump literally millions of puppies on shelters every year, telling themselves that the shelters will find homes for them. Some puppies do get adopted, but many of those are later returned or abandoned. Those that are not chosen for adoption, or have even the slightest health defects, may be put to death because the shelters must make room for the continual influx of unwanted dogs. Some private shelters can afford to have a "no-kill" policy, promising to keep every dog until it is adopted. That forces those pounds and shelters that must accept any and all pets brought to them into the position of acting as the mercy killers for their communities, thanks to people who allow their pets to breed.

Even if you found homes for the pups your female dog produced, that could mean the same number of other puppies already waiting to be adopted would go to their deaths because those homes were not available to them. Animal shelter workers often wish the misguided parents who bred their dogs for the children's sake would bring the kids into the shelter at euthanasia time so they could see the "miracle of death" that their actions brought about.

Now for the good news. Here are the medical advantages of spaying a female dog:

She will be spared heat periods.

She will be spared false pregnancies.

She will be protected against uterine infections.

She will be protected against ovarian and uterine tumors.

And especially if she is spayed before her first heat, her chances of developing breast tumors (both benign and cancerous) are virtually nil.

The benefits to both dog and owner are obvious. The only disadvantage is that you can't enter her in dog shows, except in obedience classes.

The spay operation is an ovariohysterectomy: removal of the uterus and ovaries. It can be done at any age after six months, but the longer you wait, the fewer the benefits. Ideally, it should be done just before a dog's first heat period—that is, when she is between six and nine months of age. Some veterinarians prefer to wait until after the first heat; they say the dog's feminine characteristics will be more firmly established then. But the operation should not be performed while the dog is in heat because the uterus is engorged with blood at that time.

There used to be a theory that a female dog should have a litter first, before being spayed, but that has been shown to offer no health advantages to the dog and, as we have seen, brings more puppies into a world already too replete with puppies.

For the surgery itself, the dog is completely anesthetized, her abdomen is shaved, and the procedure takes about thirty minutes. Most veterinarians prefer that the dog remain in the hospital two or maybe three days. When you bring her home, she should be kept warm and as quiet as possible for a few days. In the highly unlikely event that she becomes lethargic, loses her appetite, and seems feverish, you should notify the veterinarian immediately. But in all likelihood, she will recover quickly, and except for having the stitches removed in a week or ten days, that's it.

Your dog will not get fat and lazy unless you overfeed and underexercise her. Spaying in itself does not cause obesity or undesirable personality change.

Various other methods of birth control for female dogs, such as pills, liquid medications, or injections, are available. They act by suppressing estrus. Some have risky side effects or can be used for only two successive heat periods, after which you must let a third estrus pass without the contraceptive. Some are not recommended for lifetime use.

A dog food containing one of the contraceptive drugs has been developed and may be on the market soon, to be fed daily to female dogs. It is presumably effective and safe when properly used and might offer advantages to the professional breeder. But none of the contraceptive drugs offers the health benefits that spaying gives. For the city dog that lives as a pet, neutering still seems to be the best choice.

The Male Dog

In our culture, it is routine to castrate domestic male animals—except dogs. The word "castration" has unpleasant connotations, and perhaps the special status of dogs among many Americans makes owners reluctant to do it. While most dog owners can handle the idea of spaying a female pet, many have serious hangups about castrating a male. This seems to be particularly true of male people, and one wonders whether they have perhaps confused their dog's sexuality with their own.

Another reason it's less popular to neuter a male dog than a female is that if offspring result from a mating, they become the problem of the owners of the mother dog rather than the owners of the father, if indeed the father dog is even known. In areas where dogs are allowed to roam, owners of males often feel no compunction to castrate their pets.

It is highly advisable to castrate a male dog, however, no matter where he lives. He will be far easier to control on the street, easier to train, and more obedient. Though many intact male dogs are affectionate, most become more demonstrative after neutering. And just as spaying offers health protection to female dogs, neutering offers health advantages to a male dog:

He will be protected against tumors of the reproductive tract.

He will be protected against infections and tumors of the prostate.

He will be calmer, less aggressive toward other dogs, far less likely to get into fights.

The only disadvantage is that if he is a purebred, he won't be eligible to enter dog shows except in obedience classes. He certainly won't give a damn, but you might, so I thought I should mention it.

The castration operation is much simpler than a spay because it doesn't involve cutting into the abdomen. It is best done when the dog is about a year old. The operation, performed while the dog is under general anesthesia, involves the surgical removal of the testicles from the scrotal sac through one or two small incisions. He can usually go home the same day or the next and may seem a little sore but otherwise none the worse for wear. The stitches may be the kind that dissolve and won't have to be removed.

If he has been an aggressive or hyperactive dog, don't expect a sudden improvement in his behavior because it takes six to eight weeks for the hormone level to decline.

Contrary to general belief, castration will not make the dog fat. However, he may tend to put on weight if you feed him the same as formerly, so you may want to reduce the size of his meals or increase his exercise.

One thing about neutering: It will not necessarily stop a dog from sexual behavior. Spayed female dogs sometimes try to mount other dogs—males or females, neutered or not—and engage in clearly sexual activity, especially during play. Castrated males also may try to mount other dogs that they are particularly friendly with. Both males and females sometimes clasp people's legs and carry on the same way—often to their owners' embarrassment. This is not deviant behavior, just a normal response to the animals' occasionally sexy feelings.

At the request of some humane organizations, the American Veterinary Medical Association developed a protocol for tattooing an animal, at the time of the neutering operation, with a tiny male or female sex symbol with an X in the circle, as a permanent means of identifying those dogs and cats that have had the surgery. Since it is usually impossible to locate neutering scars under the fur, putting the little tattoo in a more visible spot provides definite evidence. It can spare a pet needless repeat surgery, both in shelters that demand neutering as a condition for adoption and in any circumstances where a pet goes to a new owner. It also might be useful in communities where a discount in the license price is given for neutered dogs.

PET HEALTH INSURANCE

If your dog needs a pacemaker, one can be had and will greatly extend its life, but it will cost you a bundle. If you are lucky enough to have several pets but are unlucky enough to have a run of serious illness among them, their combined veterinary bills can necessitate a bank loan. The increased sophistication of modern veterinary medicine, along with inflation generally, means that pet owners now spend over three billion dollars a year on medical care for their dogs and cats.

Health insurance for pets is a relatively recent phenomenon, and its practicality is still somewhat controversial. But while some companies that offered it initially have discontinued it from lack of response, several are surviving and even growing. Insurance at first was limited to clients living in California or New York, but now it is available in quite a number of states, and if the predictions of the companies are right, it will be increasingly extended.

Supporters of pet health insurance believe it will make veterinary care available to more dogs and cats who need it. Could be. But detractors claim it will just drive up veterinary bills.

Arguments can be made on both sides for urban dog owners to consider. One factor in favor of having insurance is that because of their high overhead, city veterinarians usually charge higher fees than suburban or rural vets do. Many owners simply cannot afford the costly medical care that could prevent a pet's untimely euthanasia. Health insurance will pay a large percent or all of the veterinary expenses, after deductibles, for many illnesses or injuries. If you have several pets, you pay at a reduced rate for their coverage.

However, since well-cared-for city dogs have fewer illnesses and far fewer accidents than the average, health insurance might not be worthwhile. Coverage does not include vaccinations, checkups, routine neutering, regular dental work, and hereditary or preexisting disorders.

Also, at present, plans don't cover puppies under three months old, and coverage for dogs over nine or ten years is extremely expensive.

If you live in a state where pet health insurance is available, you'll want to weigh all the factors before deciding whether or not it makes sense for you.

Dr. Hayes suggests that a pet owner might instead start an interest-bearing savings account for a pet, which would not be used for routine health care such as vaccinations, neutering, urine or fecal exams, or the like, but kept to cover serious illness or injury. As little as two dollars a week could increase nicely. If a dog never needed it during most of its life, the savings could cover its geriatric care, its burial, if desired, or could be transferred to another pet. Good idea.

CHAPTER 7

SAFETY AND FIRST AID:

Protecting Your Dog, Giving Emergency Care

Statistics indicate that accidents hurt or kill more young children than all diseases combined. I'd be willing to bet the same is true for dogs. Although not all pet accidents are preventable, a good many are, especially if you are alert to their possibility and know how to take precautions against them.

After all I've said about how dogs live with us in perfect comfort in cities and how suited they are for urban life, I want to emphasize the fact that they must be under the stewardship of responsible people. Their own survival and self-protective instincts do not help them much when they're on their own in an urban environment. This is the one instance in which their genes have not caught up with their situation. A homeless dog in the city is doomed, for it will not last long against automobiles, hunger, disease, exposure, and human cruelty. And a day spent in any busy urban veterinary hospital, seeing the dogs that are brought in, suggests that even dogs with homes don't do all that well if their owners are careless about supervising them.

The point to remember is that the burden of your pet's safety is totally yours. You can't guarantee it complete protection, of course, any more than you can guard your child or yourself against every conceivable accident, but you don't want to expose it to danger needlessly. In this chapter I'll point out common hazards.

Also, at some time in your life with your pet there could be an emergency in which you must render first aid to keep the animal alive until you can get professional help. At the end of this chapter I'll give you information on how to cope with those extreme situations, just in case. If you ever do have to save your dog's life, you should know how.

THE UNLEASHED DOG

"We had a dog but he got run over," people say. This piece of information is imparted matter-of-factly, without the slightest trace of guilt or blame, and received without surprise, as if the owner had played no part in this common method by which hundreds of thousands, perhaps millions of unsupervised dogs are killed each year.

In truth, except in the most remote countryside, where there are no busy highways for miles and miles, the time has long gone when dogs can safely be allowed to roam unsupervised. In the suburbs, rural areas, and small towns, vehicles take a heavy toll on dogs. I myself saw a beautiful Golden Retriever hit by a car, his back broken, on a country road in the exurbs fifty miles from New York. I saw a ranch dog killed on a highway in front of his home, in the foothills of Colorado. As for the city, dog owners frequently ignore leash laws, especially in residential neighborhoods, and dogs suffer and die daily because their owners don't protect them.

Yet, of all the risks people take with their dogs, none seems to be so fraught with emotion as the matter of the leash. While letting their dogs run loose seems to be a characteristic typical of irresponsible dog owners, it's also true that some people who otherwise take good care of their dogs turn brainless when it comes to the leash.

In my opinion, dog owners who walk their dogs unleashed fall into three categories, with a lot of overlapping. There are the misguided owners who believe that they're giving their pets pleasure by letting them run at their own pace and that leashing reduces the dog's fun. There are owners who believe that they have their dogs completely under control and that their pets are so well trained and so street-smart that they would only have to give a command and the animals would obey absolutely. I think there's a lot of macho among this type.

And then there are the folks whose own egos have gotten in the way somehow and caused them to view themselves as free spirits with free-spirited dogs and to think their image would be sullied if they did anything so conventional as leashing their pets. Such an owner usually walks along paying no attention to the pet at all, leaving it entirely the dog's problem to keep up. In my observation, this is the also the owner least likely to clean up after the dog.

While almost every city in the United States now has laws requiring dogs to be leashed on the street, hardly any are enforced, the authorities presumably having more important problems on their hands. All three of the above types of dog owners can get very ugly if you go up to them and ask them please to leash their dogs. So I'm not suggesting that you indiscriminately try to persuade other people to leash their dogs; I'm only going to point out good reasons why you should leash your own:

A dog cannot judge the speed and distance of an approaching vehicle and won't jump out of the way until the vehicle is right upon it. A dog at the curb cannot tell when a parked car is suddenly going to start forward or back up.

A dog seeing a friend or enemy on the other side of the street is very likely to dart across. (Unneutered pets are especially impulsive.) People who believe their dogs are too street-smart to run into traffic should spend a day in any big-city veterinary hospital and watch the injured and dying dogs brought in that have been hit by cars. I once heard an idiot dog owner put it archly: "My dog had an *unfortunate encounter* with a car!"

A dog frightened by a sudden loud noise such as a backfire, blasting, crash, or whatever will instinctively take off, and you can scream obedience commands till you're blue in the face before it will hear you or pay attention.

A dog off the leash is at the mercy of any hostile dog who is also off the leash. At the very least, it is a nuisance to other dogs who are leashed.

A dog can lose sight and smell of its owner on a busy sidewalk all too easily and chase off in the wrong direction trying to catch up. If you ever saw the panic of an unleashed dog running up and down looking for its owner, you would not want to put your pet through that. Leaving aside its emotional state, such a dog will certainly dash into traffic in its single-minded search for its owner.

A dog off the leash and out of sight of its owner can be stolen. (More about the danger of dognapping below.)

A dog running loose stands an increased chance of picking up a disease because it will sniff and lick or eat dirty stuff in the gutter. It could also be poisoned this way.

By contrast, a dog *on* a leash feels safe and can be relaxed and enjoy its walk without having to worry about getting lost or losing its owner.

There is no question that dogs do love to romp and play freely, and if you can provide an opportunity for this in a protected place, great. I once lived near a very small park with a tall wrought iron fence around it. Around eleven o'clock at night there was usually nobody in the park but a bunch of us dog walkers, so then we'd close the gate and let our pets run about with each other. One dog liked to play Frisbee, and another liked to chase a tennis ball, and there was enough light from the streetlamps so they could.

Unfortunately, such opportunities are not plentiful in New York; perhaps there are more in other cities. Some civilized places even have fenced dog runs available. The city of San Francisco has twenty-nine protected dog runs where owners can let their dogs romp freely, safely, and legally. The San Francisco SPCA published a map in its quarterly magazine showing the location of these runs.

If you do take a small dog to a dog run, be sure to check the fence to make certain your pet can't slip through.

THE UNATTENDED DOG

Next to letting their dogs run off the leash, probably the biggest risk that city dog owners take is leaving them tied up outside on the sidewalk while they go into a store, bar, or restaurant. In the first place, the animal certainly suffers anxiety. Some dogs bark nonstop, and if you look at the situation from their point of view, can you blame them? When my daughter lived in Soho, she was forever distressed by the dogs she saw and heard tied up for hours outside the trendy bars in the dead of winter. Sometimes she could get action by telephoning the managers of the bars, who would identify the owners and make them take the dogs home. On occasion, she could get the police to come—they would respond if she put the request in the form of a nuisance complaint because of the barking, though a few times she got the impression that the cops were also sympathetic to the dogs.

But the main reason it's dangerous to leave your pet is that it can be stolen. Dognapping is widespread.

Who would steal an unattended dog, and why? Dogs are stolen by people who take a fancy to them and by crazies just for mischief. If they are purebred dogs, they may be stolen by people who will sell them. And any dog can be stolen for sale to a laboratory.

Dognapping is a popular method by which "bunchers" obtain dogs. Bunchers are people who sell dogs to research laboratories, usually for prices below what the laboratories would have to pay for animals obtained from regular lab animal breeders. Unfortunately, most laboratories that use living animals in experiments are not known to be particular where they get them. And even if a research lab tries to be careful about the sources of its animals, stolen pets can easily be mixed in with a legal batch from a pound. In a well-publicized case in Minnesota in 1984, a buncher was arrested and several dozen stolen pets turned up in research laboratories at the University of Minnesota and at the Mayo Clinic. That same year, in Chicago, a sting operation uncovered a lucrative black market in stolen dogs that involved former and current animal control officers and unlicensed kennel operators.

On the subject of laboratories, by the way, an estimated seventy million animals, including some half a million dogs, are killed every year in the testing of household products and cosmetics, in teaching, in military experiments, in medical research, and in experiments conceived for purposes of obtaining grants or graduate university degrees. Dogs are battered, burned, shot, starved, exposed to radiation, and used in medical and surgical experiments that would impress even a Nazi torturer with their creativity.

They are also subjected to cruel psychological experiments. For example, in the 1970s, the University of Minnesota Department of Psychology carried out documented research called "learned help-lessness," in which dogs were taught to avoid painful electric shocks, then frustrated in their attempts to avoid them. A description of one such experimental dog reads in part: "He runs around frantically for about thirty seconds, but then stops moving, lies down, and quietly whines" while enduring them.

Harvard's School of Public Health reported in the *American Journal of Cardiology* experiments in which dogs were restrained in a "Pavlovian sling," given a series of electric shocks, and after a rest period, returned to the sling. "The sling environment evoked the behavioral and cardiac responses indicative of stress," the report of this "scientific breakthrough" read. "The dogs were restless, exhibited somatic tremor, had sphincter relaxation, salivated exces-sively, and had a rapid heart rate."

I can assure you this kind of experimentation is not unusual and goes on at research centers all over the country right now, most of it paid for by public funds. There is a constant demand for animals for the labs. Think about all this the next time you are tempted to leave your dog tied up alone somewhere.

If a lost or stolen pet winds up in the pound or public shelter, it can still be turned over to a laboratory. In many states, public pounds, or animal shelters that have the contract for animal control and function as the pound, are required by law to supply medical laboratories with living research subjects. This is known as pound seizure. The argument in favor of it is that 70 to 80 percent of unclaimed dogs and cats are going to be euthanized anyway, so it doesn't make any difference whether they die that way or in a laboratory experiment.

However, many people feel that servicing laboratories perverts the purpose of a pound or shelter. They believe that a shelter is intended to be a haven for strays, a place where lost pets can be reclaimed by their owners and where others can be offered for adoption. If a shelter animal must be euthanized, they argue, it is usually killed by painless injection. In a laboratory it may be subjected to prolonged, repeated, agonizing experiments before it dies or is killed.

Also, because the vast majority of animals in a shelter have been pets, they are assumed to suffer even more from fear and anxiety than dogs that have lived all their lives in cages without much human contact, having been bred and raised specifically for research laboratories.

Pound seizure is controversial, and not only do state laws vary, but counties and cities may have different laws. In some communities, the public pound or shelter *must* turn dogs and cats over to the laboratories; in others, the pounds and shelters are not required to do so but do have that option. In still other places, the people opposed to pound seizure have succeeded in changing their laws to make pound seizure illegal.

All pounds or shelters that accept or pick up strays are required to keep them a certain length of time—several days, usually—to give owners a chance to claim them. However, in places where pound seizure is legal, the temptation to sell them immediately is apparently more than some keepers can resist.

What this means is that if your dog is ever lost or stolen, it could all too easily end up in a laboratory and be forced to endure great suffering, and you would probably never see it again.

A practice intended to reduce the possibility of losing a dog through theft or any other means is that of tattooing the animal, usually on the inner thigh, with a number that is kept on file at a registry. A dog's collar can easily be removed and thrown away, but the tattoo provides a permanent identification. Veterinarians, pound and shelter workers, and research laboratory personnel, as well as

individuals, are supposed to notify the registry whenever a stray
tattooed dog comes to their attention, so the owner can be traced.

This is a basically good idea that has not yet been very successful.
For one thing, the public generally doesn't think to look for a tattoo
and wouldn't know what it meant if they found one on a dog. For
another, there are a number of different registries, and if you found a
tattooed dog, it might take a lot of research to locate the right one, if
indeed it was still in operation, for registries tend to go in and out of
business.

One company has devised a high tech method of permanent
identification—a microchip implanted under a pet's skin, which can
be read with a scanner. Scanners presumably would be kept by
veterinarians and shelters, and the numbers and letters transmitted
by the chips would be kept in a national data bank.

If someday there could be a network of cooperating registries and
some unified identification system, a lot of lost pets might be
returned to their owners.

I recommend attaching to your dog's collar a tag with your name,
address, and phone number on it, in addition to an up-to-date license
tag. Naturally, a person stealing your dog to sell it elsewhere will
simply throw away the whole collar, but in the event that the animal,
instead of being stolen, just got away from you and was found
wandering, this tag would simplify things for a finder and increase
your chances of getting your dog back. Also, if a dog thief decided
to hold your pet for ransom, the tag would help him get in touch with
you.

IF YOU LOSE YOUR DOG

If despite your precautions your dog is somehow lost, there are steps
you can take that might help you find it. Act immediately. The
ASPCA in New York says the first forty-eight hours are the most
crucial.

1. Notify the local animal control agency. This may be the SPCA,

humane society, or other agency. If in doubt, ask the police whom to call.

2. Put signs everywhere in the section of town where the dog disappeared, describing the dog, giving your telephone number, and offering a reward. Question neighbors, doormen, supers, tradespeople.

3. Visit all the animal shelters in the city or county, and ask if a pet answering the description of yours has been surrendered. Ask the staff to notify you if one is brought in. Call and visit daily or every few days.

4. Check the lost and found ads in the newspapers. Place your own ad, offering a reward.

I know one young man who visited the animal shelter looking for his lost dog every couple of days for three weeks. Finally, one day, there was his little mutt, looking at him as if to say, "What took you so long?"

THE DOG LOCKED IN A PARKED CAR

One crisp October day, I was at a football game when an announcement came over the loudspeaker, urgently requesting the owner of a car with a certain license number to go immediately and rescue the dog that was left in the car.

I hope the owner reached the dog in time and learned a lesson. The person must have innocently assumed that since the temperature was only in the 60s, the dog would be comfortable and safe. What he or she obviously didn't realize was that in the sun, even with the windows left open a crack, the temperature inside the car could reach over 100 degrees. A greenhouse effect is created, and it can kill.

In a car parked in the sun on a 75-degree day, with the windows partially open, the temperature inside can reach 120 degrees in half an hour. On a 90-degree day, the temperature inside can reach 110 degrees within 90 *seconds*, and 130 degrees in ten minutes. An animal trapped inside will suffer heatstroke at 110 degrees and will collapse and die in minutes.

In a car parked in the shade, with windows partially open, the temperature may not rise quite so fast, but the heat can go high enough to kill any living thing inside. Also, people seem to forget that the sun moves, and the car parked in the shade when they leave it can be in the sun minutes later.

Remember that a dog's normal body temperature is between 100 and 102 degrees. The animal cannot withstand a body temperature of 107 without suffering permanent brain damage and will die very soon.

Yet as every city dweller knows, a dog peering out the rolled up window of a parked car is a common sight. Except possibly in midwinter, in places where it's still below freezing in the noonday sun, dog owners are risking a terrible death for their pets every time they leave them in the car even for a very short time. Why do they do it? With all the warnings that have been issued on this subject by animal shelters, animal hospitals, veterinarians, and other concerned sources and widely publicized by the media, you'd think by now everyone would know better. Yet apparently many folks still haven't got the message, or have chosen to ignore it, because heatstroke is a common killer of dogs. For information on what to do in case your dog suffers heatstroke, see "First Aid," below.

A dog can get into trouble in a locked car even in cold weather. I heard about a German Shepherd whose owner left it locked in the car for a short time one winter night when he ran out of gas and walked to a filling station to get help. The dog apparently went crazy with anxiety, for it chewed up a considerable amount of the seat upholstery before its owner returned. The upholstery contained metal springs. Fortunately, the owner got his pet to a veterinarian in time to save its life. But it took quite a bit of fancy surgery to remove the fabric and twists of metal from the animal's stomach.

Bear in mind that a dog can be stolen from a parked car, even a locked parked car, since—as every car owner knows well—locked cars can easily be broken into. Gentle, friendly dogs are the most vulnerable.

For suggestions on safe ways to take your dog with you when you drive, see Chapter 12.

HOT WEATHER HAZARDS

When the temperature soars in the city, dogs especially feel it because they lack that cooling mechanism that our human bodies are equipped with: the ability to perspire on virtually every surface of our skin. The notion that dogs perspire through their tongues is inaccurate. When a dog pants, it salivates, and the evaporation of this moisture on its tongue does have some cooling effect on its blood and thus on its body. But there's a limit to how much cooling effect panting can have when the animal is exposed to severe heat. This is true of all dogs, but particularly of little short-nosed dogs such as Boston Terriers, Lhasa Apsos, Shih Tzus, and Pekingese because of their respiratory problems.

Given a choice, most dogs prefer just to lie around and not move much in hot weather, and it's an insensitive owner who will drag his or her pet out for a walk in the heat of the day. If the city has cooled off during the night, an early morning walk will be enjoyable, and if there's a breeze, late night can be a good time. But in the afternoon or early evening, a trip just to the curb should be it. This is especially true for older dogs.

A haircut such as a puppy cut offers some relief to long-haired dogs, but a dog should not be shaved in summer. It makes the animal subject to sunburn, insect stings, and more discomfort than it was in with its full coat of hair.

Obviously a scorching sidewalk will burn a dog's feet—that's another reason for keeping a dog indoors during most of the day in sunny hot weather.

A very little dog with short legs will really feel the heat rising from the sidewalks—not just in the paws, as all dogs do, but in their faces and entire bodies. Because Dandy is medium size, I'd never thought about that, but a neighbor with a Dachshund mentioned it. "For Ludvig, it's like walking on a furnace," he said.

Also apropos of little dogs, don't try to transport one in hot weather in one of those carriers with a domed, rigid plastic top. The heat buildup in those things is fast and insidious, and you could arrive at your destination with a dead or dying dog.

Never leave a dog out on a terrace in hot weather. Not only can a terrace become a hotbox if the sun hits it and cause the dog to keel over from heat prostration, but the dog can go over the side trying to escape the heat.

Make sure your dog's water bowl is filled because it may drink more than usual.

COLD WEATHER HAZARDS

It always amazes me that a person can put on a sweater, overcoat, hat, scarf, boots, and gloves and sally forth with his or her short-haired dog wearing nothing but its birthday suit when the wind chill factor makes the temperature something like 5 degrees. I've seen dogs shivering miserably tied to lampposts in bitter cold weather while their owners are in nice warm coffeeshops having brunch.

Cold weather is felt especially by dogs that live indoors most of the time, as urban dogs do. Dogs that are unfortunate enough to have to live outdoors year-round grow thicker coats as cold weather approaches, and if properly fed, add a layer of fat to their bodies that helps protect them. But the bodies of dogs that spend most of their time indoors do not change very much with the seasons, so going out in winter is, at least for the short-haired dog, somewhat like it is for us.

I think dog coats or sweaters make sense for city dogs in severe weather if they are short-haired or elderly or are going to be out very long. Also, a raincoat gives good protection in a sleet storm and makes less trouble for you in drying your dog off when you bring it in after a walk in a downpour.

Be sure to dry an animal right away when you bring it in from snowy or rainy weather. And don't dry just the back and head but legs and stomach as well. Check the feet for encrusted ice or snow and rinse immediately to prevent frostbite.

Dogs, especially young vigorous ones, need their exercise just as much in winter as any other time, so their owners should be prepared to tough it out, for the sake of their pets. But like people, dogs can slip and hurt themselves on icy pavement, so pick a nonslippery place for play.

Another big winter problem for a city dog is the chemical salt that's scattered on icy and snowy sidewalks to keep people from breaking their necks. In most urban neighborhoods, the doormen and superintendents are out there with the salt as the first snowflakes begin to drift down, and although helpful to people, this stuff is hell on dogs. It burns their footpads cruelly. I've seen dogs limping, even crying in pain. I try to walk Dandy in the middle of the street where there's likely to be fresh snow or even slush but no salt.

And that's not the end of it. If you don't wash, not merely wipe, your dog's feet when you come indoors, the animal can get sick from licking them. Chemical salt is poison when ingested.

Dog boots look funny on a dog, but in a very snowy city where sidewalk salt is widespread, they may not be a bad idea. Some dogs really hate them, but others seem to get used to them.

SPORTS WITH YOUR DOG

Vigorous play and exercise are good for most dogs, and your pet will think it's great fun to participate in almost any activity with you. But do choose the activity according to what the animal can realistically do and enjoy. Don't try to make a jock or a showoff of your dog.

Jogging

If you yourself like to run, your dog may enjoy going with you, but first, here are a few words of caution:

Bear in mind the animal's footpads. Your dog is not wearing Nikes. This is especially relevant to city people, because you may be running all or most of the way on pavement, in which case it's probably best to leave your dog home. I once heard of a man who was in the habit of walking his dog across the Brooklyn Bridge every day. Walking, not even running. The animal's footpads were torn and bleeding before the owner noticed.

Don't try to make a little short-legged breed jog with you, and especially not a short-nosed breed such as a Boston Terrier, Pug, or Bulldog.

The dog should have good chest capacity and a strong heart. Get it checked out by your veterinarian before taking it jogging, and work it into the exercise gradually. Once you take your pet on regular jogs, be alert to intermittent lameness, which is a sign the animal is overdoing it.

The dog should be over two years old and under late middle age, not elderly. Since age is relative to a dog's size and breed, be sure you know what middle age is in terms of your particular pet. For most dogs, except giant breeds, middle age is between five and seven or eight years.

The reason a dog should not become a running partner until it is over two years of age is that its bones and joints aren't mature enough. You'd be setting the animal up for serious orthopedic trouble later.

Naturally an overweight dog should start out very slowly and for short, limited runs. Otherwise your fatso pet will collapse.

Don't even think about jogging with your dog off the leash. Everything that I said against walking a dog off the leash applies to running, too.

Some hardy folks can safely run in hot weather, but a dog cannot. The body of a human jogger cools itself by sweating. A dog can only pant, which is inadequate to keep it from overheating while running on a hot day.

If your pet begins to slow down and lag behind while you're jogging, it's trying to tell you that it's overexerting, so you slow down too or stop and let the animal take a breather.

Don't let your jogging partner gulp huge amounts of water when you arrive home. The animal should drink all it wants—but a little at a time.

Bicycling

If you can train your healthy and vigorous dog to trot at the side of your bike while you pedal, fine, provided you protect it by observing stringent safety rules:

Go slowly. You may think you're going at a sedate cruise, but you can exhaust a pet who has to gallop to keep up.

If you're biking on pavement, go only short distances. The same caution about a dog's footpads applies here, too.

Never tie the dog to the bike. You want to be able to feel the animal slowing down when it tires.

And of course, never, never bike with a dog in traffic, for obvious reasons.

Swimming and Boating

It is a myth that all dogs can swim instinctively. A dog will move its feet—dog paddle—if it can't touch the bottom, but that doesn't mean it won't panic, choke, become exhausted, and eventually drown.

Some idiot people toss their dogs overboard from boats as a way of introducing them to the water. That is indescribably mean. You should never ever force a dog into the water. If you go in, let the animal enter the water and follow you if it wishes—in its own time and at its own pace.

Some dogs, and Dandy falls into this category, hate the beach. They are miserable in the heat, sun, and sand and are afraid of the ocean. Let your pet decide how it feels about the beach, lake, or swimming pool.

If your dog does love to romp in the surf, by the way, be sure to rinse its coat thoroughly with fresh water afterward.

THE GARBAGE CAN

I don't think a dog can be expected not to get into the garbage can. To the dog, the receptacle is filled with appetizing edibles, and when you're not looking, even a dog that has just finished a meal will find it hard to resist. Don't be hard on the animal for this—remember that food is just about at the top of its list of instinctive priorities.

Some dogs explore the trash can just for something to do when their owners are out. Puppies do it just out of curiosity, and in play. Most of the time, this habit is objectionable mainly for its nuisance value, since the dog won't clean up the mess it has made.

But sometimes the garbage can will have stuff in it that's dangerous to dogs—bones, for instance, and also the string that roasts were wrapped with, and scouring pads used to clean cooking pans. This sort of thing can play serious havoc with a dog's insides. Bones can stick in the throat and choke an animal, they can puncture the stomach or intestines, or they can compact and cause intestinal blockage. String can get tangled around an organ or ball up and block a passage. Scouring pads can scour an animal's inner organs.

You can train a dog not to get into the garbage by the same method that you can train it not to lie on the furniture or howl when left alone (see Chapter 4).

Or you can simply put the can where the dog can't reach it, or close the kitchen door. Whatever means you use, remember it is a sensible safety measure to keep your pet out of the garbage at all times.

POISONS

You wouldn't believe the kinds of toxins that dogs have ingested, as a result of which they have wound up in veterinary hospitals—or in heaven. The substances are as astonishing and worrisome as the known poisons that little children have consumed when their parents weren't looking. Who would think that a dog would be attracted to detergent, drain cleaner, antifreeze, toilet bowl cleanser, paint, turpentine, roach poison, cigarette butts, matches, cough syrup, boric acid, laxatives, or shampoo, for instance? Yet dogs have ingested all of these, and much much more. So help me, I once heard of a dog that ate its owner's birth control pills.

I have never had a dog that was poisoned, but Dandy once proved to me that under the right circumstances, a dog will consume just about anything. I had gone out with some friends, people she knew and liked, and she apparently took offense at being left behind. When I returned, I discovered she had eaten an entire bowl of walnuts that had been on the coffeetable. Walnuts in the shell. She'd cracked the nuts open with her teeth, scattered the shells about, and eaten the meats. Later she threw up the mess.

Walnuts of course are not poisonous, but the fact that she did this convinced me always to cover or put away anything that she or the cats could conceivably get into. I think you can train yourself into the habit of automatically putting dangerous stuff out of reach, just as you do when there are very young children around.

Dandy has never shown any interest in eating plants, but one of my cats loves to nibble now and then, so I keep only harmless plants. The following house plants can be poisonous to pets: dieffenbachia, poinsettia, caladium, philodendron, Jerusalem cherry, schefflera, English ivy, and—not house plants but common decorations—mistletoe and bittersweet.

Rather than try to list every single poisonous substance that a dog might ingest, it's more helpful and practical to advise you simply to assume that your pet (especially a puppy, for puppies are the worst in this regard) just might sample anything and everything.

Therefore, keep all closets firmly shut, especially under-the-sink cupboards, and don't leave any kind of medicine on a counter or table that the dog could possibly reach. Be sure there are no places in the house where the paint is chipping; for some unknown reason, dogs have been known to eat that, too. When you're using any paint, thinner, remover, varnish, polish, or wax, keep the lid firmly on except when you're right there on the spot using it. Keep the dog away from any insect or bug poisons you might put around. Empty all ashtrays before you leave a room; nicotine is poisonous to dogs. (I once heard of a dog that sampled the remains of a marijuana butt it found in an ashtray and got high—not funny, since the poor dog of course didn't know what was happening to it and got very upset.)

Don't let guests offer your dog anything for a lark, such as cocktails, cocaine, or coffee.

At holiday time, be sure to protect a dog from harmful stuff it could chew up—ribbon, tinsel, mistletoe, and other decorations.

Don't let a dog have any painted toys.

Dogs have been poisoned from chewing their flea collars. If you put a flea collar on your pet, fasten it just tightly enough for you to slip your finger easily between it and the dog's neck. If you leave it too loose, the dog might get its jaw under it and chew on it. Be sure to cut off and throw away out of reach any excess length so that there is no dangling end.

If you have any reason to bring your car's antifreeze into the house, keep it well out of reach. It sounds impossible, but both dogs and cats love the taste of this stuff and will go to great lengths to get at it. Outdoor cats have been known to climb up into the engines of parked cars to lick any antifreeze that has spilled over. Antifreeze (ethylene glycol) is a killer.

Sidewalk salt isn't the only poisonous substance that your dog can get on its paws when out for a walk—oil spills in the gutter are dangerous because the animal will try to lick its paws clean later. And if you let your pet run or walk on grass outdoors, be sure that the grass hasn't recently been sprayed with herbicide.

The University of Illinois College of Veterinary Medicine established and operates a National Animal Poison Control Center where veterinarians and animal owners can get immediate, emergency advice on treating animals that have ingested toxins. Dr. Harold Trammel there points out that city poison control centers are set up for people and might not be able to be as helpful in animal poisoning cases as the Center. He recommends that dog owners call their own veterinarians first; otherwise, they can call the twenty-four-hour hotline: (217) 333-3611. I suggest you put that number in your personal telephone book.

For first aid for poisons, see below.

BURNS AND ELECTRIC SHOCK

To a house pet, the kitchen is where the real action is, the most important room in the house, especially when you're there, too. That means that if you have a small kitchen, as many city people do, your dog may frequently be right under your feet.

It's important to keep the handles of pots on the stove turned toward the back, just as you would if there was a small child in the house. In fact, with the exception of sunburn, your dog can be burned in the same ways the rest of us can, and common-sense measures offer the only protection.

Some dogs, especially puppies, take an interest in electric cords, and the minute your dog shows this tendency, you have a problem. Puppies generally do it out of curiosity, or when they're teething, and will lose interest as they grow up. Older dogs may resort to it just for something to do if they're left alone for long periods, or if they're upset and anxious about something—an owner's prolonged absence, for example. An animal that chews on a cord can get not only an electric shock but a burned mouth.

If you have a determined cord chewer, the only solution is to keep an eye on the dog when you're home and either confine it when you go out or disconnect all the lamps and other appliances that have cords—an awful nuisance, but a necessary one if you value your pet's life.

For first aid for burns or electric shock, see below.

TOYS

You'd think that the manufacturers of dog toys would take safety
into consideration, but since every pet supplies shop is full of toys
that are dangerous for dogs, apparently they don't. Among the worst
are soft rubber toys and those that squeak. Any dog worth its salt can
chew up a soft rubber toy in a matter of hours, swallowing the bits of
rubber as it goes along. As for toys that squeak, the squeaker goes
down the dog's throat along with the shreds of rubber or fabric the
toy is made of.

Equally harmful potentially are toys with beads, buttons, bells, or
rubber bands attached, and painted toys.

Safe dog toys include hard rubber balls—just be sure to gauge the
size of the ball according to the size of the dog's jaws, because a too-
small ball can choke the animal. Hard nylon and rawhide bones are
okay, too. Some people give their dogs old shoes or socks, which the
animals apparently enjoy, but as I suggested in Chapter 3, this might
encourage them to assume that any shoes and socks are fair game.

The point is that before you give your pet any sort of plaything,
bear in mind that it will be chewed as well as tossed about, and
examine it for any potential harm it could cause.

FALLS

Falling from open windows is such a common type of accident
among cats that veterinarians have given it a name: highrise
syndrome. The majority of highrise victims are cats, but dogs too
suffer falls from stairwells, open windows, terraces, fire escapes,
and rooftops where their owners have taken them to play.

Every city dweller with pets should have all windows firmly
screened. And here's something else to think about: I once lived in a
ground-floor apartment where Dandy used to lie against a window

Safe: A tennis ball is a good toy for a young dog.
(Jane Sapinsky)

A groomer puts the finishing touches on a beautifully combed show dog.
(Hope Ryden)

A standard poodle shows off his sporting clip. *(Michael Bernkopf)*

Happiness is a nap with a best friend. *(Kathy Chochrun/Courtesy, Humane Society of New York)*

The dog on the right has just joined the family. The incumbent has accepted him, but grudgingly. *(Michael McCulloch, M.D.)*

Dog friends playing. Note the gaily carried tails, the pretended aggression. *(Jane Sapinsky)*

This poor cat thinks the puppy is a real pest. *(Arington/Courtesy, Humane Society of the United States)*

But this kitten loves the family dog. *(Wilson/ Courtesy, Humane Society of the United States)*

and watch for us when we were out. But one day she apparently leaned against it too hard, or bumped it, because I came home to find the pane cracked and a tuft of her fur in the crack. Had she broken the glass, she could have been cut. She also could have escaped and gotten lost had the whole pane gone. So if you have a window seat or any window where your dog likes to look out, be sure the glass is extra heavy; otherwise, put a window gate or screen on the inside.

A puppy will have to be protected from stairwells until it learns to go up and down safely. A gate (baby gate or special dog gate sold by pet suppliers) at the head of the stairs is a good idea.

It's a good practice always to check on a pup's whereabouts before you leave the house, to be sure it isn't shut accidentally in a closet, for example.

FIRST AID

First aid is to keep your pet alive during critical, life-threatening emergencies until you can get it to a veterinarian. It is not intended to replace professional medical care.

If you should find yourself and your dog in one of the situations described here, try to keep cool. It's natural to get very upset when your dog is in a serious emergency, but if you lose your head, you could do the wrong thing and make matters worse. Also, because the animal is sensitive to your feelings, if you go to pieces, you'll be unable to give it the reassurance it needs. In addition to the first aid, the will to live can make the difference for the pet.

Before listing the common emergencies that might require first aid for your dog, I want to tell you how to administer artificial respiration and cardiopulmonary resuscitation (CPR), even though you will probably never need this information. In fact, I suggest you commit the instructions to memory. If an emergency should ever arise in which your pet needs this kind of first aid, you won't want to waste time reading directions.

Dr. Audrey Hayes of the Animal Medical Center in New York City points out that either procedure is exhausting for one person alone, so if you can yell for help while administering to your dog, do so. This emergency really calls for you to do three things simultaneously: keep your pet alive by giving artificial respiration or CPR, get someone to help you, and get the dog to a veterinarian without delay.

Artificial Respiration

This procedure is for an emergency in which the dog has stopped breathing but the heart is still beating. (If the heart also has stopped, CPR is required, see below.) To determine for certain if the dog is breathing, hold a mirror up to its nose to see whether the mirror mists over.

Place the dog on its side with its neck extended. Clear its mouth of any blood or mucus. Now hold its mouth closed, place your mouth over its nose, take a deep breath, and blow into the nostrils for three or four seconds. If the dog is a puppy, blow in quick puffs.

Repeat ten or twelve times, then stop and look to see whether the animal is breathing on its own. If not, keep it up until the dog is breathing—otherwise its heart will stop. You must get the dog to a veterinarian fast; if it still hasn't begun breathing, continue giving artificial respiration en route, any way you can.

Cardiopulmonary Resuscitation (CPR)

If administered within a few minutes after a dog's heart has stopped, CPR may save the animal.

Give artificial respiration (above) for two or three seconds. Now, if the dog is small, place it on its back, put your hands on its chest, fingers clasped over the breastbone, and compress your palms quickly and firmly, once every second for ten to twenty seconds. Then give artificial respiration again for two or three seconds. Repeat. Keep alternately pumping the chest and blowing in the nostrils, stopping every few minutes to check for breathing and heartbeat.

To check for heartbeat, feel the heart at the left center of the chest, under the front leg, or in the groin, where a hind leg meets the body.

If the dog is medium-size or big, begin with artificial respiration for two or three seconds, then lay the dog on its side and place your hand just behind the rib cage. Press quickly and firmly, down and a little forward, once every second for ten to twenty seconds. Then give artificial respiration for two or three seconds. Keep alternately pumping the chest and blowing in the nostrils, stopping every couple of minutes to check for heartbeat.

Keep giving CPR while transporting the dog to the veterinarian, stopping only when the heart resumes beating. If the heart starts but the dog still isn't breathing, continue artificial respiration.

Here are some situations calling for first aid:

Bite

If your dog is bitten by another animal, clip the hair around the wound and flush it out with hydrogen peroxide or betadine solution. Then take the dog to a veterinarian. Even if the bite looks okay now, it may need stitches, and the dog should receive antibiotics.

Bleeding

Blood pouring out of a wound can be very scary, and in fact, if the animal loses a lot of blood, it can go into shock, so you should stop the bleeding if possible before you start for the veterinarian. Press a clean dressing on the wound and hold it in place for a few minutes. Don't take it off to see if the bleeding has stopped, because if the blood has formed a protective clot you don't want to disturb it. If the wound bleeds through the dressing, add more on top of the first. If necessary, keep pressing firmly with your hand to stop the bleeding. Apply a bandage over the dressings and get the dog to a vet.

If the bleeding is at a limb or the tail and doesn't stop, you might have to apply a tourniquet. Use a bandage, tie, handkerchief, or belt about one inch wide (don't under any circumstances use string, rope, or wire, which could cut the flesh). Tie it around the limb or tail above the wound, then tie a pen, stick, or spoon to the knot and twist it in such a way that it tightens the bandage or whatever you have wrapped around the affected limb or tail, just enough to stop the bleeding. Release the tourniquet for a few moments every fifteen minutes, then retighten, until you reach the veterinarian.

Burn

A dog can have a serious burn that you can't see because hair covers it, so clip the hair around the area of skin to examine the extent of the burn. If the burn looks only minor, red and sore, forget that old remedy we used to believe in—butter or grease. Modern medicine has discovered that a far better first aid is cold water or an ice pack, applied gently to the reddened area.

However, if the dog's skin is blistered or charred, don't touch it. Get the animal to a veterinarian at once, making sure that nothing comes in contact with the burn. Be on the lookout for shock (see below), a serious complication that can be caused by a bad burn.

Choking

A dog choking on something will gag, salivate, and paw at its mouth, and if the obstruction blocks the windpipe, the dog will lose consciousness. First look in the dog's mouth (this is not easy, for the animal will be frantic, and even a normally gentle pet might bite you; if you have a pair of gloves handy, put them on). If you can see what it's choking on, try to remove it with your fingers. Face the fact that you will undoubtedly get bitten, but that's better than losing your dog.

If that doesn't work, you'll have to get the animal to a veterinarian fast. Its breathing or heart may stop, so you might have to administer artificial respiration or CPR on the way.

Convulsion or Seizure

This is a symptom rather than a condition in itself. It can be caused by high fever, heat stroke, liver disease, a blow to the head, brain disease, or poisoning, for example, as well as epilepsy. The dog may fall down and twitch violently; it may stiffen, froth at the mouth, urinate or defecate, and lose consciousness. Or it may run around bumping into things and barking wildly, a state of frenzy in which it's unable to stop and unable to respond to you.

How to treat a dog having a convulsion depends in part on the cause. If it is suffering from heatstroke, you have to concentrate on first aid for that. If it has been poisoned, that calls for a different sort of first aid. But if there is no apparent life-endangering cause, then treat the convulsion by wrapping the dog in a blanket, keeping it from hurting itself, and getting it to a veterinarian immediately.

Convulsions can last from thirty seconds to about three minutes. But the animal should be taken to a vet, even when the seizure stops.

Electric Shock

If a dog has received a shock and is thrown away from the cord, it will probably go into cardiac arrest, so you should begin CPR immediately and get it to a veterinarian.

However, and this is important, if the dog still has the cord in its mouth, *don't touch it* or you might get electrocuted yourself. Disconnect the plug at the outlet. Then start CPR and rush the animal to the vet.

Dr. Hayes cautions that one effect of electric shock—pulmonary edema—can develop as long as twenty-four hours later, so the veterinarian may want to X-ray the dog's chest and hospitalize it for observation. He or she will also check for burns around the dog's mouth.

Eye Injury

If you notice your dog squinting and pawing at its eye, the first thing you want to do is prevent it from injuring itself by further pawing and rubbing its face on the floor. Flush the eye with water. You may notice a sort of extra eyelid has moved out from the inner corner of the eye and partly covered the eye; don't be alarmed by that—it's normal. But you do want your veterinarian to see if the eye has been injured and to clip the dog's nails to prevent further injury if the dog paws at itself.

Dogs with pop eyes—Pekingese, Boston Terriers, Shih Tzus, Pugs, and the like—are subject to alarming emergencies in which an eye actually comes out of its socket. Cover the eye with a sterile dressing that has been soaked in a solution of sugar and water (add enough sugar to make the solution cloudy) and keep it covered while you rush the animal to the veterinarian. Dr. Hayes says the sugar solution will keep the eye from swelling, which would make it impossible for the veterinarian to get the eye back in the socket.

Heatstroke

As I explained earlier in this chapter, the most common cause of heatstroke is leaving a dog in a closed car—I think it could be called the closed car syndrome. The dog will drool, pant, collapse, vomit, and if not rescued in time, will have convulsions. Its temperature can reach 107 degrees. You must immerse the animal immediately in cool water and keep it there for some thirty minutes. Then put an ice pack on its head while you get it to a veterinarian.

Poisoning

This is a scary crisis, but you must keep calm and act quickly. The signs the dog will show depend on the type of poison it has swallowed. The animal could be vomiting, twitching, drooling, trembling, and crying out in pain, or it could be comatose, or having convulsions. You must act promptly.

The first thing to do is to find out what your pet has swallowed. This is crucial because there are two different courses of action to take, and what works for one kind of poison is wrong for the other. If you can't reach your veterinarian for instructions, call the National Animal Poison Control Center hotline, (217) 333-3611, to find out the appropriate antidote.

If the substance swallowed is a corrosive acid or alkali or petroleum-based product (such as detergent, cleanser, drain or oven cleaner, lye, plaster, paint, paint solvent, or floor wax), or if the dog is comatose, *do not induce vomiting*. Hold the dog's head downward and flush out the mouth with water, then get it to swallow olive or vegetable oil, milk or cream, egg white, or milk of magnesia—a tablespoonful at a time. Be sure the dog swallows. When the dog seems somewhat relieved, rush it to a veterinarian. Take the container of what the dog ate with you.

If the subtance swallowed is a noncorrosive poison (for example, plants, medicine, vitamins, shampoo, insecticide), *induce vomiting*. Give the dog an emetic, such as hydrogen peroxide mixed half and half with water, or prepared mustard mixed with water, or table salt mixed with water—a tablespoonful at a time until the dog vomits. Or, if you have ipecac syrup on hand, that's also good—one and a half teaspoons for a little dog or a puppy, two teaspoons for medium-size dogs, three teaspoons for a big dog. As soon as the animal vomits, get it to a veterinarian, taking the vomitus and the container of whatever the dog ate with you.

Shock

More dogs die of shock following an accident than from the injury itself, so if your pet gets seriously hurt, you want to be alert for signs of shock and treat the animal for that as well as attend to the injury.

Any serious trauma, burn, or loss of blood can cause shock. The animal will have a fast heart rate (maybe even over 150 beats per minute), rapid breathing, and white or very pale gums. Wrap the dog very warmly in blankets or coats and lower its head, and keep it that way while you rush it to a veterinarian. If it is bleeding, do whatever you can to stop it. (See "Bleeding," above.)

There's an excellent spiral-bound ninety-six-page book devoted entirely to first aid for dogs, complete with clear how-to drawings and covering not only the emergencies I've described but many others, from broken bones to toad poisoning. Most dog owners, especially city dwellers who take their dogs to the country, would find this a useful handbook. *Emergency First Aid for Dogs*, by Sheldon Rubin, D.V.M., and the editors of *Consumer Guide*, is available from Publications International, 3841 West Oakton, Skokie, IL. 60076.

CARRYING AN INJURED DOG

Since many of us who live in cities don't have cars, since taxi drivers often refuse to take dogs, and since dog ambulances may not be immediately available, you may find yourself facing the problem of how to get your sick or injured dog to a veterinarian. A little dog, of course, you can just pick up in your arms; it's the medium-size and large dogs we have to worry about.

The good thing about living in a city, however, is that you can more quickly get someone to help you—a friend or neighbor, or even a stranger. When we once had an emergency with Benjy, my son simply stopped a passing car and asked the driver if he would take him to the vet with Benjy. That Good Samaritan didn't hesitate.

If the dog is in pain, it might try to bite you, so wear heavy gloves in handling it and muzzle it with a scarf, dish towel, large handkerchief, or nylon stocking or panty hose. (But don't try to muzzle a dog that is vomiting, gagging, or choking.) To make a muzzle, tie the dog's mouth shut with the cloth, knotting it under the dog's chin, and then bring the ends to the back of its neck and tie them. Don't make the muzzle so tight the dog can't breathe, especially if it's a short-nosed dog, but tie it tight enough so that it stays on.

To transport a dog when you have another person to help you, you should improvise a stretcher. Ideally, the stretcher should be rigid and flat like a board, but how many of us have such a thing in our city homes or apartments? Next best is a blanket or coat. Roll the dog gently onto it and immobilize the animal by tying it to the stretcher with a belt so it can't fall, especially if it is thrashing about.

Another very useful means of transport is a child's wagon. Lay the dog in it and fasten it with a belt so it can't roll off.

However, if you can't get help and can't get a wagon, you can carry the dog across your shoulders. (Be sure it's muzzled before you try this.) Lay the dog on its side with its legs facing you, grasp its front legs with one hand and its hind legs with your other hand. Now kneel down and slide your head under the animal's middle while pulling it over your shoulders by the legs as you stand up. Unless the animal is unconscious, better hang on tight, because if it struggles you might drop it or lose your balance. Still, this is a lot better way to support a big dog's weight than by trying to clutch it in your arms across your chest.

The best way to carry a medium-size dog is feet down, broadside against your chest, with one arm wrapped around its chest, the other around its rump.

Chances are you'll never need to use any of this first aid information, but I'm glad you now know it anyway.

CHAPTER 8

GROOMING:

Keeping Your Urban Dog Looking Good

When the wild dog took up with the first human beings, long ago, probably nobody noticed or cared that it was not an especially fastidious animal. Hygiene had not yet been invented, so most likely the people weren't too fussy about the dog's condition, though they might have made it sleep outside their dwelling when it had been rolling in carrion.

From what I've read of history, we human beings were a long time in cleaning ourselves up, let alone our domestic animals, but somewhere in the course of centuries, many of us began to be offended by unreasonable amounts of dirt. Cleanliness became a virtue, and that was when a dog owner must have looked at his or her house pet one day and said, "Rover, you need a bath. You also need to be combed and brushed and your ears cleaned out, and your breath is pretty smelly too—let's have a look at your teeth." Dog grooming was born.

By grooming, I don't mean have a dog's coat trimmed in the latest haircut and its nails polished as if for the show ring. I mean having a clean, well-kept, healthy-looking animal that is a credit to itself and its owner. Like it or not, a dog's appearance speaks volumes about its owner. A scruffy-looking, unkempt dog is a worse advertisement of its owner's slovenly ways than ring-around-the-collar. Such a dog is a victim of neglect almost as serious as if it were underfed or had a chronic medical problem that was allowed to go untreated.

A dog makes a stab at its own upkeep. It will try to remove mats, burrs, and parasites from its coat with its teeth; it may wipe its mouth on the rug after eating; it will scoot along on its bottom if it feels bothersome stuff clinging to it after defecation. But for the most part, it is dependent on its owner for its grooming, just as it is for food, shelter, protection, and love. When you see a pitiful filthy stray, bear in mind that living in human dirt and lacking human care are what have reduced the animal to that condition.

Regular grooming sessions accomplish other worthwhile objectives besides keeping your dog looking good. They help strengthen the bond between the two of you. Even if your dog initially doesn't like to be brushed, it will grow to appreciate and enjoy your undivided attention, especially if you talk to it.

Also, in the routine of checking on your pet's body, especially its coat, ears, teeth, and eyes, you pick up health problems that need veterinary attention. You'll spot sores, rashes, cuts, lumps under the skin, inflamed areas, and the like early, before you might otherwise notice them and before they begin to threaten the dog seriously. Jim Stewart, a professional dog groomer who owns a shop called Caniche in New York City, says that in the course of his work he quite often discovers and alerts his clients to conditions in their dogs that should have veterinary attention.

If a dog develops an unpleasant smell—not just the doggy smell that indicates it needs a good brushing or bath but a sick, foul sort of smell—this can signal a condition such as ear, tooth, or gum infection. These are typical of the problems that will be noticed during grooming, before they advance to the stage where they cause the poor dog to smell.

Get a puppy accustomed to grooming while it's still very young. Hold it on a table, not on your lap, but put a rubber mat or something nonskid under its feet to give it a firm footing. Go over its body with your hands, open its mouth and check the teeth, look in its ears and under the tail. Examine its feet, separating the toes. Brush it all over. The pup will learn to like the experience, or at least to tolerate it. Adult dogs that aren't used to being groomed can view it as an ordeal and even become hysterical at a professional groomer's. Conditioning a dog early in life can make routine care a lot easier for both of you.

The best time to groom your pet is right after a walk, when the animal has relieved itself and is ready to relax.

Every dog owner should have a few basic grooming tools: a comb and brush appropriate for your particular dog's coat, a pair of nail clippers (the kind especially designed for dogs), and a good tearless dog shampoo. I'll tell you how to use these when I give information on routine grooming.

Purebred dogs are more likely than mixed breeds to require the services of a professional groomer, either regularly or occasionally. However, grooming has nothing to do with the cosmetic surgery forced upon many purebred show dogs. Tail docking and ear cropping are performed by breeders and veterinarians. These practices are discussed in Chapter 1, in the section on acquiring a purebred dog.

BRUSHING YOUR DOG

Urban living has an impact on a dog's coat that a caring owner deals with more or less daily. Your urban dog won't collect external parasites to the extent that it probably would if it lived in the suburbs or country, but its coat brings in dust and dirt from the street. It sheds—year-round. Heating and air conditioning tend to dry it out. The city dog's coat needs regular care.

This is not to underestimate the importance of diet. If a dog is not getting the proper balance of nutrients, with enough fat, its coat will be dull and dry no matter how much regular brushing it gets. Also, the coat is one important barometer of a dog's health. If the coat is in truly poor condition, this may be a sympton of illness, and the dog should be checked by a veterinarian.

Brushing serves to remove dead hair, which reduces shedding; it stimulates the natural oils of the skin, giving the coat a healthy sheen; and it gets rid of dirt the dog has picked up. Obviously, long-haired dogs need more brushing and combing than short-haired, but every dog will benefit from at least a quick once-over with a comb and brush, daily or every few days. Jim Stewart says that combing is even more important than brushing; he advises dog owners to comb their dogs' coats thoroughly at least twice a week.

Dogs with long silky coats tend to mat badly, and you have to keep ahead of this tendency or the mats will get out of hand. A coat full of mats and tangles looks unsightly, and because mats pull and irritate the skin, they are extremely uncomfortable for a dog.

Brushing and combing should be a pleasant experience for a dog, so be very gentle with the tangles and talk soothingly all the while. Then the animal will learn to put up with having its tangles and mats removed because it will feel cared for.

It's a good idea to take a dog's collar off indoors, at least at night. With a long-haired dog, this helps prevent matting of the hair around the neck, and a short-haired dog won't have that band around its neck where hair has been rubbed thin by the collar.

Don't forget to comb out or clip off any dried matter under the tail. Dogs with furry rumps sometimes can't help getting stuff stuck on their bottoms.

Shedding is regulated by nature according to temperature and daylight; it increases in spring and fall. However, when a dog lives in an environment that is heated, cooled, and lighted artificially, this natural regulation is not needed. Consequently, although your dog may shed somewhat more in spring and fall, it will normally lose hair more or less year-round.

Some dogs, particularly if they live in very warm houses or apartments, tend to get dandruff. If your pet has this problem, you have to brush unstintingly, but don't bathe—frequent bathing can make dandruff worse. Ask your veterinarian about the dog's diet—maybe it's not getting enough of certain vitamins or fatty acids. I've heard that brewer's yeast is good for dry skin, and you might try adding half a teaspoon of it to your dog's food daily. It can't hurt. Or try polyunsaturated vegetable oil: one tablespoon for a medium-size dog every few days.

The type of comb and brush you use will depend on your particular dog:

Short-coated dogs, such as Dachshunds, Basset Hounds, Beagles, and mixed breeds with similar short, smooth coats need a fine-tooth metal comb and a medium-soft, short-bristle brush or a grooming glove. Brush gently but firmly with the grain of the hair and wipe off any loose hair afterward with a soft cloth.

Medium-coated dogs, such as Golden Retrievers, Spaniels, Setters, and dogs with similar coats need a wide-tooth metal comb and a wire or firm-bristle brush. Comb first, then brush with the grain of the hair, giving special attention to the ears, chest, rear end, and tail where the hair is especially thick.

Long-haired dogs, such as Lhasa Apsos, Shih Tzus, Wheaten Terriers, and long-haired mixed breeds need a wide-tooth metal comb (caution: a fine-tooth comb will tear the hair) and a brush with long, stiff bristles. First work out the tangles and mats with your fingers and the comb—gently. Mats form at the roots of the hair, so be sure you really separate the strands. Brush one section of hair at a time, with the grain of the hair.

Double-coated dogs, such as German Shepherds, Siberian Huskies, and other dogs with shortish, dense coats need a wide-tooth metal comb and a brush with long, stiff bristles. These dogs have a topcoat of coarse hair over an undercoat of soft dense hair. Give a light combing, then brush from the skin out, against the grain of the hair.

Curly-, wavy-, or woolly-coated dogs, such as Poodles, Miniature Schnauzers, and mixed breeds with similar coats need a wide-tooth metal comb and a short-bristle wire brush. These dogs need professional haircuts every six or eight weeks, but you can keep them in good shape in between. Comb lightly, then brush. One Standard Poodle I know, name of Chopin, wears what's called a "sporting clip" (short on body, longer on top of head and legs), which his owner brushes against the grain, daily, after combing his ears and topknot. Coco, the Miniature Poodle of a friend of mine, has a "lamb cut" and gets the same care almost as often, plus a bath every two or three months.

BATHING A DOG

Baths take on special importance to city dog owners because nobody likes living in the same house or apartment with a dirty pet. In relatively close quarters, you're much more apt to notice when your dog begins to get a bit overripe. Also, the air pollution of most cities makes bathing necessary more often.

How often? You'll probably find that your dog will need a bath at least every couple of months. Stewart has found that even a monthly bath will not deplete the natural oils in the dog's skin, and in fact some people bathe their pets more often than that with no undesirable consequences. The coat itself will tell you by its looks whether or not you're bathing it too often.

For city people, bathing a dog usually means the bathtub, though a little dog might fit in the basin or the kitchen sink. Put a lot of newspapers or towels around, because even if no water gets spilled during the bathing and rinsing, the dog will shake itself mightily at the end of, if not during, the bath.

Most dogs hate getting a bath and have to be dragged to it looking reproachful and martyred. Dandy tries to hide when I start to draw the water in the tub; somehow she knows when it's for her and not for me. In fact, when I do take a tub bath instead of a shower, she sometimes pushes the door open and comes in to check on me, looking worried, as if I had lost my mind or were in some kind of danger.

A puppy shouldn't be bathed until it is at least six months old, by the way. Don't bathe a dog right after it has eaten. And never bathe a dog when it isn't feeling well, or within a week of its having shots. Don't bathe it until a month after an operation or stitches for a wound.

Don't use soap or people shampoo on a dog; most are too strong for a dog's skin. Use a good, tearless dog shampoo.

As for how to bathe a dog:

1. Walk the dog so it can empty its bladder and bowels.

2. Comb and brush the dog's coat, removing all tangles and excess undercoat.

3. Spread towels and thick newspapers around the bathroom and lay out several clean towels for drying the dog.

4. Set out a sponge or washcloth and a large plastic pitcher or a hose attachment for the faucet, and put a nonskid mat for the dog to stand on in the bottom of the tub. (The tub mat is important because if the poor animal loses its footing and falls, getting its head under water, it will panic and thrash about and possibly escape, and all you need is to be struggling to maneuver a frightened, sopping wet, soapy dog back into the tub.)

5. Put a rolled up bathmat or old cushion at the side of the tub for you to kneel on because the floor will get awfully hard under your knees before you're through.

6. Put on old clothes that you won't mind getting soaked.

7. Draw a tub of warm, not hot, water—about the temperature you'd bathe a baby in. The water should be deep enough to cover the dog's belly when it's standing up. Don't try to put the dog in when the water is running; some are frightened of the noise.

8. Now search out your pet, who is probably under the bed. Use the leash to lead it to the bathroom if you have to. *Close the bathroom door*. Lift the dog gently into the tub, with lots of reassuring talk and praise.

9. Stuff cotton in the dog's ears to keep the water out. If for some reason you're not using a tearless shampoo, put a drop of mineral oil or a tiny bit of petroleum jelly in each eye.

10. Wet the animal thoroughly and then soap it, working from neck to back, leaving the face till last so that will be wet and soapy the least amount of time. Use a washcloth or sponge on the face, avoiding the eyes. Unless the dog is unusually dirty, one thorough all-over soaping should be enough.

11. Rinse thoroughly. This is where a hose is handy, but don't just sprinkle the water on—hold the nozzle close to the skin so the clean water gets right in there. If you don't have a hose, you'll have to risk scaring the dog by running the water to fill the pitcher many times with clean water, because just rinsing in the bathwater is not enough.

You have to get all the soap completely out, and the bathwater will be soapy by this time. If you don't get all the soap out, the dog's skin will be irritated and the coat dull and sticky. Let the water run out of the tub while you rinse with clear water so that by the time you're all through the dog is standing in an empty tub.

12. Towel the dog down while it's still in the empty tub because it will shake itself several times, spraying water. When you lift it out, or let it climb out, it will shake itself some more, but at least you'll have gotten some of the water out of its coat.

13. Keep toweling the dog until it is as dry as you can get it. If your pet will tolerate the hair dryer, use it, directing it on one area at a time and brushing as you dry. According to Jim Stewart, it's important not to direct the hair dryer on one spot more than a few seconds—keep it moving. If you have a long-haired dog, combing will prevent tangles and hasten the drying process, but be careful not to hurt the animal by pulling hard on tangled strands. Use a wide-tooth comb and work gently.

14. Tell the dog how gorgeous it looks. Give it a dog biscuit or other treat.

15. Keep the dog in a warm, draft-free room for several hours. Make sure it doesn't lie in a direct draft from an air conditioner. And don't take it outside until it's thoroughly dry, not only because it might catch cold but because the damp coat will attract dirt and dust from the street.

If you have a white-coated dog, you might want to give it dry shampoos of cornstarch, baby powder, or commercial dry dog shampoo in between the real thing. Stand the dog on newspaper and work the substance into the coat, then brush thoroughly. If you don't brush all the powder out, the dog will trail it all over the house. Dry shampoo is also good for puppies too young to be bathed and old dogs who live in a very cool or cold house.

A good bath removes grime, irritants, and bacteria from a dog's coat, but shampoo and water are not effective against tar, car oil, paint, chewing gum, and other comparable substances a dog occasionally gets in its coat. Don't use any dry cleaning fluid—it will burn the dog's skin and is highly toxic! You have to use a solvent like turpentine to remove paint; nail polish remover works on chewing gum; baby oil or vegetable oil might soften tar and automotive oil enough for you to comb them out. Don't get turpentine or nail polish remover near the dog's eyes, ears, genitals, anus, or any cut or scratch. After you've got the offending substance off the dog, including the equally offending stuff you used to remove it, wash the area with soap and water, rinsing well.

If you take your dog on holiday with you where it enjoys going in the ocean, or likes (and is permitted) to jump in a swimming pool, be sure you rinse the salt or chlorine out of its coat after each dip. In fact, the rinse should be supplemented with a real bath at the end of the vacation, to assure that the salt and chemicals are totally out of the coat.

If you take your dog to the country and it has a confrontation with a skunk (and city dogs, being unsophisticated about wildlife, may provoke one), you'll want to act quickly for your own sake as well as the dog's. The traditional antiskunk shampoo is tomato juice, but a vinegar-and-water or baking-soda-and-water solution might work also. If the dog's eyes and ears are affected, wipe them with a soothing ointment. Whatever you use, it will take a lot of bathing to get rid of the smell to the point where you can live with the dog. The dog will be confused and upset, so give it a lot of reassurance and don't make it feel more humiliated than it does already.

YOUR DOG'S EARS

Part of every routine grooming session should be an ear check. A dog's ears can get dirty just from being outside, rolling on the rug, lying under the bed, or simply existing in polluted city air. That being the case, you'd think that a dog with hang-down ears would be better off than one with stick-up ears. But a dog's ears need air circulation to remain healthy, and dogs with floppy ears are more susceptible than others to ear infections.

You can clean a dog's ears with a washcloth or cotton-tipped swab dipped in mineral oil, baby oil, or vegetable oil—not alcohol or any substance that will sting. (Don't use peroxide either, because the dog might not like the fizzle it makes in its ear.) Gently wipe all the crevices, going downward as far as you can go in the ear. A dog's ear canal is designed so that it goes downward for a short distance, then makes a sharp horizontal turn toward the eardrum, so as long as you only clean downward, you won't injure the eardrum. Don't under any circumstances ever use a syringe to clean the dog's ears—then you could really damage the eardrums.

Don't clean every day unless the dog's ears are dirty—a normal amount of wax is needed to protect the skin.

Be sure to check your dog's ears after it has been running in a park, through bushes, or rolling in the grass—it could have picked up burrs, seeds, or other foreign matter. Remove anything like that with a cotton-tipped swab dipped in mineral, baby, or vegetable oil. And be sure to check the ears if your dog has been in a dogfight, even a play fight, because serum and blood make a good medium for bacteria.

If your dog has a lot of hair growing at the entrance of its ears, you probably should keep that trimmed. A groomer sometimes plucks excess hair out of a dog's ears—this is fine as long as he or she puts an antibiotic on the plucked spot afterward to prevent infection.

When a dog has an ear infection, it's likely to hold its head on one side or rub its head on the floor. The ear will be tender, usually red and swollen. There may be a bad smell and dark brown wax or a discharge. This condition calls for immediate veterinary attention.

Foreign bodies in the ears such as ear mites or ticks can damage a dog's ears. Puppies are more susceptible than adult dogs to ear mites, which are microscopic, cause intense itching, and are very contagious to other animals. The puppy will scratch and shake its head and is usually pretty uncomfortable. You can't see the mites except under a microscope, but you'll see a brown or black waxlike substance in the ears. The pup should be taken to the vet for diagnosis and medication—and the trick with using the medication is to keep it up. What can happen is that the puppy gets relief quite fast, and often the owner, seeing that the ears look okay, stops using the medicine, and before he or she knows it the mites are back. Be sure to go the whole way with the medication for as long as the veterinarian instructs.

You can usually get rid of ticks yourself, if they're in a part of the ear that you can reach easily. First use a cotton-tipped swab to put a drop—just a drop—of alcohol (whiskey will do) right on the tick, and then use your fingers or tweezers to grasp it and pull it out. If the head remains in the skin, the spot may be inflamed for a few days but will rarely cause infection. (See Chapter 6, the section on external parasites.)

ROUTINE EYE CARE

For most dogs, routine eye care means only wiping dirt or normal discharge from the corners of their eyes with a tissue or cotton moistened with water or mild boric acid solution. Be sure to wipe only at the corners next to the nose, and don't draw the wiper across the lids.

Tearing is a problem of old dogs; their eyes might have to be wiped several times a day. Dogs with white faces don't produce more tears than other dogs, but the tear stains show up more, so they need more frequent wiping just to look good.

Dogs with protruding eyes, such as Pekingese, Lhasa Apsos, Pugs, and Boston Terriers, are subject to eye injuries, so owners of such breeds should examine their pets' eyes daily. Also, dogs that have a lot of hair hanging over their eyes need special attention because overlong facial hair can scratch the eyeballs. It's a good idea to keep the hair over the eyes clipped.

Cloudiness of the eyes in an old dog is normal and does not impair the animal's vision. But redness, inflammation, a yellow color, or discharge in the eyes of any dog should be called to the attention of a veterinarian.

FOOT CARE

Every routine grooming session should include a quick check of your dog's footpads. You'll want to look for cuts, scrapes, and deep cracks or fissures that are prone to infection. Check between the toes for mats and disentangle them before they cause discomfort.

You'd think that city dogs just walking around the block would wear their toenails down enough not to need trimming, but this doesn't seem to be the case. While your dog's regular home grooming sessions won't include nail trimming, you should check the length of the nails frequently and trim them when they grow overlong. The nails should just clear the floor when the dog is standing upright. Otherwise they can cause the toes to spread in an abnormal fashion, and the dog will be uncomfortable, walk funny, and eventually limp and become lame. Jim Stewart says that unless a dog is heavy and is walked a lot on pavement, its nails should be trimmed every two months.

Be sure to use clippers specially designed for dogs. If you try to use your own nail clippers or fingernail scissors, you'll hurt the dog, because its nails are too tough for anything but the right tools.

Work in a good light and speak quietly and reassuringly to your dog when you trim its nails. Trim only the tips. If you cut too much off and hit the quick (the pink line coming down into the nail from the foot), you'll hurt the dog and the nail will bleed. Some dogs have black toenails in which you can't see the pink quick; with those, you obviously have to be very cautious. Cut almost to the groove on the underside or just to where the nail starts to curve downward.

Don't forget to trim the dewclaws—those useless nails on the legs just above the feet. If they become too long, they can curl and cut into the flesh.

Have peroxide and styptic powder or pencil on hand when you trim your dog's toenails, because if you accidentally cut too much and the nail bleeds, you should disinfect it with peroxide and then apply the styptic to stop the bleeding. If the bleeding is excessive, you may have to apply cold wet compresses for ten minutes or so, before the peroxide and styptic. Also soothe and stroke the dog, because it will be very upset.

Dogs hate to have their feet touched—that's why it's a good idea to get a puppy used to it early. As I said previously, I wish Dandy had been conditioned to having her feet handled when she was a puppy, because now there's no way I could cut her nails by myself. My gentle, passive pet turns into a thrashing, bucking, hysterical beast on whom I have to get a stranglehold while Jim Stewart, with all the patience in the world, manages to do the job.

If your dog is still patient by the time you finish trimming its nails, smooth the tips with a nail file or emery board.

Dogs sometimes tear their nails in playing or running around. A nail catches on a rug, floorboard, or some protrusion and begins to bleed. First aid consists of pressing cold compresses on the spot, but if the nail is really torn, the dog must be taken to the vet.

With a long-haired dog, it's a good idea to keep the hair on the feet clipped fairly short. Otherwise the dog will be forever tracking dirt, mud, snow, and ice into the house.

If it seems as though under the heading of grooming I've recommended a time-consuming examination of your dog's body, plus a lot of regular work, let me add that it will go fast once you get into the routine. And this kind of care will pay off in better health and comfort for your dog and lower veterinary bills, in addition to keeping your pet looking good.

PROFESSIONAL GROOMERS

Some breeds with stand-out, long, or wiry coats need professional haircuts once in a while, not to look fashionable but simply to look neat. If you've ever noticed a Bichon Frise, Poodle, or Miniature Schnauzer whose coat has gone to seed, you'll see what I mean.

I'd be the last to suggest some of the weird hairdos I've seen on certain show dogs. The trim that makes a Poodle a walking ball of fur from neck to waist but leaves its hindquarters naked is grotesque, in my opinion. The dog can't be comfortable with a burden of hair around its front half and exposed around its flanks. But a Poodle with a nice basic "lamb cut," which Stewart says requires professional attention only every six to eight weeks, looks adorable.

Also, dogs with thick hair that live in hot climates or where the summers are intense are probably more comfortable if their coats are trimmed and thinned. A "puppy cut" seems to help these dogs through hot weather.

If you have a puppy of a breed that will be getting a professional trim regularly or even once in a while, it's advisable to get it used to the grooming parlor early, so it feels comfortable there. Leave the pup in a cage at the groomer's for an hour or so from time to time and just let it watch. Then when its turn eventually arrives, it won't be scared.

Dog groomers are not licensed, so you're on your own in choosing. How to judge a groomer? By asking friends whose judgment you trust, as I suggested in choosing a veterinarian. Jim Stewart points out that some dogs have very definite preferences for being groomed by women instead of men, or vice versa. Also, look for a person who really likes dogs, and check on how the dogs that are being worked on are behaving. It's reassuring to be able to see the grooming shop in action: If the groomer does his or her work in a basement or back room where the client is not allowed, that's a bad sign.

Some working people drop their dogs off at the groomer's on their way to work and pick them up in the evening. This is fine for dogs that are comfortable at the groomer's. When they're not being worked on themselves, they watch the others, or sleep. But if your pet feels unhappy and anxious at the groomer's, you might try to book a time when it can be taken as soon as you bring it in. Ask how long your dog will be there and pick it up as soon as it's ready.

In big cities like New York, there are many groomers who will make house calls. You'll have some cleaning up to do afterward, but the pet will have the comforting advantage of being in its own home. Also, you'll be spared taking it to the groomer's and picking it up.

But go by your animal's reactions. Some dogs may regard the experience as an invasion of the sanctuary of their own home.

One friend told me that her dog developed an eye irritation that her veterinarian recognized at once as "groomer's eye." From irritating soap, the doctor said. If your dog's eyes are red and sore after a bath in a grooming parlor, call it to the groomer's attention— or change groomers.

Some groomers routinely give dogs tranquilizers before they work on them, to reduce anxiety and make them calm and tractable. Stewart believes that this kind of groomer should be avoided unless he or she works for a veterinarian, right in the clinic. Not all dogs tolerate tranquilizers equally, and drugs should be used only with medical advice and supervision.

One thing a professional groomer will do is empty a dog's anal sacs, which are on each side of the base of the rectum. It's a good idea, because if anal glands become blocked, this can lead to discomfort and possibly infection. Normally, the sacs are emptied every time the dog defecates, but sometimes they can become impacted. Groomers and veterinarians know how to empty a dog's anal sacs by pressing on them. I personally don't recommend that dog owners attempt to do this themselves unless they are taught exactly how by a professional.

A good professional groomer's contribution to your dog's care can be much more than cosmetic.

CHAPTER 9

TWO'S COMPANY:
A Friend for Your Dog

Dedicated dog lovers sometimes have a hard time stopping at just one. You hear of a dog that desperately needs a home, you find one on the street, you pass a pet shop, or you see a dog on TV that's up for adoption from an animal shelter, and you melt. These are all good reasons for taking in a second, third, or tenth dog. There are so many millions of dogs needing homes in this world that it's almost a moral obligation to have several.

There's another, very sound, humane motive for acquiring a second dog—or perhaps a cat. If nobody's home at your house during the day and sometimes in the evening, a single dog can get very lonely. As we discussed in Chapter 4, a dog can be taught not to bark and howl when it's left alone, but often just the presence of another creature is a good solution to the problem of a pet's separation anxiety. It seems to me that giving your dog a buddy to keep it company is a loving thing to do for it anyway.

You might think that two pets would be twice as much trouble as one. Actually, in some ways they are less trouble. When you have to work late, for example, or decide to go to dinner directly from the

office, or are having fun somewhere and wish to stay longer, the
disturbing image of your pet at home alone waiting and waiting can
make you very uncomfortable. This can put a damper on good times
and be distracting during business obligations, and with good
reason, because for a single pet, you're It—you're all it has in the
way of regular companionship. But knowing there are two or more
social animals at home to while away the time together can make
you feel a lot less concerned and guilty.

Also, it is definitely cruel to leave a single dog alone over a
weekend, even if a sitter comes in daily to tend to its needs. But two
or more animals, given daily care by a sitter, can keep one another
company till you return. As one who has often been a sitter for
absent friends' pets, I can tell you there is a huge difference in
behavior between the single animal and the pair, trio, or more. The
solo dog or cat exhibits far greater anxiety.

Many dog owners firmly believe their pet would be outraged if
another animal were brought into the household. Some have even
tried it and been convinced, by the incumbent's initial reaction, that
it would never work. This may be true in rare cases in which either
the resident or the incoming animal is highly aggressive or insecure.
But it is hardly ever the case among normally sociable, neutered
pets. While not all will welcome another with open paws immediately, and some may grumble for weeks, nearly all dogs will adjust to a
newcomer eventually, and most will be much happier having a
friend. And in fact, even if the animals never learn to love each
other, they nevertheless seem to get some satisfaction just from the
other's presence.

One tip in introducing a second pet, whether it is a dog or a cat:
Never force the two animals on each other. Some pet owners
mistakenly drag the two creatures right up to one another, make
them touch noses, and restrain them in close contact. Instead, you
should respect each animal's space and let the initial contact be more
natural. If either takes one look and wants to run and hide, let it, and
allow them to meet each other in their own time.

Another tip: Whether you adopt a cat or another dog, don't treat
them like Siamese twins, but reserve some time each day for a one-
on-one relationship with each. A pet needs to have you all to itself

sometimes, even for just a little while. Dandy being my only dog, she gets plenty of my time alone, but each of the cats seeks me out alone at certain times, and I pretend for the moment it's my only cat.

BRINGING IN A SECOND DOG

I once heard a wonderful, true story about a woman who had an elegant purebred Standard Poodle that she walked in Central Park. One day her spayed female pet met up with a pitiful, scruffy-looking stray, obviously down on his luck. The Poodle apparently decided that the stray was the greatest dog she'd ever met, and the two cavorted around together in as many games as the Poodle's leash would allow. If dogs can fall in love, these two did. When the lady and her dog headed for home, the stray followed.

"Peaches kept looking at me as if to say, 'Please, Mom, can't we keep him?'" the Poodle's owner related. "I simply didn't have the heart to drive the dog away, so he came on home with us, and I figured I'd call the ASPCA later to come and pick him up. Of course, it never happened. The change in Peaches was dramatic. Where before she had been a gentle but rather timid, very dependent dog, crestfallen and often destructive when left alone, she turned into a sunny, exuberant animal, much more affectionate toward us as well as devoted to Buddy, as we named the new dog. And she stopped chewing up things when we were out."

Peaches and Buddy made a somewhat odd couple, the pedigreed apricot Poodle and the ungainly animal who, even after his body filled out and his coat became clean and healthy, was no beauty. But Buddy, neutered and made to feel at home, clearly enriched Peaches' life and cured her of her separation anxiety.

I applaud this tale wholeheartedly. Many dogs will not only choose a friend for themselves but will be perfectly agreeable to your bringing in another. I have never detected any jealousy in Dandy when another dog has been staying with us, nor any regret when it leaves—she simply seems perfectly content either way. I think that's because of her amiable temperament and the fact that she always has my cats for companions.

But I do want to add one note of caution: If your pet should select a stray dog for a friend, by all means take it in—but have your veterinarian check it out *immediately* to be sure it's healthy. A poor dog that's been forced to scrounge for food and shelter is an easy victim for canine diseases, so even if your pet's vaccinations are up to date, you want to protect it from catching anything contagious the stray might have (worms, for instance). And of course you'll want to have the new dog vaccinated and neutered as soon as possible.

Many dogs that bark when left alone will stop the habit as soon as a companion dog is acquired for them. But Dr. Peter Borchelt, consultant at the Animal Behavior Clinic of the Animal Medical Center in New York City, warns that if you have a dog that is a confirmed howler or barker when left alone, bringing in a second dog might mean you'll end up with two vocalizing dogs instead of one. Or you could have one dog that's quiet and one that howls. There are no guarantees. But I have known enough dogs that were cured of separation anxiety when another pet entered the household to pass the suggestion on to you as an option to consider seriously.

Let's say you have a normally well-adjusted dog and wish to bring in another for whatever reason. You want the introduction to go as smoothly as possible. Here are a few suggestions:

Your resident dog will more quickly take to a puppy or younger dog than to one its own age or older.

If you are getting a new puppy, its sex doesn't matter, because your resident dog will be dominant anyway. But if your dog is an adult and you're bringing in an adult, choose one of the opposite sex.

Both your resident dog and the new one of course should be neutered. If for some strange reason you have not had your pet neutered, it could be risky to bring in an unneutered adult dog of the same sex—you might have one hell of a dog fight on your hands. And you don't want two unneutered adult dogs of opposite sexes for obvious reasons.

Unless your dog is extremely mellow and self-confident, it will probably be happier with a new dog that's smaller or of equal size, not a whole lot bigger than itself.

Have someone else bring the new dog to your home, or have the two dogs meet on neutral ground and go home together after they've had a chance to check each other out. It could get things off on the wrong foot if you were to walk in on your dog with another dog in tow.

Have both dogs leashed when they meet, but let them explore each other normally. Act natural and calm yourself, and let the dogs know that you don't anticipate any problems between them.

Remember everything you ever knew about introducing a new baby to an older sibling. Give your resident dog lots of affection so it knows it isn't being replaced. If the new dog is a puppy, resist the temptation to cuddle it and fuss over it while ignoring the older dog, and be sure visitors also give the older dog equal time. Be sure to give treats, toys, and attention equally.

On the other hand, don't lean over so far backward lavishing attention on the resident dog that it gets the idea that the new one doesn't belong and the new dog feels left out. Make it clear that the newcomer is welcome and has rights of its own.

In very rare instances, an incoming dog will try so hard to make a place for itself that it will bully the resident pet and attempt to dominate it in a threatening way. If the older pet is clearly upset and even frightened, the situation calls for professional advice from a dog trainer or behavior counselor, or—in extreme cases—actually giving up that particular second dog. If, after a fair trial period and sincere efforts on your part, the two personalities are just not compatible, you should make another arrangement for the new dog, because it isn't fair to your original pet to subject it to continual harassment. Try another, different sort of dog, or a cat, as a companion for your resident dog.

INTRODUCING A CAT TO A RESIDENT DOG

Sometimes when I mention to people that I have a dog and several cats, they are surprised. "Do they get along?" they'll invariably ask.

It is a firmly established notion that cats and dogs are natural enemies, one that is hard to dispel. One explanation is that if they haven't been raised around cats, some dogs—especially certain hunting breeds—chase them because they apparently mistake them for small game. Also, a lot of dogs have been taught by stupid, cruel people to attack cats. The redneck way of inculcating cat hatred in a dog is to say "Sic 'em" whenever a cat comes in sight, so the dog gets the message. Living kittens are often used, tied and dangling from a mechanized carriage, in the training of Greyhounds and other racing dogs, who are eventually allowed to tear them apart. Cats are often thrown to Pit Bull Terriers to give them a taste of blood in training them for the "sport" of dogfighting.

But the idea that dogs are born to chase cats can be perpetuated even by perfectly nice people so that it becomes a self-fulfilling prophecy. Because dogs pick up and act upon even subtle attitudes in their owners, they can absorb the notion that they're expected to attack every cat they meet just from their owners' body language. If the owner believes that it's the nature of dogs to hate cats, he or she doesn't have to say a word. Just by the tension of the leash and its owner's uncertain behavior, a dog knows that meeting a cat is creating a certain amount of concern. Then the dog may decide the cat is something it must defend its owner against, so it behaves in a hostile manner, thus confirming the owner's original belief.

Sometimes the cat plays a role in the confusion. If a cat has had unpleasant and even life-threatening encounters with dogs, it won't trust them and may take immediate defensive action when it meets one. It may lash out against even perfectly gentle dogs who actually like cats. Naturally, some dogs won't turn the other cheek, as Dandy will when she meets such a cat, but will respond with barking and snapping, thus contributing to the myth about cats and dogs.

It is not true that dogs and cats are natural enemies. There is no innate or instinctive competition between the species—wild canines and felines have separate hunting preferences and generally ignore each other. It is a great pleasure to have both as pets, to enjoy the beauty, intelligence, affection, and special characteristics of each. So unless you have a confirmed cat-killer, or a dog with a poor track record regarding cats, you shouldn't hesitate to acquire a feline pet. Your dog doesn't have to have a proven liking for cats, just an open mind.

The ideal way to set up a dog-and-cat household is to adopt both animals together when they are very young. Just be careful, if the puppy is big and boisterous, that it doesn't hurt the kitten in playing with it. A hefty three-month-old pup with the most innocent intentions in the world could break the back of a kitten, just in fun. Some people recommend that the puppy be old enough to understand basic commands, such as "No."

Both animals should be neutered the minute they are old enough, not only for their individual health but for the benefit of their relationship. No matter how loving they have become toward each other, their friendship could be strained if the behavior of either animal was changed by puberty.

If you are introducing a kitten to an adult dog, you also want to protect the kitten from accidental harm if the dog tries to play with it. The kitten should be fourteen to sixteen weeks old, strong enough to run, jump, and climb successfully.

You should feed the cat on a counter or somewhere the dog can't reach, by the way. Dogs eat a lot faster than cats, and the cat will never be allowed to finish its meal if the dog can get at its bowl.

Cat therapist and author Carole Wilbourn recommends that you don't adopt a shy cat or kitten if your dog has a high energy level, or impose a bouncing, extroverted cat or kitten on a passive, retiring dog. In other words, do try to match their personalities.

According to the Wilbourn method, you should bring the cat into your house in a see-through carrier and leave it where the two animals can observe each other for a while before you let the cat out. Keep the two in different rooms for a few days, preferably separated by a gate or screen so they can watch each other through it. When they finally do meet, be sure the cat can escape to a high piece of furniture if it wants to, where it can contemplate the dog until it feels confident enough to come down. Confine them separately whenever you leave the house until they have become completely accepting and nonchalant about each other.

Keep an eye on them, but just as I advised in introducing two dogs, don't communicate any anxious thoughts you might have. Act relaxed and natural, as if the cat's arrival were the most normal thing in the world.

Wilbourn says you should pretend that you've acquired the cat as a present for the dog. If you act as if you were giving the dog a marvelous gift that it is going to love, the dog might buy it. Make a big fuss over the dog, and mention its name every time you touch the cat for the first week or two, so the dog feels included. This has been known to work.

A couple I know has a dog named Samuel Johnson whose best friend is a cat named, appropriately, Hodge. Sam is a Rhodesian Ridgeback, a powerful hound breed originally used for hunting and today known for its aggressive loyalty and superior qualities as a guardian and watchdog. You might think Ben and Julie would have had reservations about adopting a cat, but they knew their particular dog and they knew cats.

Sam was ten months old and weighed nearly eighty pounds when his owners introduced ten-week-old, two-pound Hodge into the household. Sam had seen cats on the street but never up close and was goggle-eyed over the kitten. Julie held the kitten and let Sam sniff but not touch at first. Sam's owners made it clear—and I think this was the key factor—that Hodge was somebody they valued, somebody to be protected and nurtured. Gradually, Sam was allowed to come closer and closer, all the while being cautioned firmly that he must be very careful with the small creature. The kitten was afraid of Sam at first but was continually reassured by the owners.

The next day, Hodge was put on the floor and the two animals were allowed to get acquainted under close supervision. Soon Hodge was trailing Sam around, and it was apparent that mutual love was developing. Today, when Ben and Julie return from work, the two pets meet them at the door—together. When Sam is taken for walks, Hodge tries to follow, frisking about the big dog, jumping up and boxing his ears. The two sleep in Sam's bed—together. Hodge licks the dog's muzzle; Sam in turn grooms the cat, particularly his face and ears.

So much for your "fight like cats and dogs" stories.

INTRODUCING A DOG TO A RESIDENT CAT

You won't have a problem introducing a puppy to a household with a kitten as long as you take their relative sizes into consideration and protect the kitten from rough play. It's when you already have an adult cat that you have to take steps to assure that the introduction of a dog or puppy goes smoothly.

I'm assuming your cat is neutered, reasonably well adjusted, and not a confirmed dog-hater that will attack any and all dogs on sight. Even cats that have had terrifying experiences with dogs can learn to trust individuals, but you don't want a new dog harmed by eight pounds of clawing, snarling fury within its first hour in your home.

An adult cat will be thoroughly disgusted by a puppy and needs to be reassured that you haven't lost your mind. It's wise to cuddle and make a fuss over the pup when your cat isn't looking, so you won't hurt its feelings and arouse jealousy. The sex of the puppy is not important.

Trim your cat's nails before bringing in a puppy or dog.

If you're adopting an adult dog, be absolutely sure that it has a good attitude toward cats. Ideally, it should be one who has lived with cats before, or at least has learned to respect them.

Carole Wilbourn believes an adult cat will accept an adult dog of the opposite sex more quickly than one of the same sex. This holds true, she says, even though both will be neutered.

And according to the Wilbourn method, you should have someone your cat doesn't know bring the dog to your home, so the cat won't feel you have betrayed it.

Just as I suggested about bringing a cat into a household with a resident dog, your own body language will influence the integration process. If you are convinced your darling cat will die of jealousy, you're setting up a situation that is bound to fail. Let your cat know that you love it as much as ever, but that you wish to have this new animal and that the dog is welcome and has rights of its own.

Be sure to feed the cat somewhere that the dog can't reach—on a table or counter, for example. And Wilbourn says to give the cat a quiet roost to call its own—a box, basket, or pillow on a piece of furniture that's completely inaccessible to the dog.

Unless your cat likes dogs, or at least is used to them, be prepared to put up with a certain amount of hissing and snarling from your cat at first. In all likelihood, this will pass in a few days. It's worth enduring it for the pleasure you will enjoy in having both animals, and they will be better off for each other's company—and may grow to love one another.

And by the way, whether you add a cat when you already have a dog or vice versa, don't be surprised if the cat becomes the dominant animal. A cat can turn out to be the boss pet, even lording it over gigantic dogs, who don't seem to mind.

OTHER PETS

As an urban dweller, you probably won't be acquiring rabbits, ponies, goats, or other wonderful outdoor animals, but you may have birds, and households with children are especially likely to have cute little pet rodents such as hamsters and gerbils. Most of the time these creatures will be in their cages, so you don't have to worry about their interaction with your dog or with a dog that you wish to introduce into the family.

But do use a lot of common sense if you let these pets out of their cages to stretch their wings or legs from time to time.

Remember where your dog is coming from. If it is a hunting breed, or a mixed breed with "sporting dog," hound, or terrier ancestry, it will very possibly regard a bird or small mammal as something it is supposed to catch. The first time your parakeet takes wing when your setter, pointer, or retriever is in the room, don't blame the dog if it springs into the air after it. And you can't expect even a well-behaved and gentle hound or terrier to refrain from snapping up that little hamster scampering across the room.

I have had no experience with dogs and parrots, so before you mix these two species, do some research. Large parrots could inflict bodily harm on dogs of most any size, and dogs of hunting breed ancestry could confuse a parrot with a pheasant or mallard. Also, the sounds parrots make might spook a dog. So it's important to gather all the information you can before you adopt either creature to cohabit with the other. Chances are they'll just ignore each other and be no problem.

Many, many dogs reside in perfect harmony with birds of all sizes and in fact with all other creatures large and small. I once knew a nice Golden Retriever who lived with two parakeets that he was apparently fond of. They would roost on his head, even on his paws when he was lying down, and he wouldn't even blink. Our dog Benjy never showed any interest in my son's hamsters, who used to run about on the floor sometimes. (But we never left him alone with them.)

It's best to keep everyone safe by not having unrealistic expectations of a dog. Even if your dog shows no interest in these other species, don't let it out of your sight with an uncaged pet bird or rodent.

As for whether pets of these types can be companions to a dog, I'm inclined to doubt it. I think a dog needs a comparatively social animal like itself—another dog or a cat—for a buddy.

CHAPTER 10

THE THERAPEUTIC DOG:
How Dogs Help Us

Ever since the primitive dog cast its lot with our ancestors, it has played many different roles in our lives. Hunting and herding helper, guardian and protector, companion and playmate, workmate and guide, child-substitute and source of love. Thanks to its infinite flexibility, the dog has gone along with our demands throughout history. We've relied on its loyalty, willingness, and intelligence and turned it into whatever kind of animal we needed.

The dog has been so taken for granted that dog lovers now view with some amusement a phenomenon of recent years: the scientific interest in this animal and its relationship with us. Researchers are now investigating what many of us have known in our bones forever—they've discovered that dogs can be beneficial, even essential, to human health and well-being. Their studies give credibility and respectability to what we have long intuited.

THE BOND

A half-dozen years ago, scientific interest in what is now termed the human/companion-animal bond was sparked by the discovery that pets may perhaps help to extend human life. This was a quite serendipitous finding. A group of university researchers were investigating people with coronary artery disease: Why did some live longer than others? The scientists took in-depth profiles of about one hundred heart attack victims; a year later, they compared the charts of patients still living with those who had died over the year. All variables were examined—age, occupation, marital status, general health, income, lifestyle, and the like. To the research team's puzzlement, one factor that consistently proved out on the computer was that most of the people still living had pets, while most of those who had died did not.

That raised questions: Is there something in the personalities of people who keep pets that acts as a survival factor? Yet, a subsequent study comparing the psychological status of pet owners with that of non-pet owners uncovered no significant differences. So, is there something in the relationship between people and their companion animals that in itself may tend to promote health? The evidence from ongoing research suggests that the presence of a loved pet in a person's life can offer emotional and physical benefits.

A group of veterinarians, social workers, psychologists, anthropologists, and other researchers at the University of Pennsylvania were the first to launch an organized investigation into the human/companion-animal bond. An early study revealed that petting a dog or cat lowers blood pressure. It had been known for some time that petting a dog lowers *its* blood pressure, but until now, no one had thought to measure the blood pressure of the human doing the petting.

Furthermore, it was learned that normally when you talk to another person, or read aloud, you experience a rise in blood pressure. But if you talk to someone, then pet your dog or cat, and then resume speaking, your blood pressure rises less during the second conversation, indicating that the soothing effect lasts a while.

And speaking of speaking, the researchers learned that when you talk to your dog or cat (as most pet owners do), the rise in blood pressure doesn't occur. In fact, stutterers don't stutter when they talk to pets.

For one thing, most of us, in talking to our pets, touch them and use a pattern of speech similar to that we use when we talk to babies—an intimate and affectionate "motherese" that has been associated with lowered blood pressure. Also, because the animal is noncritical and nonjudgmental, there's no reason to worry about how we're coming across. And even though most of us believe that our pets understand at least some of what we say, and our mood, we can assume they won't give us an argument or think we're fools.

One experiment involved bringing children into a living room, one by one, with a researcher present. At some point during each child's interview, a dog was let into the room. In every case, the child's blood pressure dropped. Just the presence of the dog, without necessarily any tactile involvement of the child, apparently reduced the child's tension. The reason is unknown, but one interpretation might be that on some primitive level, the dog communicated a sort of reassurance.

Another study was conducted in the waiting room of a veterinary clinic where men and women sat with their pets. Virtually every client fondled his or her pet, either attentively or absentmindedly, whether or not the pet appeared anxious. The behavior of the people seemed to indicate that stroking their dogs and cats was done as much to soothe themselves as the animals. Just as infants fondle a favorite blanket, or as people in some cultures finger "worry beads" or stones, the very act of touching the familiar creatures seemed to reduce stress.

Now, similar research is going on at other universities—Minnesota, Kansas State, and Washington State among them. Several symposia have been held, including some in Europe, for interest among scientist in other countries has risen as well. An organization of professionals, the Delta Society, has been formed as an educational and service resource on the human/animal bond.

THE FAMILY DOG

"Max is a member of the family," a person may say, indicating the canine "relative" who, for better or worse, is firmly entrenched in the household. Studies of this common attitude indicate that the family dog is regarded as an in-between creature—not quite human, yet more than an animal.

Psychologist Herbert Nieburg points out that the dog indeed qualifies as a family member by many of the accepted criteria by which we define family. A family can be identified as a group related by blood, by sharing a home, or by reciprocal affection; it is a relationship that is entered by birth, adoption, or marriage, persists over the years, and is left only by death. While some dogs are forced out of their families not by death but by abandonment, many meet the definition, and in fact, some qualify as the only family their owners have.

One family therapist believes that a dog may be a barometer of the level of anxiety within its family. "Problems involving human relationships may become apparent in the context of animal-human interaction where they would not be clearly visible otherwise," says Ann Ottney Cain. "Pets can provide important information about how the family system is organized or disorganized." Dr. Cain advises any family therapist to include the pet in an investigation of the way family members interact.

In some families, it is not uncommon for the dog to be used in a process called triangling, a way of dealing with intense feelings. In triangling, one family member gets a message to another not by expressing it directly but through a third person—or a pet. A family member may yell at the dog instead of at the person he or she is really angry with. A spouse may take the side of the pet when the other is scolding the animal for some misbehavior, as a way of provoking an argument and bringing out anger over something unrelated to the pet. Needless to say, it can be very confusing and upsetting to an animal to be dragged into human conflicts in this way. Dogs, who are honest about their feelings and anxious to please, don't deserve this.

Children regard the family dog as a playmate, confidant, and perhaps protector. The dog is never cross when it wakes up, it's always ready for a game, and it may be the only family member who doesn't scold or try to improve the kids or tell them what to do.

The dog is waiting when the child comes home from school, and if both parents work, keeps him or her company in the empty house or apartment. The animal may be a reassuring constant in a single-parent family or in one that frequently moves its home base. If the child loves the dog and treats it well, the dog returns the love without qualifications. The child can count on it even in the face of a bad report card or other trouble. This positive approval raises a child's sense of self-worth.

The early adolescent period in a youngster's life can be a sort of emotional wasteland in terms of affectionate touching. To a boy or girl too old to be cuddled like a baby but too young for satisfying sexual relationships, the pet may be the only creature he or she can stroke and hug with perfect social and psychological impunity. With the dog, the child feels free to express the very human need for touching.

A pet can be a good teaching tool through which parents can help a child develop some of the most civilizing qualities—empathy, self-control, compassion, awareness of and consideration for the needs and feelings of another creature. If the parents treat the dog with affection and respect, the child will be inclined to follow suit. Some psychologists believe that a child who has learned to take care of a pet is more likely to grow up to be considerate of other people.

One mother in a family with a beloved dog reported putting the children's affection to good use. When her kids become unbearably boisterous, they won't always calm down when she tells them to, but if she says, "Stop that racket, you're upsetting Max," they quiet down immediately.

The relationship of children to companion animals can also be significant in an opposite and quite ominous way. Studies have shown a correlation between animal abuse on the part of children and eventual criminal behavior. Interviews with criminals serving time for violent crimes have revealed patterns of animal abuse in childhood, leading psychologists to conclude that cruelty to animals by a child is not an innocent, trivial activity that he or she will outgrow. It can be a signal of serious emotional trouble that should not be neglected but given full professional attention.

Dogs are common pets among rural and suburban families, but they are especially valuable to urban children, who lack contact with other animate life forms. City children see pigeons and squirrels, perhaps the captive animals of a zoo, but unless they have pets, they have no chance to observe fully and understand a nonhuman species. Yet increasingly we are forced to recognize that an enlightened stewardship of other species and a sharing of the planet with them are essential to our own survival.

THE CHILD-SUBSTITUTE DOG

Conventional wisdom has it that people who make a pet a substitute for a child are off the wall. This so-called eccentricity receives a good deal of ridicule, especially from folks who offer the opinion that pet owners should instead be lavishing attention, money, and time on fellow human beings. Interestingly, however, persons who make those criticisms are rarely involved, themselves, in doing anything for others.

There's also a widely voiced cliché that people who have intense affection for pets have problems relating to other humans. Their pets are presumed to be the object of displaced attachments that normally are reserved for other people.

This notion may reflect our cultural bias that claims that love for people is the only legitimate one, that affection for pets is sentimental and trivial. It may also result from the observable fact that sometimes persons who are very shy, disabled, extremely eccentric, or for some reason rejected by other people may indeed turn to companion animals for the love and fellowship they are denied elsewhere.

There is no hard evidence to support the theory that strong love for animals means dislike for people. There is one university study that revealed the opposite: It found that low affection for dogs was accompanied by low affection for people. I have a personal bias that makes it difficult for me to form warm personal relationships with people who dislike animals. Even though intellectually I try to allow for exceptions and tell myself that many kind and decent human beings simply cannot relate to other species, in my heart I am suspicious of them.

Non-pet owners are perhaps understandably turned off by pet owners who buy jeweled collars and fur coats for their animals. Some dog owners, city folks especially, it seems, do buy needless luxuries for their pets. I once attended an embarrassing display of this at a dog show entitled "Pampered Pets." A Dalmation dressed in a ruffled red chiffon jacket with matching hat is not my idea of how a dog should look.

But the trouble is that to some people even the spending of money on a legitimate necessity for a pet can seem an outlandish luxury. A special diet, expensive medicine or surgery, or careful provision for a pet's care when the owner goes out of town can look to someone else like a ridiculous indulgence. In between a mink-lined designer raincoat for a dog at one extreme and unconscionable neglect at the other, there's a wide range of care, some of which is bound to seem unnecessary to somebody.

I believe that unless it has been suppressed somehow, the nurturing quality exists, to varying degrees, in all human beings, men and women alike, and that the happiest of us find outlets for that need to cherish. I have a friend, a single woman, who signs her Christmas cards from herself and her "fur baby." This woman is rational, talented, successful in her work and friendships. What's wrong with her regarding her cute little dog as her "baby"?

That brings up another advantage of the dog as a child-substitute: While it will grow old, it will never grow up—it can always be its owner's baby.

A veterinarian I know remarked that people whose pets are their babies are often the worst clients, for treating dogs like humans is not always best for the animals. Obviously, one should keep a rational perspective when it comes to diet, medical care, and the like.

But I am talking about feelings, not about treatment. The way I see it, when people regard their pets as child-substitutes, it does the people good, it usually benefits the animals, and it doesn't harm society.

THE COMPANION DOG

Loneliness has always been a human problem, for we are perhaps the supremely social animals. We know now that this insidious disorder can make us not only unhappy but unwell. While loneliness can afflict persons living in the midst of a large family, it is most prevalent among people who live alone, and it seems to occur in its most poignant form in cities.

A pet, particularly a dog, can be a good defense against loneliness for any single person. Some people claim that just having somebody who's glad to see them when they come home from work is reason enough to keep a dog. A comforting presence at the foot of the bed, a responsive sentient creature to talk to, somebody to take care of, a companion to go for walks or on trips with, somebody to play games with and laugh at, a warm body to hug—a dog can be all those things and more.

"Our dogs will love and admire the meanest of us, and feed our colossal vanity with their uncritical homage," wrote the American essayist Agnes Repplier—and who among us couldn't use a little uncritical homage now and then? A dog is not put off by physical disability or homeliness; it doesn't notice inadequate education, poor social skills, lack of success. If you're good to your dog, it will never divorce you or leave you for a younger, richer, smarter, sexier, or more successful owner.

It is a truism that walking a dog offers you a chance to meet other people. In my New York City neighborhood, for example, it can take me an hour just to walk Dandy around the block because we meet so many people and dogs we know. Summer evenings, a bunch of us may stand around and talk while our pets socialize. Friends who sometimes walk Dandy for me are amused by the number of people they meet who say hello to her—and one courtly gentleman even tips his hat.

The late Michael McCulloch, a psychiatrist, pointed out that a dog can be a great social facilitator, especially for shy people. Strangers who strike up a conversation because of a dog are usually on the street or in some other public place where social demands are low and where the conversation can be easily ended. Also, noted Dr. McCulloch, it's the dog who's the focus of attention. A person who lacks poise doesn't feel he or she is being examined.

In a few studies of how people with pets are perceived by strangers, pet owners have come off rather well. In one, psychologist Randall Lockwood showed a group of subjects pictures of people with and without pets and asked them to rate the people in terms of such qualities as friendliness, happiness, dependency, aggressiveness, comfort, intelligence, and so forth.

In general, the people pictured with animals—walking, sitting, or playing with them—were rated more positively than those without. A woman walking a dog was perceived as richer and more comfortable; a man walking a dog was viewed as not only wealthier and more at ease but friendlier, more intelligent, more sympathetic, and safer to approach than a man walking alone.

PETS AND THE ELDERLY

One of my fellow dog-walkers is a nice, very elderly gentleman with a sweet but uncommonly homely dog. His dog and my dog always stop and greet each other as dogs do, so the man and I make small talk. I never fail to admire his dog, which seems to please him; in truth, it has a lovely temperament.

He once mentioned to me that he and his dog had Thanksgiving dinner together, just the two of them. This brief glimpse of the man's life points up the role a companion animal can fill in the life of an elderly person who lives alone, perhaps without close family or friends.

Many elderly people tell me that they would dearly love to have a pet, but they worry about being able to take care of it. In bad weather, an old person naturally would find it difficult to get out to walk a dog or buy pet food. They also worry about what would happen to their animals if they had to go to the hospital, or if they died.

In a more humane world, networks of volunteers, perhaps associated with a senior citizens center, block association, or even an animal shelter, could serve as supports for the elderly who wish to keep pets. Then, on those occasions when an old person could not walk his or her dog, buy pet food, take the animal to the veterinarian, or whatever, help would be available. No single, older person who wanted a companion animal would be deprived of one for lack of assistance.

In the last few years, it has been the practice of SPCAs and humane societies in major cities to conduct "pet therapy" programs, which consist of taking small animals—usually puppies and kittens, sometimes also rabbits, hamsters, and pet birds—to visit the patients in nursing homes and hospitals. I have had the opportunity to go along on such visits in cities all over the United States. I've seen the impact of the animals on the patients, whose lives are often cheerless and boring. Anecdotal evidence of the success of these programs is rich and plentiful, and research studies have confirmed it. The benefit the patients derive from holding and petting, even just watching, the small creatures is dramatic.

Once I was with a humane society group on its first visit to a particular nursing home. One old lady immediately clasped a puppy. "I haven't held anything warm and young and alive in my arms in twenty years," she said.

Some of the old people visited talk nostalgically about pets they had when they were young. Often, the surprise to the staff is not what they talk about but that they talk at all. It is not unusual for a withdrawn or depressed elderly patient to speak for the first time in months or even years when a pet is placed in his or her arms. "Puppy!" exclaimed one eighty-year-old stroke victim, to the amazement of the nurses. It was his first spoken word.

Occasionally, a patient will burst into tears, as if emotion long unused had surfaced. "I don't know why I'm crying," said one lady in a wheelchair as I helped her cuddle a puppy. "I love dogs!" Even those who are severely disabled respond. Whatever the reason, "pet therapy" helps fill the need to caress, to nurture, and confirms the almost mystical connection we have with the companion animals that have shared our lives for thousands of years.

Because of the publicity these therapeutic and certainly appealing programs have received, the recognized benefits to the patients, and the pressure from humane society and nursing home staffs who believe in them, a number of custodial institutions now allow resident pets. Some thirty states have passed laws permitting them. The laws vary from state to state—some limit the number of pets, all limit the areas within the institutions where the pets are allowed.

A cat named Lisette was donated to a nursing home in Brooklyn by the Humane Society of New York. Lisette lives in the recreation room but makes rounds twice a day in the arms of a nurse to bedridden patients and sometimes can be seen strolling down a hall alone on her way to visit a favorite patient by herself. "This animal has brought life to this place!" one patient summed it up.

The animals not only dispense love and amusement and make institutions seem more homelike, but according to staff members they sometimes help get patients' minds off themselves. An old lady I met in a nursing home in Boston was very proud of the fact that she was able to take the mascot, a Boston Terrier, for his morning walk.

"Do you take him out even in bad weather?" I asked, for Boston winters can be bitter cold, snowy, and icy—risky for a frail old lady to be out in.

"Oh, it's all right," she replied with a twinkle. "He has a coat."

Just when pets are increasingly allowed to visit and even reside in nursing homes because of their recognized value to human health and morale, it is outrageously cruel that elderly people who live at home (as most do) are so often denied the life-giving companionship of pets because of the no-pet rules in urban housing (see Chapter 11).

The time may be not far off when doctors will routinely prescribe pets for their patients who could benefit from them, especially the urban elderly whose lives may be restricted. As Dr. Leo Bustad, veterinarian and author of the book *Animals, Aging, and the Aged*, has said, it would be unwise to withhold or withdraw doctor-prescribed medicine from an aged man or woman; what if that medicine is the companionship of a loved pet?

Many changes need to be accomplished to make ours a more compassionate society. Guaranteeing the right to own a dog or cat should be one of them.

CHAPTER 11

THE LEGAL DOG:

The Rights and Responsibilities of Dog Ownership

Ironically, just at the time when there's a growing awareness of our need for companion animals, as well as scientific evidence of their importance to human health as well as happiness, it has become more difficult to keep that quintessential companion animal—the dog—in the place where most of us live—the city. Increasingly, urban rules and legislation are threatening to regulate our dogs right out of our lives.

Not all of the laws that govern the way we live with our urban dogs are wrong. Leash laws, for instance, protect their lives, and clean-up laws make cities a lot nicer to live in for all of us. However, one fairly recent type of regulation, which is virtually standard in every city in the United States today, is turning dogs into urban endangered species and denying pets to many would-be dog owners: the no-pet clause in the leases of rental housing.

In direct contrast to these laws that seem to discourage or restrict our relationship with animals is the rising concern for animal rights—a philosophical point of view that ascribes inherent rights to animals beyond their value to humans. This premise has increasingly captured the interest of lawyers.

There have always been some laws to protect some animals from abuse, but they have been largely ignored. Monstrous cruelty to animals—dogs, cats, horses, farm animals, zoo animals, wildlife—was until quite recently public and pandemic, and we have heard about the way animals are treated in laboratories and slaughterhouses. But public attitudes are gradually changing, and with this consciousness come new and amended laws and more vigorous enforcement of laws already in place. You don't have to feel helpless when you see an animal being abused. In addition to offering suggestions for what you might do about the no-pet clause, I'll give you some pointers below on what you can do about animal cruelty.

CAESAR'S WIFE'S DOG

For starters, one way to prevent more laws from being passed against city dogs is to be sure that your pet's behavior, and yours as a dog owner, is impeccable. You must both be, like Caesar's wife, above suspicion. A country dog can be a noisy, misbehaving roughneck and get away with it because it's less likely to bother other people. But in the city, a dog's (and dog owner's) personality traits show up glaringly.

One of the greatest annoyances to neighbors is the dog who barks or whines incessantly when left alone. This can be equally distressing to dog haters and dog lovers. Dog haters would like to throttle the beast, while dog lovers worry about it and feel sorry for it. As discussed in Chapter 4, this habit can and should be stopped with proper training.

Housebreaking should be absolute. Even if your pet behaves okay in the public halls and only has repeated problems in your apartment, sooner or later neighbors, the super, and the landlord will become aware of an unpleasant smell in your place, and though you might not notice it yourself, they will object.

Some housing units limit the number of pets a household can

have—in fact, in some cities there are ordinances that limit the number of pets even people in private homes can keep! These laws are muddleheaded, because standards of pet keeping, just like those of housekeeping in general, are highly individual. Some people can keep twenty pets in cleanliness and harmony; other folks can't seem to keep even one decently.

The cruel no-pet clause is said by the real estate community to be the result of years of irresponsible behavior on the part of dog owners. While this argument is open to question, it should be stressed that there is no excuse for any of us to keep a pet that's a problem to others. People are frightened by hostile dogs. People are annoyed when a tenant keeps an inappropriate number of animals in unsanitary and odoriferous conditions. People are disgusted by dogs who mess on their property or in public places. People are irritated by dogs that are permitted to yap or bark on the street late at night.

The first tactic of any dog owner for stemming the tide against dog ownership in cities is to clean up our act so there is no justification for complaints against us.

SCOOP LAWS

A paramount objection to urban dogs is, of course, the waste matter on the streets, sidewalks, lawns, and flowerbeds. It's crucial that every city dog owner observe the clean-up laws faithfully. In my doggy neighborhood, some of us habitually cleaned up after our dogs even before New York City's scoop law went into effect, just to try to reduce the pandemic and unpleasant presence of dog dirt.

Really, cleaning up is no big deal! There are several methods that work: You can use one of the commercial pooper scoopers on a stick. There's also a disposable contraption consisting of a paper bag and cardboard scoop; some city humane societies sell packages of these.

Or, you can use a simple plastic bag—just slip it over your hand and pick up the matter (imagine you're picking up sod or mud), turn the bag inside out so the waste is inside, and deposit it in the first public trash can you come to. Another method, if your dog doesn't object, is to slide a folded newspaper under its rear end at the crucial moment, then roll up the paper when the dog is finished and throw it away. This method is especially practical for a dog that has occasional soft stools.

Some dog owners have the offensive habit of being oblivious to where their dogs urinate. I've seen male dogs permitted to lift their legs against people's front steps, bicycles, trees, and flowers. Trees on a city block with a high concentration of dogs will eventually perish from the constant depositing of acidic urine against their bark. Flowers and ivy can be turned brown and killed.

It goes without saying that people should be most vigilant with their dogs in city parks and keep their pets out of playgrounds altogether. At a playground near me, parents have had to plead with inconsiderate dog owners not to let their animals relieve themselves in the sandbox, for heaven's sake. That's an offense that makes all decent dog owners feel ashamed.

LEASH LAWS

One of the most puzzling practices of dog owners that offends many city people is letting dogs run off the leash. It's puzzling because it not only bothers other people but endangers the dogs.

A common city sight is a dog trotting along the sidewalk apparently quite alone, with no owner evident. All too often such an owner goes his or her way without paying any attention whatsoever to the pet, expecting the dog to take responsibility for keeping up. Or perhaps this is a way of avoiding the clean-up law; after all, if a person is clear at the other end of the block, he or she can't even notice when the dog relieves itself, leaving passersby in the dark about whose dog the offending animal is.

As I have said, some dog owners mistakenly think they are making their pets happy by giving them off-the-leash freedom, but it can be very stressful for a dog. The crowds, noise, and confusing jumble of scents on a city street make it easy for a pet to lose sight, sound, and smell of its owner.

And how about the feelings of other people on the street? It can be unnerving to have a strange dog come upon you suddenly, off the leash and uncontrolled. It can terrify some people, and they have rights too, which should be respected.

A free-running dog can also upset a dog walker whose pet is on the leash. Very often, a confrontation takes place between the two dogs. On a few frightening occasions, I've had to actually beat off unleashed hostile dogs who dashed up and provoked quarrels with my mild-mannered (and leashed) Dandy.

A dog off the leash can turn neutral people into dog haters who will be the first to support laws to deprive us of our pets.

LICENSE LAWS

The attitude that city license laws are merely an unfair tax on dog owners, to be avoided like other taxes, is completely mistaken and dumb. An up-to-date dog license gives an owner a fighting chance to retrieve his or her pet if the animal becomes lost. If the dog is picked up by an animal control officer or brought to the police or a shelter by a sympathetic citizen, the license serves as identification.

If an unlicensed dog is injured—say, hit by a car—and brought to a pound or shelter, it may not be given any medical attention. It may just suffer in a cage until its owner comes for it, or it dies or is euthanized. Many shelters that function as the pound, where stray dogs are brought, cannot afford to provide medical care for an injured dog whose owner is unknown and might never turn up to pay the bill. Persons who don't bother to license their dogs should be aware of this.

Even if it is not injured, a lost dog suffers tremendous stress and fear, especially in a city. Look at the panic in the eyes of the next lost dog you come across and ask yourself if you would want your pet to have that expression.

Even if you never walk your dog off the leash and you believe it would never leave your side, no matter what, remember that accidents can happen. Caring and responsible people do lose their dogs sometimes in a variety of unforeseen circumstances. The license alone is no guarantee you will get your dog back safely, but it is one extra, inexpensive protection. A license could reduce considerably the time your dog is separated from you and might save its life.

Lastly, even if you buy a license every year throughout your dog's life and it is never needed to restore your pet to you, the fee supports animal control, which helps other dogs. Whether your local dog pound, or shelter that performs animal control, is a good one or a dump, a dog is better off in one than roaming the streets. It is sheltered instead of homeless, fed instead of starving, protected instead of terrorized and possibly tortured by crazies, and even if it is eventually euthanized, that death is better than the almost certain death it would meet from starvation, exposure, disease, accident, or atrocity.

THE NO-PET CLAUSE: HOW IT WORKS

A harsh and callous consequence of a tight housing market, the no-pet clause has become a standard fixture in rental and even cooperative housing nationwide. It denies the joy, companionship, and protection of pets to possibly several million people. It swells the numbers of pets in animal shelters or abandoned on the streets. And it often forces pet owners who are fortunate enough to live where they can have animals to stay put, even when they can no longer afford the continual rent increases.

Landlords claim the no-pet clause is a reaction to irresponsible pet owners who permit their animals to destroy property or annoy other people. They cite cases of dogs who bark all day, cats who mess in public halls, and so on. Even if all their complaints were true, and in isolated cases they might be, landlords are, through the no-pet clauses, making *a priori* judgments about pet owners. The assumption is that your pet is automatically and surely going to deface property and offend others. The no-pet clause acts to punish the many for the crimes of the few.

The flaw in the landlords' argument is that every standard lease *without the no-pet clause* gives a building manager all the power he or she needs to deal with those tenants whose pets truly do cause problems. The no-pet clause is not needed for this purpose. The nuisance clauses in leases, and the nuisance laws of every community, assure landlords of the legal means to force tenants to control their pets or give them up.

So why, then, the no-pet clause? For one thing, it saves landlords the trouble of dealing with tenants on an individual basis. If nobody is allowed to have a pet, that's one less potential hassle for the landlord. Building owners often refuse to rent to families with children for the same reason. They probably would, if they could get away with it, also put no-stereo clauses into leases—surely loud stereo music causes complaints which landlords or superintendents have to handle on an individual basis.

The no-pet clause is also a weapon for landlords to use to intimidate tenants in order to keep down complaints, even to punish tenants who demand their rights. If a pet owner has a lease with a no-pet clause that has not been enforced, that tenant is going to think twice before asking for more heat, secure locks, clean halls, or repairs.

Because of the low vacancy rate everywhere, people tend to stay put far more than they used to when housing was plentiful. But since many city landlords can charge higher rents from new, incoming tenants than the regular increases allowed in rents of existing tenants, they naturally prefer frequent turnover. The last thing they presumably want is stable tenants. It is therefore very tempting for landlords to use every means at their disposal to empty apartments, especially those with longtime residents and especially those still covered by rent limitations. The no-pet clause provides many a landlord with a legal weapon to get people out: "Get rid of your pet or move."

Private landlords are by no means the only villains in this picture. Operators of government-subsidized housing—federal, state, and city—are just as bad. In some ways, they are worse, because often the people who need subsidized housing are the same ones who have a great need for companion and protective animals—the elderly. Untold thousands of senior people who live in subsidized housing still grieve for the pets they had to give up when they moved in. Or they long for the new ones they aren't allowed to have.

In addition, other elderly people who happen to be allowed to keep pets where they live are sticking it out in rentals they can no longer afford, or in neighborhoods that have deteriorated and become unsafe, just to keep their dogs or cats. One couple wrote to me that they chose to skimp on food in order to pay their rent in private housing because they could keep their beloved Poodle. They were eligible for subsidized housing but couldn't bear to give up their dog.

Many cooperatives and condominiums also refuse to allow pets, but at least in some cases owners might have input with the elected boards and seek to change the rules.

THE NO-PET CLAUSE: HOW TO AVOID IT

Other than by having the incredible luck to find an apartment where pets are permitted, are there ways to avoid the no-pet clause? In rare instances, yes.

Sometimes you can persuade a landlord, or a building agent, to strike the clause from a lease you are about to sign. This might be possible if he or she is friendly and reasonable and if you can convince all concerned that you are a responsible pet owner. Perhaps you can provide a letter of recommendation from your previous building owner or superintendent. You might even offer to introduce a prospective landlord, or agent, to your pets so he or she can see how well behaved they are. A course of action that's even more likely to work is to offer to pay a security deposit, or even a small monthly fee, in exchange for permission to keep your pets.

It's safest to ask, tactfully, to have such a waiver in writing, especially if you have a dog or dogs. Or, if the landlord won't agree to that, at least ask to have the no-pet clause crossed out of the lease and initialed. Be cautious about all this, because you don't want to give the impression of being a troublemaker. But if the ownership of the building should change, you would need some proof other than your word that you have permission to have pets.

When I was signing the lease for my Greenwich Village apartment some years ago, I noticed the no-pet clause. Back then, it was not as common as it is now. I was appalled.

"But I have a dog and several cats," I protested in alarm.

"Don't worry about it—that clause is just there in case problems come up," said the agent. But nothing was put in writing.

There are many resident dogs and cats in my building, and nobody seems to mind a bit. I mention this only because it illustrates the fact that some no-pet clauses are only selectively enforced. Or a building may have a grandfather policy, allowing people to keep pets they already have when the lease is signed, but forbidding new ones. Oral permission is no protection for a tenant, however, nor is the presence of other pets in a building. Unless a local law says otherwise, a no-pet clause can generally be enforced or not enforced by landlords at will.

It's never advisable to sign a lease with a no-pet clause and then smuggle in your pet, or secretly acquire one later. Landlords, like the rest of us, don't like to be deceived and are more likely to take revenge against a tenant who has lied. Better to be up-front in your dealings.

A very enlightened building owner (or cooperative or condominium board), instead of forbidding pets altogether, might establish firm rules for pet owners to observe. Such rules could protect the rights of all tenants fairly. A huge apartment building in Chicago, for instance, requires that all dogs be taken down the back elevator and that the owners avail themselves of pooper bags provided by the management! The regulations are meticulously obeyed, and everyone seems satisfied. Perhaps, if you're moving into a building, you might suggest that rules be set up along these lines.

The management of one large housing complex in Massachusetts not only provides a separate dog-walking area but goes so far as to insist that all pets be neutered and have their shots. A volunteer board of tenants is set up to enforce rules and handle complaints. The board idea seems especially good, because it not only provides a way to permit tenants to keep pets but assures non-pet owners that their rights are protected.

It is difficult to get a fair and creative idea put into action sometimes, especially where real estate is involved, but worth the effort.

THE NO-PET CLAUSE: HOW TO FIGHT IT

Most people, threatened with eviction from their homes unless they give up their pets, are intimidated. Many submissively give away their animals, or surrender them to pounds or shelters.

Some pet owners, however, have hired legal counsel and gone to court—and often won.

According to members of the Animal Legal Defense Fund, a national group of attorneys who will advise or defend pet owners in many types of cases, a discerning lawyer can often find careless wording in a lease that renders the no-pet clause legally unenforceable. Jolene Marion of the New York chapter of the organization says that rental real estate attorneys are sometimes overconfident in preparing leases and leave discrepancies in the wording, perhaps because they are unused to being challenged. After one tenant's case which Ms. Marion won, the landlord's counsel vowed to rewrite all the leases for his client's properties, to plug up the loopholes she had found in the no-pet clause.

In another case, Counselor Marion was able to prove that a rental agent had enticed a woman into moving into a building that he was having difficulty renting. The apartments weren't filling up fast enough, so the agent gave the woman verbal assurance, in the presence of two witnesses, that she could keep her dog. A few months later, after the building was fully occupied, he then sought to evict her because of the dog.

In court, the judge not only found for the tenant but awarded her damages for having been deceived. And, to give you an idea of what the public thinks about the no-pet clause, when the judge announced his decision, the entire courtroom full of strangers applauded!

It's very important to hire an attorney who has some knowledge of no-pet clause litigation. Most lawyers have not had experience in this area and are not even aware of the ways and means of defending such cases. However, in recent years, lawyers interested in animal rights, and tangentially the rights of pet owners, formed the organization that addresses these issues, among others. The Animal Legal Defense Fund has members in a growing number of U.S. cities. If pet owners threatened with eviction can't locate a lawyer in their community with experience in defending tenants in cases arising from no-pet clauses, they or their attorneys can contact this group: Animal Legal Defense Fund, 205 East 42nd Street, New York, N.Y. 10017.

The message to urban dog owners told to give up their pets because of a no-pet clause is this: Don't automatically give up your pet—you might win in court.

THE NO-PET CLAUSE:
HOW TO MODIFY OR ABOLISH IT

In New York City, the no-pet clause in leases was only minimally and selectively enforced by the real estate community until the real crunch in rental housing came in the 1970s. Then, landlords began to turn to it as a means of emptying apartments and putting them on the market. People who had lived openly with their pets for years, pets about whom there had never been any complaints, were suddenly facing eviction unless they gave them up. In many pathetic instances, elderly men and women whose pets were their sole companions were told to get rid of them or move. But move where? They had no place to go, no affordable housing available to them.

Tearfully, some of the elderly pet owners, along with others, began to seek legal advice from Elinor Molbegott, the ASPCA counsel, and from the few attorneys in private practice who were sympathetic to such cases. As the litigation began to reach the courts, judges realized there was more going on than the mere fact of pet ownership. It became apparent that an overzealous real estate community was trying to stir up a very sluggish market by invoking the no-pet clauses, realizing that many people would move before they gave up their pets, thereby making their apartments available.

When enough of these instances were brought to the attention of the city lawmakers, hearings were held in the New York City Council. The members became convinced that in reality, many eviction orders had nothing to do with pets. The no-pet clause was being used simply to empty apartments. So, to the intense relief of the city's pet owners, a law was passed that provided that tenants who had lived openly with their pets for three months or more without complaints could not be ordered to give them up, even with a no-pet clause in their leases.

This local law does not challenge the basic premise of the no-pet clause, nor is it any help to pet owners moving into new buildings with leases that forbid pets, nor to people who have no pets but wish to acquire them. But it does give protection to people living with existing pets.

In 1983, bills passed in Congress stating that senior citizens living or moving into certain types of housing that receive federal subsidy could not be denied the right to keep pets. This is now technically the law of the land. If you or someone you know needs information about senior citizens' housing and pets, contact the Animal Legal Defense Fund.

Even those of us who are not elderly or needful of subsidized housing have a stake in this. Any law that guarantees the right to own pets recognizes the principle that companion animals are an intrinsic part of human well-being. While it has yet to be decided that owning a pet is a constitutional right that can't be abridged, we can at least make some headway against the no-pet clause.

Every urban pet owner should be aware of any pending legislation that would limit or abolish the no-pet clause or other restrictions on responsible pet ownership. You can find out whether any such legislation has been introduced in your community (city or state) by calling your representatives in the city government or state capital. If there are no such bills, form a committee of fellow pet owners and sympathizers and try to get your lawmakers to sponsor some. Politicians will listen—they may be pet owners themselves, or they at least know that animal lovers are a large, passionate, and important group.

As urban dog owners, we have our work cut out for us. First, we have to be unfailingly considerate and law-abiding pet owners ourselves and encourage—insist, if possible—others to be so, too. Then, we have to change the laws to make the no-pet clause illegal.

ANTICRUELTY LAWS

No discussion of the laws that affect companion animals should omit mention of those that give them some protection against abuse. All dog owners—in fact, everyone who loves dogs or even cares about justice—should be aware that laws against cruelty to animals exist in every state, and we can use these laws in helping to put a stop to it.

It is impossible to care about animals and not feel a surge of sickening rage at the sight of a neglected or beaten pet. Yet, few people are aware that they can do anything about it. Cases of neglect can sometimes be solved if you speak to the animal owner in a friendly way and point out what he or she is doing that's harmful. But you may be met with just a shrug, and in some cases you may be taking a risk, because people who abuse animals are very often violent toward other people as well. Another problem is that the authorities treat cases of animal abuse as a relatively low priority matter.

Nevertheless, laws are on the books, and the extent to which they will be enforced depends largely on how much the public cares. Lawmakers, district attorneys, animal control officers, SPCAs, and even the police are responsive to pressure from citizens. While anticruelty laws are not very stringent, at least we can see that those we do have are enforced and violations punished.

Cruelty to animals is defined two ways: active cruelty, such as beating, shooting, or torturing; and passive cruelty, such as failing to provide proper shelter, medical care, or food. Both are crimes in every state. Even if a person is unintentionally harming an animal, he or she is still generally considered to be breaking the law and can be stopped.

A person neglecting or abusing an animal may be warned, or

taken to court and fined, and in very rare cases imprisoned. If the neglect or abuse is extreme, the animal may be confiscated by the authorities.

If you know of a case of cruelty, *don't hesitate to report it*. Where to report it varies from one locality to another, but start with the police. If cruelty investigation is not within their jurisdiction, they will tell you whom to call. That may be the animal control department, humane society, SPCA, or other animal protection society.

If possible, back up your cruelty complaint with some other complaint, especially one concerning property, which seems to be more sacred in some quarters than animals. For instance, if you know of a dog that is chained up all day and night and barks or whines, add the noise complaint to your objections to the cruelty. Or if you hear a dog screaming because it is being beaten, insist that the noise bothers you, as well as your objection to the treatment of the animal. If someone's half-starved dog gets into your garbage, don't tell the authorities only that the dog is ill fed, but add that it tips over your garbage cans or treads on your flower beds. The object is to help the dog, so use everything you can think of to get the attention of the authorities.

When you make a complaint, give as much accurate, specific information as possible: name and address of the person abusing the dog; date the abuse took place (or time period if it's a long-term abuse such as starvation or failure to provide adequate shelter or medical care); description of the animal; type of object used to cause harm; license number if a vehicle was involved; names and addresses of other possible witnesses; your name, address, and phone (which will be kept confidential if you request it). Many well-supported urban humane societies or animal control agencies will willingly prosecute cases of animal abuse, and often win, but they do need accurate input from you if you are the instigator of the report.

Once you've made the report, don't just sit back and assume everything will be taken care of. Follow up to see what has been done. If the appropriate agency has failed to act, report this to your district attorney's office. Be pleasant but firm; insist that the situation be corrected.

Don't hesitate to tell the news desk of your local newspapers and TV stations, especially if the law enforcement agency seems to be dragging its feet. The media will usually welcome animal stories, and often the light of publicity—or the threat of it—will inspire authorities to act.

It is always a good idea to join your local humane society, SPCA, or other animal protection society, just on general principles. Then, if you do ever have to report a case of animal cruelty to this agency, you might be more likely to get fast action if you're a member, especially if you're an active member. These organizations not only care about the welfare of animals, but depend on the good will of their membership.

CHAPTER 12

TRAVEL:
Taking or Leaving Your Dog

As a city person, you probably put opportunities to escape fairly high on your list of leisure-time priorities. If you lack your own weekend retreat, you treasure the invitations to those of your friends, or you manage trips to your favorite vacation spots whenever you can.

Perhaps you travel on business. And possibly you are contemplating a move across the state or to another part of the country.

Where does your dog figure in these plans? In this chapter, the different modes of travel will be examined in terms of taking the pet along. Unfortunately, you're pretty much limited to driving or flying, because most rail lines (such as Amtrak) and bus lines (Greyhound, Trailways) won't allow pets on board at all. For information on other train or bus lines, inquire well ahead of time, but don't be disappointed if you're told, "No pets." For those times when your pet can't go with you, alternatives for its care while you're away will also be explored in this chapter.

Although it's not always possible or advisable to take the dog along on a visit or vacation, taking it when you move is not even debatable. Ask the staff at any animal shelter anywhere in the country what reasons are most frequently given by people surrendering pets. Right up there among the top five is "moving." This excuse is offered as though it were so perfectly understandable that no further explanation is necessary. It's a mystery to me how anyone can abandon a pet, especially for no other reason than the perceived inconvenience of taking it along. I think leaving a pet behind is despicable.

The subject of moving with pets reminds me of my friends Gretchen and Leo Scanlan, lifelong pet owners who naturally took their ten dogs and cats with them when they moved across the country. Because they had so many animals, the most practical thing for them to do was to rent a mobile home for the journey. They planned and plotted the trip carefully, allowing eight days, with stops at campgrounds that they knew permitted pets. They kept their dogs leashed and walked them frequently. Since cats of course are known to be great escape artists, the Scanlans had their six travel in safari cages, two compatible cats per cage, with litter boxes and bedding in each. The entire family made the trip in comfort, with no problems.

People who really care about their pets can work out a way to take them when they move and won't feel inconvenienced or put upon for doing it.

You do want to be prepared, by the way, for the fact that most dogs tend to get very upset at the sight of packing cartons and their familiar home being dismantled. A pet has no idea what is going on and may display anxiety symptoms such as breaking house-training, barking when left alone, or other undesirable traits, even if it has never done so before in its life. Once when I was getting ready to move, Dandy took to chewing up books and sofa cushions whenever she was left alone. I had to stash her in a local kennel for day care while I was out of the house at my office. As soon as we were ensconced in the new apartment, she settled down and was herself again.

It helps if a dog can be taken to visit its new home as often as possible before moving day. Then the new place won't seem so strange.

Actor William Hickey with his best friend. *(David Cupp)*

A child regards the family dog as a playmate and confidant. *(Debbie Elbaum/ Courtesy, Pets Are Wonderful Council)*

The nurturing quality exists in men as well as women. *(Douglas T. Weir/ Courtesy, Pets Are Wonderful Council)*

Big armful for an elderly lady, who seems to like it.
(Don Pollard/Courtesy, Humane Society of New York)

The newspaper method of obeying the city clean-up law. *(David Cupp)*

This dog, allowed to run loose, fell down a steep rocky hillside and was stranded on a ledge. The humane officer was lowered by rope like a mountain climber to rescue her. *(Jane Hutchison/Humane Society of Santa Clara Valley)*

"So when am I going to get out of this boring travel crate?" *(Hope Ryden)*

Suitable outdoor costume for a 14-year-old dog to wear on a freezing day: owner's sweater. *(Jane Sapinsky)*

A highly territorial dog may take offense at movers who come in to carry out the furniture and household belongings. This type of dog should be parked with a friend or put in a kennel on moving day.

BASIC TRAVEL TIPS

Here are a few suggestions that would apply no matter how your dog is traveling or what the destination.

A health checkup beforehand is in order, including a heartworm test. A pet that is not in the pink of health shouldn't travel at all, but should wait until it's well.

All immunizations, including rabies, should be up to date. Ask your veterinarian to furnish you with a certificate stating that your dog has had these shots, and take it with you on the trip. In addition, if you're flying, be aware that individual airlines have their own health certificate requirements, as do the states or nations you plan to visit, so you'll need to find all this out well in advance.

Remember to take a supply of any medication your pet needs regularly, enough for the duration. It's also a good idea to take a bottle of Pectolin or Kaopectate, in case it gets an upset stomach.

If your dog is highly nervous or timid, tranquilizers might make it more comfortable. A veterinarian who knows the animal well can advise you. Otherwise, they should not be necessary.

Take familiar things from home such as your pet's blanket, favorite toys, food, and water dishes.

If you're traveling by air, try to book your flight at mid-week, when traffic in the airport is relatively light.

One thing that is of no use when you are away from home with your pet is, obviously, an identification tag with your home address and telephone number on it. Put a new identification tag on your dog's collar giving the address and phone where you are staying.

However, that won't help you when you're en route, so here's a plan the Scanlans worked out for their pets' protection: Have your dog wear a tag on its collar giving the phone number of a trusted, nontraveling friend who has agreed beforehand to take collect phone calls. The tag should read, "Please call collect (area code and number)." Then if you should lose your dog, alert the friend and keep in continual touch while you're searching the area where it disappeared. Your pet may be lucky enough to be picked up by someone who will contact your friend and leave a name and location where you can reclaim it.

TRAVELING BY CAR

Once when I was a teenager, I was driving my father's car with my dog Laddie in the back seat. The car windows were open, and Laddie was not only looking out, he was apparently leaning out. I turned a corner and out the window he went into the street. Fortunately, I noticed immediately and stopped for him, and fortunately he wasn't hit by another car or hurt by the fall, but it was a close shave and I've never forgotten it.

Now that I'm much older and wiser, I know that Laddie shouldn't even have been permitted to ride with his head out the window in the first place—people let their dogs do this all the time, with many resulting eye injuries from dust or cinders flying in or from windburn.

In fact, I don't think it was wise for me to let Laddie ride unconfined in the car with nobody to supervise him. Today, I would keep the windows at least mostly up or get window gates, and if I was traveling far, I'd put him in a portable kennel or safari cage to keep him safe. I might even investigate getting him a car seat, like those they make for babies. Don't laugh—I've seen car seats that are made for dogs. Well-stocked pet supplies stores sell protective devices for traveling pets.

It might be best to have your pet ride in its carrier. But if the trip will be long, the carrier should be big enough for the dog to stand up in and lie down full length.

One of the cruelest and most dangerous things to do is to have a dog rattling around loose in the back of a pickup truck. I'm sure you've seen dogs riding this way, struggling to keep on their feet or whipped by the wind as they lean over the side. Even if the animal doesn't fall out, it is thrown about and can be injured.

You'd have to be a moron to make a dog ride in the trunk, but people have done that, too. A dog can die from heat prostration, asphyxiation, or dehydration, and at the very least can be injured from jolting about.

Don't feed your dog for at least six hours before departure, and unless the weather is hot, withhold water for a couple of hours. Then walk the animal before you leave, and at several stops along the way—always, repeat, always—on the leash. If it's an all-day trip, the dog should be given water after each walk en route. But never put food or water in the carrier, portable kennel, or safari cage while traveling—it will just spill and make a mess, and no dog should have to sit or lie in that.

Please reread everything I said in Chapter 7 about the dangers of leaving a dog locked in a parked car. Naturally, when you're on the road for any length of time, you have to stop to eat, stretch your legs, go to the bathroom. If you're traveling with another person, one of you should stay with the dog while the other goes in to have a meal or to pick up food to eat in the car, or whatever. Other options are picnics and drive-ins. If you're driving alone with your dog and have to make a very brief stop, at least leave the motor running with the air conditioning on, and try to keep your car and the dog in sight.

Bear in mind that the greenhouse effect of an overheated car is not the only risk you take in leaving your dog alone—it can be stolen. As you know, there is no such thing as a car that can't be broken into, and dognappers are everywhere. I once met a couple who had left their Poodle locked in their car at night while they went into a restaurant for dinner and found it missing when they returned. Your dog may be a seasoned traveler and enjoy riding in the car with you, but be sure to protect it against heat exhaustion and theft.

Careful planning is essential for overnight trips if you'll be stopping at motels or inns, because you'll need to know in advance whether they accept pets. When you're a guest, keep your dog always leashed except in the room, and if you must leave it alone in the room, keep it in its carrier or portable kennel. And listen outside the door to see if it starts to bark, because if it does you can't leave it alone.

The best advice I can give anyone planning a motor trip with a pet is to obtain a copy of *Touring with Towser*, a valuable directory of some seven thousand hotels and motels, listed state by state, that accommodate guests with dogs. The booklet also indicates whatever restrictions an inn may impose, such as "Small dogs only," "Small extra charge," "Dogs must be housed in hotel's kennel," and the like. *Touring with Towser*, updated every two years, is available for $1.50 from Gaines TWT, P.O. Box 8172, Kankakee, IL 60902.

Some campgrounds permit dogs, if they are kept leashed, but you'll want to find out in advance. The leash law, among other things, protects dogs from getting lost or injured, or from possibly getting bitten by a wild animal or snake. City dogs do not necessarily take to the wilderness—and remember that not all dogs are swimmers or even like to go into water.

And here's an extra word of caution: Stay out of the woods during hunting season. Hunting is allowed in most state parks, all national forests, and ironically, in over half of all wildlife refuges. Thanks to prohunting groups and their powerful lobby, and the silence or lack of awareness of voters on the subject, the number of public lands on which hunting is allowed increases every year. Also, hunters often go onto private, posted land. Hunting seasons vary from place to place, so find out before you and your pet go traipsing around the countryside, or you could both get shot.

Your dog could also get caught in a trap in places where trapping is allowed—that is, most state parks, all national forests, etc. It is a relatively common occurrence in rural and wilderness areas for unsupervised dogs and cats to lose their legs, or their lives, in traps. City people are the ones most likely to be unaware of hunting and trapping dangers.

TRAVELING BY AIR

The rules and regulations for taking a dog with you on a flight vary considerably.

Let's start with the assumption that you have a small dog and want to take it in the cabin with you on a domestic flight. Forget it, say some airlines; all dogs must go in the cargo hold. But most airlines will allow one or two dogs per cabin—usually one in first class, one in tourist—provided the animals are in sturdy carriers that fit under the seat. If you have a choice of several airlines, shop around first to find out which ones offer the best service in regard to pets.

Don't forget to ask what is required in the way of health certificates for your dog, whether it's going in the cabin with you or in the cargo hold. Also ask about the type of carrier; some airlines have definite regulations, and very few will allow you to use your dog's own carrying case.

You have to make a reservation for your dog at the same time that you make your own, and pay for it, usually at the excess baggage rate. Don't be surprised if there's some screw-up and you arrive at the airport to find they have no record of your dog's reservation. It's a good idea to get to the airport well ahead of time.

A word to the wise: Once in a crowded airport, I saw a little Poodle leap from the arms of its owner, who had made the mistake of taking it out of its carrier. The frightened dog fled into the crowd with its owner in pursuit. Fortunately, a quick-thinking bystander intercepted it before it got lost or into trouble.

By the way, your dog doesn't have to go through the X-ray at the gate.

Whatever the rules and regulations, much that applies to traveling with a pet in the cabin seems to depend on the attitudes of the airline personnel on duty at the time you and your pet are flying. For instance, whether or not you can take your pet out and hold it in your lap during the flight may depend on whether the flight attendants, and the passengers near you, like dogs. In any case, it's supposed to stay in its carrier when food is being served.

However, if you have a big dog that won't fit in an underseat carrier, or the airline you want to go on won't allow dogs of any size in the cabin, then the poor animal is relegated to the cargo hold. It must travel in a crate large enough for it to stand up and lie down comfortably in. Some airlines require very specific types of crates. The airline you'll be traveling on will instruct you about the crate and how it should be labeled.

Seems to me a short-haired dog might be uncomfortable on a long flight, because while cargo holds are pressurized, they're not heated, and the air can get awfully cold up in the clouds, even when it's summer on the ground. Nevertheless, dogs do seem to survive in the cargo hold.

Always try to book a direct flight, if possible. But if you must change planes, or if there's a layover or delay along the way, don't assume that your dog will make the connection safely or, for that matter, be comfortable in the cargo hold for very long in hot weather. A few years ago there were occasional horror stories of dogs that died in their crates that had been unloaded from the planes but left on baggage carts on the airfields in broiling sun and hundred-degree temperatures.

If you find you're going to be delayed in an airport after your pet has already disappeared behind scenes along with your luggage, go to the airline desk and ask for your dog so you can keep it with you until loading time. Be polite but firm. Airline employees are busy, but if you make clear your concerns, you can get their cooperation.

Don't get on the plane until you're sure your pet is being loaded. You don't want to arrive at your destination to discover that the dog was bumped or forgotten. There are no tried-and-true procedures to pass on to you; all I can advise is that you be on top of each situation as it arises and not take anything for granted.

For overseas flights, the airline regulations regarding dogs vary from one airline to the next, and the type of health certificates it will need depends on the country of destination. Some countries also require import permits, visas, and the like. And even before you start to think about those, find out whether or not the place you're flying to will put your dog in quarantine.

You can't take a dog to Britain at all because you'd have to subject it to a six-month quarantine, which no one in their right mind would do. If you're going to Europe, however, I've heard that once you get there it is in some ways easier to travel with a dog than it is in the United States. Many Europeans travel with their pets, apparently, and railroads and hotels in many European countries are much more lenient than they are here. Check with the consulates and tourist bureaus.

Don't feed your dog for twelve hours before a flight, and walk it as close to departure time as possible. Whether or not you should sedate it depends on its temperament and your veterinarian's advice.

LEAVING A PET WHILE YOU TRAVEL

There are many different types of arrangements you can make for your dog when it can't travel with you, but far and away the ideal solution is to leave the pet in its own home with a trusted live-in sitter whom it knows and likes. You might know someone who will sit for you out of friendship, but if you have to ask him or her frequently, I think it's better to have a business arrangement. When you pay someone for this valuable service, you feel more free to ask for it when you need it.

Or if the person you use as sitter also has a pet that your dog likes well enough to live with temporarily, you can have the live-in arrangement on a reciprocal basis. In exchange for sitting with your dog, he or she can count on you and your dog to do the same.

If you have more than one pet, they can be left at home for periods of a few days without a live-in sitter, just as long as someone comes in three times a day to walk, feed, and keep an eye on them. There are people in most cities who offer this service for hire, but this is also a situation in which a reciprocal arrangement works well, especially among people who live in the same apartment building. Several of my neighbors and I dog-walk and pet-feed for one another on a short-term basis.

I do feel sorry for single dogs left alone, even for just a weekend. The nights and days without their owners can seem awfully long to them. If you have no other pets and are not having a live-in sitter, ask the person who will be coming in to walk and feed your dog if he or she will spend a little time just keeping the animal company.

By the way, if you have a very territorial dog, be sure it has a chance to get to know the sitter before you leave. Otherwise, your pet might not let the person in the door when he or she comes to take care of it.

Another possibility to consider is leaving your dog in someone else's home. If the person with whom you leave your pet is someone you know and trust, and your dog is comfortable in his or her home, that can be almost as satisfactory as having a sitter in your house. However, if there's nobody like that whom you could ask, there are people who advertise, in newspapers or on the bulletin boards of veterinarians' offices, that they will board pets in their homes. These can be just fine, or they may be risky. Visit several of them and check them out. Ask for references and follow up. Ask if there will be other pets in addition to yours, and if so, how many and what kind. Find out if the person's standards and attitudes about dog care are like your own. Also, if the person is fussy about health and wants proof that your dog's vaccinations are in order, that's a good sign.

If all else fails, there are always boarding kennels. I regard them as a last resort not because they are automatically bad places but because I think a dog that lives as a house pet will be unhappy in a kennel, even if the place resembles the Versailles Palace. However, if you do kennel your dog, choose carefully. Try to pick one that trustworthy, dog-owning friends have used and approve of, or that your veterinarian recommends.

If you don't have any word-of-mouth recommendation and must pick from the Yellow Pages, see if your city has a Better Business Bureau. Such an organization might know if there have been any complaints lodged against any of the kennels listed.

Before you make a final decision, visit the kennel you are considering and check it out for cleanliness, upkeep, ventilation, safety, the attitude of the staff, and the behavior of the dogs that are being boarded when you visit. The sleeping and exercise areas should be of suitable size, with high, strong fences between the runs. I know of a Cocker Spaniel that was killed by two Pit Bull Terriers in the run next to hers. The Pit Bulls, the breed commonly used in dogfighting, leaped over a six-foot fence to get her. Check the security of the kennel from the outside, also. Although it's unlikely, there's always the possibility that crazies might try to vandalize a kennel, including the dogs in it.

Make a reservation well in advance, particularly if you're going to be leaving your dog over a holiday. Some kennels have pick-up and delivery service. When you make your reservation, ask what health certificates are required. Let the kennel know what medication or special food your dog needs, if any. Give the kennel the name and phone number of your veterinarian, and find out what veterinarians the kennel uses in an emergency. Leave your itinerary or a number where you can be reached if necessary and the name and number of a nontraveling friend who could be contacted if an emergency arose in which you couldn't be reached.

It might be wise to leave your dog for one or two short stays in a kennel before you leave it for a long time, especially if it is an only pet and extremely attached to you. Have it spend a weekend or two there before you take off for a two- or three-week period. Take its bed from home and a few favorite toys.

When you drop your dog off at the kennel or turn it over to the person picking it up, be cheerful and relaxed. Don't pass any anxiety or regrets you might have on to your dog—that will only make the separation from you hard for the animal.

There's a useful booklet called *How To Select a Boarding Kennel* that's available for $1.25 from the American Boarding Kennels Association, 311 North Union, Colorado Springs, CO 80909.

CHAPTER 13

THE GERIATRIC DOG:
Caring for Your Elderly Pet

When is a dog old?

Though it's widely believed that each year of a dog's age corresponds to seven human years, this notion, as I pointed out in Chapter 1, is inaccurate. A one-year-old dog is sexually mature, comparable to a human adolescent, not a seven-year-old child. A two-year-old dog is more like a person in his or her mid-twenties. After that, the comparison gap narrows considerably, and you might estimate a dog's year equals four human years. But as I pointed out, there's a big difference in the life expectancies of dogs, depending on breed and size.

Giant breeds are lucky to live to eight or nine, big dogs may live to ten or twelve, medium-sized breeds even longer, and little dogs may live to see their seventeenth or eighteenth birthdays. Mixed breeds of course reflect the life expectancies of their parents and ancestors. If a dog comes from a long line of mixed breeds, then you can guess its life span will probably depend on whether it is huge, big, medium-size, or little.

Therefore, a Great Dane or St. Bernard qualifies as a geriatric dog at about six; a German Shepherd or Labrador Retriever will usually begin to show signs of aging at eight or nine; a dog weighing thirty to perhaps sixty pounds will be middle-aged by ten; but a little Poodle or Yorkie won't be considered geriatric until around twelve or so.

These estimates are only rules of thumb. Obviously, a great deal depends on the care a dog gets, its health, and its individual heredity. Among your own canine acquaintances, there are sure to be exceptions both ways. You probably know dogs that are old before their time, as well as those that defy the averages in longevity.

If you are the owner of a geriatric dog, you deserve congratulations and respect, because it indicates that you have given loving care to your pet for many years. The fact is that the lives of most pet animals, dogs and cats alike, are terminated long before they reach old age—through neglect, abuse, or some other form of human intervention. Dogs that are allowed to run loose, dogs that are chained year-round to doghouses in the yard, dogs whose owners are slow to notice signs of illness or injury, and dogs that are abandoned are among those that don't live long enough to grow old.

However, better knowledge of canine health care among dog owners in general, in addition to increased sophistication in small animal veterinary medicine, has given rise to a new class of dog— the geriatric. And city dogs, for all the reasons discussed in the chapters on health and safety, are on the average those that outlive others.

As a dog grows old, the first signs of aging are usually rather subtle—a little gray around the muzzle, a cloudiness of the eyes, slowness of pace, stiffness in the joints, perhaps increased thirst. Unless the animal falls victim to one of the more serious illnesses related to aging, the process is probably gradual, just as it is with people. The changes occur both in physical ability and in personality.

An elderly dog is not only susceptible to the disorders of aging but if it contracts any of the regular canine diseases, it will probably be affected more severely than a younger dog. Even in good health, it should have regular checkups by a veterinarian every six months. And of course if it does become ill, it needs close medical monitoring.

SIGHT, HEARING, AND SMELL

Cloudiness of the eyes is not necessarily cataracts (opacity of the lenses) but a normal condition in old dogs and does not interfere with vision. However, dogs do sometimes get cataracts and gradually go blind. Dogs seem to cope better with blindness than human beings do—they don't read, watch television, paint, sew, drive cars, do carpentry work, look at scenery, or go to the movies, for instance, so perhaps they don't feel they're missing as much as people naturally do. Also, of course, they rely a great deal on their sense of smell, so blindness is not as disabling. If a visually handicapped dog is kept in familiar surroundings and given a lot of protection and love, it can adjust quite well.

Some dogs develop a slight discharge from the eyes. If your veterinarian finds nothing that requires treatment, just wipe around your dog's eyes gently every day with clean facial tissue or dry cotton.

Hearing loss is almost inevitable, and for that reason you might want to start teaching your pet hand signals along about middle age. And because sight loss may follow, make the signals broad and sweeping enough for the dog to see easily. Instead of a beckon of the hand for "Come," for example, make a circle toward yourself with your whole arm.

Another way to get the dog's attention is to stamp on the floor. The animal will feel the vibrations of the floorboards.

Partial deafness can quite disorient a dog—it may vaguely hear a noise such as a siren on the street, or someone calling its name, but can't tell where the sound is coming from. In case you have ignored my warnings and the law about always walking your dog on the leash, now is certainly the time when you really must protect it by never letting it loose outdoors. You may have a very well obedience-trained dog and have always counted on it to obey, but as the dog ages its deafness could go unnoticed until one day you give it a command on the street that is necessary for its safety and it won't be able to hear you.

Dandy is now quite deaf and sometimes doesn't even hear me when I get up in the morning, even though her basket is right beside my bed. When I touch her gently to let her know the action in the household, such as breakfast, is about to begin, she always looks somewhat sheepish. She can sometimes hear higher-pitched sounds but not those in a low register. My friend Bill Berloni suggested I start teaching her hand signals, and she has learned to respond to them.

A dog's sense of smell seems to be the last to go, but it can happen, and the only problem this might present is if the animal loses its appetite as a result. Then you'll want to coax it with favorite foods and hand-feed it if necessary.

TEMPERATURE SENSITIVITY AND EXERCISE NEEDS

An elderly dog might feel the cold more than it did when younger. Even if your pet has thick long fur and has never worn a coat or sweater, now may be the time to get it one. In very cold weather, a geriatric dog should have protection if it's going to be out any longer than ten minutes.

I'm assuming your urban dog has never had to sleep outdoors anyway, so I don't have to tell you that an elderly dog should not, even if it has had to do so all its life. If it sleeps in your room at night and you like your windows open year-round, put a blanket over your short-haired dog or have it sleep in its sweater on very cold nights. Be sure its bed is away from drafts, and—equally important—not too close to a hot radiator either.

Be sure to dry your dog more thoroughly than ever after a bath. Use a hair dryer if your pet will tolerate it—only don't direct it too long on one spot because that can cause dry skin. And don't take the dog outdoors for several hours afterward on a cool or cold day.

An old dog's coat is very susceptible to dry weather, hot or cold, and needs regular, frequent brushing. An overheated house or apartment can dry out the coat of any dog, but as a dog ages, its coat needs your attention even more.

I wouldn't take an old dog out in extremely hot weather at all, except to the curb and back, and then only in the morning, evening, and night. As I've said, city sidewalks reflect too much heat; an animal close to the ground gets a blast like an open furnace in its face.

An elderly dog should get regular exercise, however, and should not be allowed to lie around all the time. Take it for shorter, slower walks than you did formerly. Let the animal set its own pace. Play quiet indoor games that give it exercise, such as fetching a ball rolled across the floor.

Most dogs like to be where their owners are, so if your aging pet follows you from room to room, encourage it. Dandy will not stay five minutes in a room that I'm not in, so she is forever getting up to traipse after me when I move about. It makes me feel sorry for her sometimes when she's lounging comfortably but pulls herself to her feet just to accompany me—after all, I'm not going more than a few yards away. But I suppose the exercise is good for her.

Your aging pet may stumble going up and down stairs and need help. It's not unusual for an old dog to attempt gymnastics that it used to do with ease and fall flat on its face. You want to prevent it from overdoing or from actually hurting itself.

DIET AND ELIMINATION

The best diet for an older dog is outlined in Chapter 5, but I want to caution you again about abrupt changes in the food you feed it. If the store is out of the brand of canned or dry food that you normally give your dog and you have to buy another, phase it in slowly. An aging dog may have trouble digesting a food that is even only slightly different from what it's used to.

Also, I think giving an old dog two small meals a day instead of one big one is a very good idea. That way you never overload its food-processing system.

Your aging pet may very likely drink more water. The line between a normal increase in drinking water and the excessive thirst that signals trouble is a fine one. Many old dogs' kidneys function perfectly well throughout their lives. But you should report increased water consumption to your veterinarian, who will probably want to run a urinalysis and blood test to determine kidney function (see below). If there is real impairment in kidney function, the dog should be put on a special diet. There are prescription dog foods specially formulated for dogs with kidney problems.

Naturally, increased water consumption will most likely mean the dog has to urinate more frequently. Do not under any circumstances cut back on its water supply in an effort to prevent this. A dog of any age should have access to fresh drinking water at all times. However, if your veterinarian approves, you might try salt-free dog foods (canned and dry), because they may reduce excessive thirst and drinking and lower the dog's urge to urinate.

If you regularly put in long days away from home, it might be a good idea to hire someone to come in to walk your dog, just as with a puppy. However, you can also train an older dog to use newspapers, in addition to going out. As I mentioned earlier, Dandy used to try to use the cats' litterbox in emergencies, so I adopted the practice of keeping a layer of papers on the floor next to the box, and now if she has to go when I can't get her out, she uses them. If you have cats, you might try putting newspapers by their box—your dog might get the idea.

Otherwise, put papers in a spot where the dog has made a puddle before, or in some other place you think might inspire the right response. Take some papers with you when you walk the dog, get them a little wet, and put the wet papers with the dog's urine smell on top of a clean layer in the place you want to train the dog to go.

By the way, a city dog that is accustomed to urinating at the curb will probably be more inclined to use a spot in the house that feels like concrete under its feet. I think it would be unusual for it to go on the rug, as a puppy might. If the dog hasn't chosen its own place to go in the house, try putting the newspapers in the bathroom or any place with a tile or cement floor that feels right under the paws.

Some very aged dogs become incontinent, unable to control their functions at all. They may urinate in their sleep and wake up in a puddle. If your pet has this problem, try lining its bed with extra-large disposable diapers at night, or put a layer of newspapers on the floor or rug where it likes to sleep.

You may have to be very inventive and patient, caring for an elderly dog. Never reproach or punish it for relieving itself in the house. The dog can't help it and is humiliated enough as it is.

One definite change I've noticed in my fourteen-year-old dog is that the urge to defecate comes over her in a hurry. Where before she would signal by leading me to the curb when it was time, now she simply stops wherever she may be, such as in the middle of a sidewalk. I always clean up, of course—in fact, I usually get the newspaper under her in time. But it can be very embarrassing to have your dog do that on a sidewalk crowded with passersby. Now I try to anticipate this by spending more time at the curb when I first take her out. A tip: When a dog is getting ready to defecate, it raises its tail a few seconds before it squats. That can give you time to pull the dog to the curb, or at least to slide a newspaper under it.

If you live in an apartment building, you may find that once you have the leash on and are headed for the street, your geriatric animal gets excited, can't wait, and has accidents in the hall, elevator, or lobby. If so, you might buy one of those belts designed for unspayed, menstruating female dogs, and use it to hold a disposable diaper in place on your dog. Have the dog wear it just to get through the building. Then you can remove it at the curb, throw it away if wet, and walk the dog normally.

One creative dog owner I know fitted her geriatric pet with a pair of little boy's jockey shorts, worn backward, tail through the flap, and lined it with a disposable diaper. Served the same purpose.

You may find your geriatric dog becoming constipated. As I mentioned in Chapter 6, you want to distinguish between intestinal obstruction and occasional constipation. An intestinal obstruction, which is life-threatening, will cause the dog to strain in obvious discomfort, to vomit, and soon stop eating. Constipation is characterized by hard or inadequate stools. If your dog occasionally needs a laxative, give it a little milk, a teaspoon of milk of magnesia, or a teaspoon or two, depending on the dog's size, of mineral oil. (Caution: Because mineral oil is easily aspirated, don't pour it down the dog's throat but mix it in the food.) But the dog should see a veterinarian if the constipation persists because that might be a symptom of a serious problem such as a tumor.

DISORDERS OF AGING

An elderly dog can get virtually all the same disorders that were discussed in Chapter 6, but some are more likely to occur in old age and deserve repeating here. I have also added a few that are rare in younger dogs but quite common in seniors. Don't forget—regular twice-yearly veterinary checkups, even if your pet has no overt symptoms of illness.

Arthritis. Just like old people, dogs can develop arthritis, particularly in the hip, shoulder, and knee. The dog will be stiff and lame, with weakness and trembling, and possibly the affected limbs will be misshapen. Stiffness is especially bad in the morning. A dog that had hip dysplasia or patellar luxation when it was young is especially susceptible.

Aspirin can help, but your veterinarian should prescribe the dosage. There are also stronger medications for dogs suffering a lot of pain.

By the way, if while reading this book it occurs to you that a bit of aspirin or Tylenol might also help your elderly arthritic cat, don't try it without close veterinary supervision. For some reason, cats are much more susceptible than dogs to aspirin overdose and could die from a dosage that's okay for a dog of the same weight. And never give a cat Tylenol.

Kidney disease. Be on the lookout for this in an older dog, since it is not unusual for kidney function to decline markedly just from the aging process. An old dog that is severely stressed by anxiety or trauma can develop kidney disease quite rapidly.

As mentioned above, if your dog begins drinking excessive amounts of water and urinating large volumes, these symptoms could indicate kidney disease. Your veterinarian should take a urinalysis and blood test to determine how the kidneys are holding up. If the tests indicate abnormal function, the dog will need a prescription diet.

When the kidneys are really in bad shape, the dog will lose its appetite, lose weight, vomit frequently. By that time, it may be too late to save the dog.

Heart disease. Dogs rarely have heart attacks or sudden cardiac arrest, but valve problems and degeneration of heart muscle are common in geriatric cases. Symptoms include coughing (especially at night), breathing difficulties, fatigue, possibly decreased appetite. Little dogs may also be restless at night. Your veterinarian will want to perform an electrocardiogram and take a chest X-ray, among other tests, and may put the dog on medication and a special diet.

Liver disease. This is usually a secondary infection, caused by a virus, bacteria, or tumor elsewhere in the body. The symptoms include increased water consumption, poor appetite, weight loss, and vomiting, sometimes a yellowing of the whites of the eyes. The dog needs antibiotics, special diet, and plenty of home nursing.

Tumors. According to Dr. Audrey Hayes, whose specialty is oncology, the most common tumors found among old dogs are benign or malignant tumors of the skin, bone, and mouth. Lymphosarcomas (cancer of the lymph nodes) are also common, as are benign or malignant mammary gland tumors in unspayed females or females spayed after they were a year old. Treatment for tumors is usually surgery or, in the case of malignant tumors, chemotherapy, perhaps in combination with surgery. A large animal hospital or one associated with a veterinary college may offer radiation therapy.

Dr. Hayes suggests that before you automatically euthanize an animal with cancer, ask your veterinarian to refer you to an oncologist for consultation. Even a highly skilled veterinarian may not be up to date on the latest advances in this specialty.

Cushing's disease. A not uncommon endocrine disease among older dogs, Cushing's disease causes the adrenal glands to over-produce a hormone called cortisol. Symptoms are excessive thirst and urination, increased appetite, weight loss, weakness, hair loss, often a distended belly, and sometimes excessive panting. It is diagnosed by a blood test and can be controlled with medication. Without treatment, the disease is fatal within one to two years.

Diabetes mellitus. Older female dogs are especially susceptible to this disorder. The animal will have increased appetite but lose weight; it will drink more water and have to urinate more frequently. In advanced stages, there may be vomiting and diarrhea, lethargy and depression. The owner will have to give the dog insulin by injection (anybody can learn to do this for his or her pet).

Tooth problems. Crust and tartar on a dog's teeth are unavoidable but, if neglected, can cause infection in the gums. The dog will have bad breath, eat carefully as if it hurt, drop food from its mouth, and may rub its face with its paws or against the floor. Keep a close check on an aging dog's teeth, and have your veterinarian examine them regularly. In severe cases, the tartar must be removed while the dog is under anesthetic.

PERSONALITY CHANGES

A geriatric dog needs a lot of tender care and affection. When we ourselves grow old, at least we have some understanding of what's going on with our bodies, but aging can be confusing and stressful to a dog. We are not sure of the level of self-awareness that dogs have, and all we can go by, in terms of their psychological needs, is what they tell us in their own ways. Owners of old dogs should be alert to all signals coming from them. Now is the time to be patient and indulgent with them for the years of love and companionship they have given us.

Naturally, an old dog will be less alert, slower to respond, easily confused. It will sleep more than usual and sometimes seem befuddled when it wakes up. Occasionally Dandy stands and stares at something or gazes into space absentmindedly.

Personality changes in elderly dogs are said to take place in one of two ways: The animals either become irritable and crotchety, or they become very dependent. A dog that becomes cranky should be allowed to live a simple life with as few disturbances and discomforts as possible. Be careful not to startle it or wake it suddenly, because it may snap.

Dandy is an example of an old dog who has become unusually dependent and habituated. I first noticed it when I took her for a walk one day into a neighborhood that was unfamiliar to her. Instead of being curious and enjoying the adventure, she was miserable. She trembled and glanced around nervously when I took her into a store on an errand. She walked so close to me on the street that she almost tripped me, and she didn't relax until we got back on our block.

Now I try not to disturb the normal routines of her life and to keep everything the same for her. She is in good health, and I hope she will never have to be hospitalized—that apparently stresses an old dog severely.

SAYING GOODBYE

Every owner of an elderly dog, even a healthy one, lives with the knowledge that the pet's days are numbered. You must watch carefully for every change, every sign of discomfort or disease. You should protect, indulge, clean up after, make allowances for, and pour on the affection—it's the least you can do in exchange for the gifts your dog has given you.

Most books on dog care, including this one, will advise you that when the quality of your geriatric dog's life has deteriorated to the point where pain and discomfort outweigh its pleasure, you should have the pet euthanized. Your friends and your veterinarian alike will tell you the same thing. This is easy advice to give, or even agree to, in the abstract. But when you actually have a very old dog, a friend who has shared your life and given you joy and companionship for many years, it's a whole other matter.

Sometimes the moment to euthanize your dog is fairly obvious. In an extreme situation where it's plain to see that your pet is suffering greatly and the veterinarian assures you that nothing more can be done, you can make the decision quickly and it's over before you have a chance for agonized inner debate as to whether you're doing the right thing.

But then there are the situations when an old dog needs expensive surgery that could prolong its life but involves much pain, lengthy hospitalization, extensive care, and at its age, sizable risk. Or the pet develops a chronic illness that is not life-threatening but keeps it in permanent discomfort with no hope of relief. When do you decide enough is enough? There simply are no easy answers.

The trouble is that with a well-cared-for elderly dog, the clear-cut moment when you really have no humane choice rarely arrives. What usually happens instead is that the animal goes downhill slowly. It is confused, arthritic, deaf, blind, and perhaps incontinent, but still eats, still wags its tail and licks your hand. Does it want to go on with its life in this condition, or is it ready to pack it in and is just responding to you out of habit and affection? Has its life become a burden, or does it still enjoy small pleasures? You have always been able to judge with reasonable accuracy how your pet feels, but now the bottom line has arrived and you have no idea.

Your vet can make an educated guess about whether the animal is in pain. But to what degree? Animals have different thresholds of pain, just as we do. There's not a caring dog owner among us who doesn't wish that every aged pet could die peacefully in its sleep, in its own bed at home, instead of continuing a joyless and painful existence.

I wish I could tell you how to recognize the moment for euthanasia when it comes, how to decide in your heart with absolute certainty that you must ease your aged pet into eternity today instead of tomorrow, or next week or next month, if ever. As the owner of a fourteen-year-old dog myself, I can't give you any glib insights.

If you have a family, the choices should be discussed and the decision made together, with your older children included. It seems to me cruel for parents to go behind children's backs and spring it on them later, perhaps with some fairy tale about where their pet has gone. Kids should have a chance to say goodbye to the pet.

By the way, don't tell a small child that the dog is going to be "put to sleep." This euphemism can be confusing. Then when the child, or a family member, has to have an operation and is told that it won't hurt because he or she will be put to sleep, the child will understandably react with terror.

Susan Phillips Cohen, a counselor for people whose pets are

severely ill or dying at the Animal Medical Center in New York City, and Dr. Carole Fudin, a psychotherapist, presenting a joint paper at a symposium on euthanasia in veterinary medicine, offered some suggestions for helping children deal with the euthanasia of a pet. They suggested that children under five or six years old should be spared the details but can be told that the pet feels very bad, that it can't get well again, and that the euthanasia will help the pet to die painlessly. After age six, they say, the child should have the reasons for and the process of the euthanasia explained to them. If they become angry with the parents or the veterinarian, their feelings should be treated with respect and patience. And they should be permitted to see the dead pet afterward and kiss it goodbye if they want to.

Both counselors say that the way parents handle a pet's death will set an example for children. If the parents act with dignity, compassion, and sensitivity, it will help the children deal with the death of a loved person later on.

Veterinarian Mark Lerman had an episode in his practice in which he was faced with euthanizing the pet of a handicapped child of about thirteen. The dog was brought to him hemorrhaging; it had cancer, but the child was weeping bitterly, certainly not ready to say goodbye to her pet. So Dr. Lerman operated, patched up the dog so it could live comfortably for a few weeks, and spent several sessions with the little girl, explaining her dog's illness and preparing her for its death. In the end, the child was able, at her own request, to hold her dog calmly in her arms when the veterinarian euthanized it.

THE ACTUAL EUTHANASIA

A pet euthanized by a private veterinarian is given a lethal overdose of anesthesia by injection. There is the prick of the needle and after that, the animal feels nothing. If you are present at your dog's euthanasia, don't be alarmed if its body should twitch or its tongue hang out, because it is not suffering. Its eyes do not close when it dies, by the way.

Ideally, one should have a veterinarian who will come to the house and administer the fatal injection to the animal in familiar surroundings. Many dogs are so scared at the veterinarian's that it would be a kindness to spare them their fear at this point. In some cities, there are veterinarians who will make house calls, and I suggest you use one for this purpose, even if he or she is not your regular vet.

Whether you have to take your dog to the veterinary clinic for euthanasia or have it done at home, your own behavior can help the dog a lot. Don't communicate your pain to your pet. Have a close, sympathetic friend with you for moral support. Act natural with the animal and be reassuring—this is not the time to throw your arms around the dog's neck and weep. You can fall apart later if you have to, but now is the moment to rise to the occasion.

Veterinarians are divided on whether or not to let a client be present at the euthanasia of a pet. Some encourage it, some won't allow it under any circumstances, and others will permit it if the client requests it (and if the vet thinks the client can handle it). I feel that the owner's presence is comforting to a pet, provided the owner is capable of putting the pet's emotional needs above his or her own at the moment. Many caring dog owners want to stroke and hold their pets, soothing them and letting them know they are loved as they slip into unconsciousness and breathe their last.

Veterinarians are not taught in vet school how to cope with a client's emotions, and I've heard some complain that they feel unequipped to be grief counselors. So don't expect too much from your vet. You may have one who is just naturally empathetic and supportive, but if the expressions of sympathy you need are not forthcoming at this moment, remember that the doctor may feel bad too and be having trouble with his or her own feelings.

COPING WITH GRIEF

The late Michael McCulloch, a psychiatrist, told of a young teenage boy who was referred to him for possible therapy. This youngster had been sunny and outgoing, a top student, a good athlete, active in school affairs. Suddenly he had lost interest in his school work and sports and had become unusually withdrawn and quiet. His parents, concerned, had sent him to the family doctor, who couldn't find anything physically wrong with him.

Dr. McCulloch interviewed the boy, who was cooperative but subdued. Then one day, about the second or third time the child was in McCulloch's office, it came out that his dog had died.

"How is it that you never mentioned this to me before?" asked the doctor, suspecting immediately that he was dealing with a classic case of unresolved grief.

"Everyone told me it was too bad but not important," said the boy. "They said Sam was just a dog, and that I should forget about him." The poor kid had been carrying around a huge burden of grief, and nobody had understood or helped him.

The death of a companion animal is still trivialized by society generally. If a man, for example, were to call his office and say he was unable to come to work because a close family member had died, expressions of sympathy would pour forth and no supervisor, department head, or chief executive officer would expect him to show up for a week. But if it was his dog that had died, his need for time off would be regarded as wild eccentricity and treated with puzzlement, amusement, or exasperation—even though in point of fact, the dog may have been his best friend, closer than any family member. In our still quite sexist society, a woman, unless she was a top executive, might be treated with more sympathy because we are allowed to be more "soft" in these matters. Still, she would be wise not to push it.

Some psychiatrists and others in the helping professions believe that the bereavement process after the death of a beloved pet is much like that which follows the loss of a significant person. According to Dr. Herbert Nieburg, author of *Pet Loss: A Thoughtful Guide for Adults and Children*, the degree of grieving is normal in proportion to the affection that the pet owner felt for the animal.

However, the death of a pet under certain conditions can produce a morbid reaction in the owner, depending on what else is going on in his or her life at the time. If a person is suffering from other severe loss—of a mate, parent, child, job, or home, for example—the death or euthanasia of a pet can be catastrophic. This might be the time to seek help from a professional, a group, or some wise and trusted individual—and not to feel ashamed for doing so.

Attitudes toward pet loss and human grief are changing slowly. If your dog should die or have to be euthanized, you can probably expect more understanding on the part of your colleagues, friends, and acquaintances than you could formerly. Above all, don't think there's anything wrong with you if you feel extreme pain and a sense of loss for quite a while.

People vary in the manner and length of bereavement. You may feel like crying for weeks or months, but try to have faith in your normal, human ability to heal.

One nice thing to do that will make you feel better is to make a donation in your dog's name to your favorite animal shelter. In helping the shelter care for dogs that other people have discarded, you honor the species that has given you happiness, and you also strike a blow against human neglect and cruelty to animals.

YOUR DOG'S REMAINS

What to do with the body of your dog after it has died is a greater problem for city dwellers than for others—you can't just bury your pet in the backyard. Even if you have a city garden, there are probably zoning laws against it.

Your veterinarian will dispose of the body if you wish, or have it cremated for you. If you look in the Yellow Pages of your city, you will probably find pet cemeteries and crematories that will pick up a pet's body from home. Also, some SPCAs and humane societies offer cremation or disposal services. Should you have your pet cremated, you can have the ashes delivered to you if you wish.

Some people derive a lot of comfort from having the pet's body or ashes buried where they can visit the grave. This is why pet cemeteries exist. They are usually beautiful, peaceful places, a testimonial to our bond with our companion animals.

At the symposium on veterinary euthanasia, mentioned above, veterinarian Margaret Young told a lovely story about a four-year-old child who insisted on putting the family pet's ashes under the flowers growing on her grandfather's grave. "Now grandpa has someone with him so he won't be lonely," she said.

LOOKING AHEAD

Some people who have loved and lost a dog, especially one that lived with them for many years, and especially one whose euthanasia they presided over, vow never again. The loss was an experience they prefer not to repeat, so they resolve that's the last dog they'll ever have.

It seems to me that every emotional attachment is full of risk, and whenever you let yourself form strong feelings for a mate, parent, child, or friend, there are no guarantees that you will love or be loved by that person forever. But if you never take the risks, you'll miss the whole ball game.

The human heart has unlimited room for love, and in this case, any number of dogs. I urge you to get another. Give yourself time for mourning—people vary in the length of time they need. I adopted Dandy ten days after Benjy died because I not only missed him, I was lonely for a dog. But it may be weeks or months before you're ready, and that is not unusual. Children especially should not be given the impression that the dog who died can be immediately replaced, like a broken toy.

Dogs are not interchangeable—each one is unique in the world. But while you can never duplicate the peerless pet you've lost, dogs fortunately share certain qualities of dogginess. Each one has its own special traits, but they also have characteristics in common. Dog lovers like myself not only love deeply our individual animals but the race in general.

So don't look for a carbon copy of the dog that died. That puts a burden on an unsuspecting new dog of having to live up to a memory, and you may be disappointed in it through no fault of its own. When my neighbor Cathy lost her beloved, sedate, gentle Husky, she grieved for a few months, and then, to the delight of the whole neighborhood, she went to a shelter and adopted. Her new dog is smooth-coated, adolescent, awkward, and exuberant—

nothing like the dear departed Volga. But Cathy loves Ruffian just as much.

One point to keep in mind is that it may be many years since you had a puppy, so you may have forgotten how much trouble they can be. Perhaps a grown dog would be more what you are used to—and remember that adult dogs are the ones that most need homes.

Don't let too long a period elapse before you embark on the adventure of getting to know another of these marvelous creatures and of establishing another love affair that could turn out to be just as happy, in its own way, as the one that has ended. Perhaps the first chapter of this book will encourage you. I hope so.

INDEX